Curriculum and Assessment in English 11 to 19

Curriculum and Assessment in English 11 to 19: A Better Plan provides an overview of the subject in considerable breadth and depth, and offers a clear, balanced and forceful critique of the current English curriculum and its associated examinations for 11- to 19-year-olds in England, and of developments in the area during the past thirty years.

The book restates fundamental truths about how students speak, read and write English with confidence and control. It describes how English can be taught most effectively, calls for an urgent review of some aspects of the current National Curriculum and its examination arrangements, and – crucially – proposes viable alternatives. This invaluable resource for those working in English, media and drama education has a wide perspective and takes a principled and informed pedagogical approach.

Based on a series of much-admired booklets released by the UKLA in 2015, this accessible guide to both theory and practice will be of interest to teachers, student teachers, teacher-educators, advisers and policy-makers in the UK and internationally.

John Richmond has a breadth of experience as a classroom English teacher and advisory teacher in London, a local-authority English adviser, an officer on the National Writing Project and the Language in the National Curriculum Project (both in the UK), and a commissioning editor in educational television in the UK and the USA.

Andrew Burn has worked as a teacher of English, media and drama in schools in Cambridgeshire. He is Professor of English, Media and Drama at the UCL Institute of Education, UK.

Peter Dougill has been an English and drama teacher in schools in the south of England, a local-authority English adviser, Chief Inspector in the London Borough of Wandsworth, an HMI and an adviser to the government's education department. He is Senior Visiting Research Fellow at the University of Sussex, and an independent ed... ...K.

Angela Goddard has taught English in all the educational sectors, from primary school to higher education. She is Chair of A-level English Language examiners at a national examination board, Professor of English Language at York St John University, UK, and a Higher Education Academy National Teaching Fellow.

Mike Raleigh has been an English teacher in Leicestershire and London, Deputy Warden of the ILEA English Centre, a local-authority English adviser and Deputy County Education Officer in Shropshire, and an HMI. He was Divisional Manager in Ofsted, Regional Director of the National Strategies in England, and an adviser to the Department for Education.

Peter Traves has been an English teacher in London, a local-authority English adviser, headteacher, and Director of Children's Services in Staffordshire. He is an independent educational consultant in the UK.

Contents

Preface

Most of the words in this book have had a former life; some have had two. The book draws on the contents of a series of ten booklets, published in June and September 2015 by the United Kingdom Literacy Association and Owen Education, an independent school-improvement agency. The series was entitled *English, Language and Literacy 3 to 19: Principles and Proposals*. This book, as is clear from its title, is addressed to teachers in secondary schools and colleges. It is published simultaneously with a volume addressed to teachers in Early Years settings and primary schools, entitled *Curriculum and Assessment in English 3 to 11: A Better Plan*.

The idea for the series was brought to me by Peter Dougill and Mike Raleigh, then directors of Owen Education. They saw the need for a restatement of basic principles about the learning of English throughout the years of schooling, for a detailed critique of some aspects of government requirements in England to do with the English curriculum and with testing and examinations in English, and for the putting forward of practical, educationally better alternatives. Eve Bearne and David Reedy then kindly agreed on behalf of UKLA to jointly finance the publication of the booklets with Owen Education. The four people named here have greatly influenced and guided the project at every stage.

Later in 2015, the Centre for Literacy in Primary Education, the National Association of Advisers in English, the National Association for the Teaching of English and the United Kingdom Literacy Association jointly sponsored the online publication on their websites of summaries of some of the material in the ten booklets. These appeared in 2016. Louise Johns-Shepherd at CLPE, John Hickman at NAAE, Barbara Conridge, Paul Clayton and Bethan Marshall at NATE, and Eve Bearne, Andrew Lambirth and David Reedy at UKLA were responsible for this initiative.

I have been the lead author on the series of booklets and the online publications, but three of the booklets – those entitled *Reading 7 to 16*, *Media* and *English 16 to 19* – were written by Peter Traves, Andrew Burn and Angela Goddard respectively. Shorter versions of these booklets have become Chapters 2, 6 and 11 of this book; their authorship is acknowledged there. Andrew Burn is also responsible for the media element of the alternative curriculum in Chapter 9.

As well as thanking those already named for their invaluable help in bringing the project to fruition, I – on my own behalf and that of my fellow authors – should make some further acknowledgements.

For comments on drafts of one or more of the booklets, thanks to: Myra Barrs, Eve Bearne, Barbara Bleiman, Ronald Carter, Margaret Clark, Henrietta Dombey, Joe Elliott, Deirdre Finan, Rosie Flewitt, Veronica Frankland, Peter Harris, John Hickman, Lesley Lancaster, Bethan Marshall, Myfanwy Marshall, Bronwyn Mellor, Nicholas McGuinn, David Reedy, Helen Savva and Claire Widgery.

I owe long-term debts to Ronald Carter (grammar and knowledge about language) and Claire Widgery (drama) for their influence on my understanding in those areas, over and beyond their immediate help with drafts of the text.

Frank Monaghan closely guided all the writing about the needs and achievements of learners of English as an additional language.

Pamela Dix supplied detailed information for the section on libraries in Chapter 2.

Theo Bryer, David Buckingham, James Durran, Craig Morrison, Becky Parry, Anthony Partington, John Potter, Mandy Powell and Mark Reid greatly influenced the ideas which Andrew Burn advances in Chapter 6.

Gillian Gibson supplied detailed information on qualifications at 16 to 19 other than A-level in Chapter 11.

Bronwyn Mellor proofread the text of all ten booklets; her careful work is evident in the text here.

John Hardcastle, first, and Andrew Burn, later, arranged for me to receive a Visiting Research Associateship at the University College London Institute of Education, which gave me access to the Institute's library and its comprehensive collection of books and research papers.

I thank Tony Harrison for permission to reprint his poem 'Dark Times'.

I thank Nicholas McGuinn, whose book *The English Teacher's Drama Handbook* supplied all the information in Chapter 5 on the history of the theory and practice of drama teaching.

I thank the English and Media Centre for permission to quote extensively from *Spotlight on Literacy: Creative Interventions in English and Across the Curriculum*. I thank the Centre for Literacy in Primary Education for permission to quote extensively from *The Reader in the Writer* by Myra Barrs and Valerie Cork.

My deepest gratitude is to my wife Helen Savva, who has supported and sustained me in every way throughout the project.

John Richmond

Introduction

John Richmond, Peter Dougill and Mike Raleigh

The purpose of this book is easily stated. There should, in the second decade of the twenty-first century, be a professional consensus amongst those who teach English to young people, or who teach young people *in* English, as to how to help them most effectively gain confidence and competence in the use of English. Although this consensus should exist, in practice it does not. The book aims to describe a desirable, intellectually sound and practically achievable consensus around which those who teach English or teach *in* English could unite.

By 'those who teach English or teach *in* English', we mean teachers of the subject English in secondary schools and colleges serving young people between the ages of 11 and 19; and teachers of a range of other subjects in those secondary schools and colleges, for whom it is essential that students have sufficient confidence and competence as readers, writers and speakers of English to access and benefit from the curriculum in those subjects.

There is a particular urgency in our purpose, since all contemporary commentators agree that, whatever progress has been made overall in raising the achievement of learners in English, there is still a large gap between the highest and the lowest achievers. There are still far too many young people who are failing to become competent and confident users of English, when there is no valid reason, in terms of their potential, why they *should* fail. Those most at risk of failure are learners from socio-economically poorer backgrounds.

Key principles

We believe that the best work on the development of language and literacy draws on seven basic principles.

1 There is no intellectual achievement more intimately connected to a young person's overall sense of worth as an individual and as a social being than the achievement of competence and confidence in the use of her or his language or languages.

2 The achievement of competence in any aspect of language is prior to and more complex than the achievement of the ability to analyse that aspect of language. Learners nonetheless continually engage in acts of reflection on aspects of the language they encounter and use.

3 The achievement of competence in any aspect of language is principally owed to the enjoyable *experience* of that aspect of language. *Instruction* in an aspect of language has a secondary but nonetheless very significant role to play in this achievement.

4 The learner's brain makes dynamic generalisations from enjoyable experiences of language. These generalisations prepare the learner for new encounters with and uses of language.

5 The motivation for any productive or receptive encounter with or use of language is the desire and need to construct meaning. Producers and receivers of language are both engaged in the construction of meaning.

6 Examples of language and literacy in use in English and of potential value and interest to learners are vast in number and diversity. Some of that diversity should be evident in the selection of examples which teachers present to learners.

7 Learners' experience of language in education should both value and confirm their linguistic, cultural and social backgrounds, and introduce them to cultural and social contexts beyond those they are familiar with.

The seven principles are stated here at a level of generality and abstraction which probably seems high-flown and dry. We shall try to invest them with a living practicality later on. In the meantime, it may be asked: What is so remarkable about them? Are they not self-evident, uncontroversial? The answer is: They should be, but they haven't been. The reason why they haven't been has something to do with the history of the contest for control of the teaching of English in our schools over several decades. It also has to do with the fact that worthwhile professional knowledge can sometimes be forgotten or get lost in the welter of new initiatives and changes of direction – often politically driven – affecting the curriculum.

The argument: truths restated

The rest of this book puts detailed flesh onto the bare bones of the seven principles. It makes no great claims to originality. It attempts to restate, sometimes even to exhume, truths about the effective learning of English which have, as we have just said, been forgotten or got lost, have indeed frequently been sidelined, sneered at, buried by those in power. The book represents the realisation that ground gained is not ground won forever; that truths can easily be overturned, ground can easily be taken back by forces of ignorant, retrospective reaction with the power to do so.

The National Curriculum for English

Chapters 1 to 6 also contain detailed discussions and critiques of the latest version of the National Curriculum for English, statutory in state schools in England other than academies and free schools as from September 2014 or September 2015 (Department for Education, 2014a). (We return below to the point about academies' and free schools' exemption from the legal force of the National Curriculum.) Here, we offer some general remarks.

The English orders then . . .

In the late 1980s, when the idea of a National Curriculum was proposed, we welcomed the principle that all children and young people in state schools have a common entitlement to a range of knowledge, understanding, competences and skills in the major school subjects.

The first version of the National Curriculum for English (Department of Education and Science and the Welsh Office, 1990), which was statutory as from 1989 and 1990, was over-detailed and contained some absurdities, notably to do with its system of ten attainment levels. But there was also much to praise: the document demonstrated an overall understanding that the learning and use of language by children and young people, both as producers and receivers, are essentially to do with the making of meaning. It disappointed the government of the day, which had seen its introduction as an opportunity to return classroom practice to an imagined golden past in which 'rigour' had prevailed: a time before the spread of sloppy, optimistic notions of 'creativity' which the so-called 'education establishment' was supposed to have smuggled into schools more recently.

. . . and now

We knew then and we know now that dualisms like 'rigour versus creativity', slogans like 'back to basics', bandied about by Secretaries of State for

Education then and since, have no basis in reality. Language, possibly the most advanced and delicate of human inventions, is both profoundly creative *and* profoundly structural. In spite of and in wilful opposition to this simple, central insight, governments of all colours since 1989, in the course of many revisions of the National Curriculum for English, have returned to the site of their disappointment: determined to impose an English curriculum freighted with detailed instructions to do with *method* and drawing its inspiration from the same regretful, simplistic vision of the way things had once been that had motivated the government a generation ago. This vision was and is a fantasy, but a politically advantageous one: 'back to basics' plays well in large sections of the media and burnishes ministers' credentials as tough, no-nonsense defenders of standards, as scourges of 'trendy teachers'.

Some of the most important instructions in the new National Curriculum for English are plainly wrong. For example, as John Richmond argues in Chapter 1, the use of spoken language in the classroom should not be confined to oral performance; it should also include the more exploratory and collaborative uses of talk in learning. As he argues in Chapter 4, the government's requirements on grammar teaching have precisely the wrong emphasis in putting the heavy load of learning about grammar onto primary-school children, and leaving secondary students simply to 'carry on the good work' in grammar, applied to more demanding texts.

The references to drama in the orders (see Chapter 5) carry no coherence to do with the range of dramatic activities which a learner should be encountering.

As discussed in various chapters, the orders decisively turn their back on the multimodal, digital, electronic world of information, communication and entertainment in which almost all children and young people now participate. Media education (see Chapter 6) has been expunged.

An alternative curriculum

This book is not the first critique of the new English orders. But it may be the first to propose, in detail, a different way of doing things. Chapter 9 is an entire alternative curriculum for English 11 to 16: more rigorous, in the proper sense of that word, than the government's effort, and much better balanced. Our alternative English curriculum derives its principles from the work of some of those who have, over many decades, thought most deeply and written most persuasively about how effective language development in English occurs, and whose work is reviewed in Chapters 1 to 6.

The non-National Curriculum

England is currently (2017) in the incongruous position of having a majority of state secondary schools and a growing minority of primary schools – those that are academies and free schools – which have been released from the obligation to follow the National Curriculum at all. Why go to all the trouble of designing a legally enforced National Curriculum and then abandon the principle of general entitlement? This is an incoherent and inequitable position. Either have legal enforcement for all – and the logic of this position, utopian as it may seem, would be to include independent schools within the scope of the legal enforcement – or achieve a broad national consensus on the knowledge, skills and understanding which children and young people are entitled to have gained in each curriculum subject at various stages of their schooling, without the need for legal enforcement.

By the purest of ironies, this was, for a brief moment, exactly the implication of the government's announcement in its March 2016 Budget statement, followed up in detail in a White Paper, that all state schools in England must, by law, become academies by 2022. The White Paper said:

> *We will embed a knowledge-based curriculum as the cornerstone of an excellent, academically rigorous education up to the age of 16, establishing the national curriculum as an ambitious benchmark which autonomous academies can use and improve upon.*
> (Department for Education, 2016a: paragraph 1.55a)

Two months later, the government changed its mind about requiring all schools to become academies, in the face of hostile opposition from the teaching profession (which it might well have ignored) and its own rebellious back-benchers and Conservative local councillors (whom it could not ignore). But it still sees universal 'academisation' as an 'aspiration'. In these circumstances, the invitation to 'use and improve upon' the National Curriculum is intriguing: Chapter 9 is a detailed proposal for the direction such improvement might take.

Assessment and examinations in English

Unfortunately, the eventual liberation being offered to all state schools in England with regard to the content of the curriculum is not being equivalently offered with regard to tests and examinations. As the government undoubtedly

understands, legally binding tests and examinations on which schools' effectiveness is judged will constrain teaching much more effectively than will
curricular requirements, particularly if those requirements are transmuted to a
'benchmark' to be 'used and improved upon'.

Even more unfortunately, there is a good deal wrong with the new arrangements for assessment and examinations in English 11 to 19. Coursework
has been abolished at GCSE and its weighting at A-level reduced, despite
clear evidence of the value of developing habits of independent study in
older students. At GCSE, students' achievement in the spoken language no
longer counts towards the main grade in English Language. AS-level has
been 'decoupled' from A-level, a decision bringing with it numerous practical
difficulties for teachers. The excellent and popular Creative Writing A-level
has been abolished.

Alternatives in assessment

Critiques of assessment and examinations 11 to 19 appear briefly in Chapters
1 to 6, and more extensively in Chapter 11. We propose alternatives in assessment at GCSE in Chapter 10.

As will be seen, we are not 'anti-exam'; we recognise that a government has
a right, indeed a responsibility, to know how well its schools are performing.
Our proposals, however, are based on the principle that assessment should
follow the curriculum, not lead it. Government and professionals should first
decide on a curriculum which embodies what we know about effective learning; then design assessment arrangements which discover, as delicately as
possible, the extent to which effective learning is taking place. Some of the
new arrangements for assessment and examinations at GCSE operate on
the reverse of this principle.

16 to 19

Although the National Curriculum and assessment and examinations at Key
Stages 3 and 4 receive the lion's share of attention in the book, in Chapter 11
Angela Goddard discusses in detail curriculum and assessment 16 to 19.
There is no single 'National Curriculum' at this phase, with its diversity of
courses leading to A-level and to other qualifications (although there are
Department for Education subject criteria that define both course content

and assessment for each qualification in English). It would be inappropriate to attempt to propose a single alternative curriculum as at 11 to 16. Because the curriculum is effectively the syllabus of whichever course a student is following at 16 to 19, and since each syllabus is expressed both in terms of content and of assessment arrangements, curriculum and assessment are dealt with in one place in this chapter. Chapter 11 contains comment on the content of several of the courses available to students, criticises aspects of recently introduced assessment arrangements, and makes practical suggestions for improvements, including in some cases returning to positions which the government has abandoned.

Learners of English as an additional language and speakers of non-standard varieties of English

Similar but not identical things may be said about each of the major elements of English as they apply to learners of English as an additional language and to speakers of non-standard varieties of English. To avoid repetition across the other chapters, the needs and achievements of EAL learners and of speakers of non-standard varieties of English have their own chapters – 7 and 8.

A desirable consensus

It should have been possible nearly 30 years ago, and it should be possible now, to achieve a consensus uniting professionals and the government on the question of how children and young people come to learn English most effectively. That, as we said in the first paragraph of this introduction, is the purpose of this book. Its authors share a passionate concern that our young people's schooling should equip them with a confident control of English – whether as first or additional language – and show them the pleasure that is to be had in its use. To have confidence, to exercise control and to take pleasure might be regarded as *the* essential characteristics of successful speakers, readers and writers of English or any language.

No one will disagree with these last remarks. It remains a matter of deep regret, however, and a disservice to our young people, that the professional opinions represented in this book are so often at variance with legislation on the curriculum and assessment in English in England. In the book, we express our criticisms of aspects of government policy in terms that are sometimes robust but we hope never destructive. Every negative criticism is accompanied by a positive suggestion for an alternative way of doing things. Whether, in the immediate term, our alternative suggestions have any effect on the policy of the government in England is a matter of doubt. But we hope that they will be seen as a constructive contribution to the debate in the medium and longer term and, for the present, as an encouragement and a support to those many practitioners – in England, in the United Kingdom as a whole and in the English-speaking world more widely – who share our passion and our concern.

1 Talk

John Richmond

Summary of main points

Speech, and attention to speech through listening, are fundamental to learning.

The spoken language is the mode of language from which competence in all the other modes springs. Literacy could not have come into being historically without the prior existence of speech; it cannot take root and flourish in the human competence of every potentially literate person without that prior existence.

The teacher has a crucial role in guiding learners' use of the spoken language and in setting contexts in which learners can practise and extend their competence in spoken language through acts of learning.

To be productive, group talk – in groups of whatever size – needs a clear structure and purpose, which it is the teacher's responsibility to provide. That structure and that purpose may be very simple: one open question and a time limit. Or it may be more complex, involving a series of tasks to be undertaken. Sometimes the teacher will be an active participant in learners' talk, sometimes not.

Group talk may well involve the other modes of language: reading and writing. But it should not become an automatic preliminary to writing. Talk should be regarded as work of equivalent status and seriousness to other kinds of work.

A key aspect of the teacher's skill is in setting tasks for learners which make demands at the edge of but not beyond the reach of students' existing state of knowledge or grasp of concepts. When that happens, the value of collaborative talk, in terms of insights gained and difficulties overcome, may most clearly be seen.

Student talk should, over time, embrace a range of purposes and take a range of forms, from the more exploratory through to the more presentational, from the more tentative to the more declaratory, from the more collaborative to the more individual.

Some 17 per cent of the UK school population now speak English as an additional language. These speakers range from new arrivals speaking no or very little English to advanced bi- or multilingual speakers who outperform their monolingual English peers. Support for these learners should take the form of an adapted version of the means by which teachers support the development of monolingual English speakers, not a different kind of pedagogy.

The teacher's approach to learners who have access to a variety or varieties of English other than Standard English must be based on respect for the language of the learner's culture and community. In the secondary school, it is also possible and quite legitimate for teachers to introduce students to the standard equivalents of non-standard forms they use in their everyday speech. This is best done in the context of the study of language variety itself.

The government's new legal requirements on the spoken language are over-preoccupied with formal and presentational uses of the spoken language in the secondary years. The alternative curriculum in Chapter 9 offers a better balance between the more individual and formal and the more collaborative and exploratory uses of the spoken language.

Voices from the past

Seven admirers on learning to talk

Linguists, psychologists and educationists compete with each other in expressions of wonderment at the intellectual achievement of almost all children in the first two or three years of life. Here is Roger Brown, the American social psychologist and expert in children's language development, writing in 1968:

> Most children, by the time they are ready to begin school, know the full contents of an introductory text in transformational grammar. One such text is a bit more than 400 pages long and it covers declaratives and interrogatives, affirmatives and negatives, actives and passives, simple sentences, conjoined sentences and some kinds of embedded sentences. The pre-school child knows all this. Not explicitly, of course. He has not formulated his grammatical knowledge and he cannot talk about it in transformational or any other terms. His knowledge is implicit, implicit in the range of sentences he understands and in the range he is able to construct.
>
> (Brown, 1968: v)

Here is Lev Vygotsky, the Russian psychologist, writing in the early 1930s (but published in English in 1962) and referring to the work of the German psychologist William Stern:

the most important discovery [made by previous investigators about the genetic roots of thought and speech] is that at a certain moment at about the age of two the curves of development of thought and speech, till then separate, meet and join to initiate a new form of behavior. Stern's [1914] account of this momentous event was the first and the best. He showed how the will to conquer language follows the first dim realization of the purpose of speech, when the child 'makes the greatest discovery of his life', that 'each thing has its name'. [We might add that, for the bi- or multilingual child, each thing has more than one name.]

This crucial instant, when speech begins to serve intellect, and thoughts begin to be spoken, is indicated by two unmistakable objective symptoms: (1) the child's sudden, active curiosity about words, his question about every new thing, 'What is this?' and (2) the resulting rapid . . . increases in his vocabulary.

(Vygotsky, 1962: 43)

Here is Korney Chukovsky, the Russian children's poet, in a work published in English in 1963:

To be sure, in order to learn language, the child imitates adults in his word creativity. It would be nonsense to claim that he adds to a language in any way. Without suspecting it himself, he directs all his efforts, by means of analogies, toward assimilating the linguistic riches gradually developed by many generations of adults. But the young child adapts these analogies with such skill, with such sensitivity to the meaning and significance of the elements from which words are formed, that it is impossible not to be enthralled by the power of his understanding, awareness, and memory, so apparent in the very arduous efforts he makes every time he speaks.

(Chukovsky, 1963, quoted in Rosen and Rosen, 1973: 55)

Here is Michael Halliday, the British-born linguist, in his famous 1975 study of his son's language development, *Learning How to Mean*:

It seems sensible to assume that neither the linguistic system itself, nor the learning of it by the child, can be adequately expressed except by reference to some higher level of semiotic organisation [by which Halliday means a system-based resource for meaning] . . . The child's task is to construct the system of meanings that represents his own model of social reality. This pro-cess takes place inside his own head; it is a cognitive process. But it takes place in contexts of social interaction, and there is no way it can take place except in these contexts. As well as being a cognitive process, the learning of the mother tongue is also an interactive process. It takes the form of the continued exchange of meanings between self and others. The act of mean-ing is a social act.

(Halliday, 1975: 139–140)

And here is James Britton, the British educationist, writing in 1970:

It is, everyone agrees, a colossal task that the child accomplishes when he learns to speak, and the fact that he does so in so short a period of time chal-lenges explanation. We can imagine ourselves cast up on a remote island and living with people whose language we did not know, whose alphabet we could not read: in the course of time, in the course of a great deal of activity where action and speech have gone together, we might succeed in resolving the stream of spoken sound into segments with meaning – given of course that we have infinite curiosity and patience and that the people around us have infinite patience and goodwill! But the endless streams of undifferenti-ated sound represent only one of two problems that face an infant learning his mother tongue. There is for him also the endless stream of undifferen-tiated experience. This is something we can imagine only imperfectly, for once in any language we have organized experience to form an objectified world we can never reverse the process.

(Britton, 1970: 36–37)

It was Andrew Wilkinson who coined the term 'oracy', and proposed in 1965 that oracy is to speaking and listening what literacy is to writing and reading. Wilkinson extended his definition as follows:

Oracy comes from practice in specific situations, whether these occur nat-urally in the classroom, or elsewhere, or are created as a specific teach-ing device. It is helped by unconscious invitation, it is stimulated by the response of others, and speech becomes clear in the necessity of commu-nication. The main job of the teacher is to provide situations which call forth increasing powers of utterance [and, we might add, of comprehension].

(Wilkinson with Davies and Atkinson, 1965: 63)

Our final admirer is one who qualifies her admiration with a warning: it is that we should not be so overwhelmed by this admiration for the preschool child's achievement in learning spoken language that we assume that the job is done by the time the child comes to school. The job is very far from done. Katharine Perera, in *Children's Writing and Reading: Analysing Classroom Language* (1984), which despite its title has plenty to say about spoken language too, has a chapter on the acquisition of grammar. This shows, with detailed examples, that development towards mastery of more complex grammatical structures continues throughout the school years. Perera concludes the chapter thus:

> *During the Seventies, it was commonplace for books on language acquisition to suggest that, apart from vocabulary, children had virtually completed the learning of their mother tongue by the age of five; for example, Slobin (1971: 40) wrote: 'a little child . . . masters the exceedingly complex structure of his native language in the course of a short three or four years' . . .*
>
> *although children have acquired a remarkable amount of language by the time they start school, the developmental process continues, albeit at a slower rate, until they are in their teens.* [For the speaker of English as an additional language, we might add, the developmental process may begin at any time during schooling.]
>
> *There are many grammatical constructions that are more likely to occur after five than before – some, indeed, that are not at all frequent until adolescence.*
>
> (Perera, 1984: 156)

Five points of agreement

Whatever detailed differences there may be between the many thinkers who have studied early language development, there is agreement on at least these five points:

1 'Language' and 'thought' are not two words to describe the same thing, either in a new-born baby's head or at all. However, a moment (or perhaps a series of moments, or perhaps a period) arrives when the two become linked and interpenetrating in the child's conscious and unconscious mental activities. This linkage is immensely significant, and an essential gateway to future learning.

2 The learning of spoken language is not merely a continuing act of imitation. Imitation is there, to be sure, but far more powerful is the continuing generalising act which young children perform, whereby they infer patterns, tendencies and rules from the raw material of the language they hear, and apply those inferences to the making of utterances whose collections of words, arranged in certain orders and in some cases varying their form according to context, they have never heard before.

3 The learning of spoken language is essentially social and dialogic. Language awareness and competence grow as a result of a constant process of language exchange and interaction with others.

4 Full meaning precedes full linguistic expression of meaning. When a child says 'Milk!', the adult can interpret that single word as 'I would like some milk', or 'Please give me some milk'. But to the child, the whole meaning (which the adult needs several words to express) is held within one word. As development proceeds, single-word and very short utterances give way to grammatically more complex utterances. At the same time, the child learns the subtleties of phonology, of sound: for example, the differences of intonation between a statement and a question, between mild request and emphatic insistence. For an adult to shout 'Milk!' when he or she wishes someone to pass the milk jug would be regarded as offensive. The child learns that there are various patterns of sound in which to express the wish to get hold of some milk.

5 The sheer scale and complexity of what the preschool and school-age child (whether mono-, bi- or multilingual) learns is testament to the astonishing powers of the learning brain operating in normal and generally happy circumstances.

The Bullock Report on talking to learn

The Bullock Committee was not set up in the early 1970s to say anything about talk. It was brought into existence because two educational psychologists had claimed, on the basis of some tests they had done, that children's reading standards were falling. The claims came to the attention of the government, which did what governments tend to do when they are unsure of what else to do: it appointed a committee to look into the matter.

The committee chose not to confine itself to answering the question which it had been set up to answer. It went on to offer a description of the state of language, literacy and English teaching in schools in England and to make recommendations. The Bullock Report, *A Language for Life* (The Bullock Committee, 1975), had a good deal to say about talk. It discusses in some detail the challenges facing the teacher as he or she attempts to communicate information or concepts to a class of students:

> *By its very nature a lesson is a verbal encounter through which the teacher draws information from the class, elaborates and generalises it, and produces a synthesis. His skill is in selecting, prompting, improvising, and generally orchestrating the exchange. But in practice the course of any dialogue in which one person is managing 30 is only partly predictable . . . It has also become clear what difficulties face the teacher if he is to encourage genuine exploration and learning on the part of his pupils, and not simply the game of guessing what he has in mind. What the teacher has in mind may well be the desirable destination of a thinking process; but a learner needs to trace the steps from the familiar to the new, from the fact or idea he possesses to that which he is to acquire. In other words, the learner has to make a journey in thought for himself. The kind of class lesson we have been describing has therefore to be supported by others in which the pupils' own exploratory talk has much more scope.*
>
> (*ibid*.: paragraph 10.2)

That is the heart of it: not in any sense to take away from the teacher's central role, but to see 'pupils' own exploratory talk' as a bridge by which their new knowledge or grasp of a new concept can be securely connected to knowledge or conceptual understandings they already have.

We could extend the bridge metaphor by referring to a bridge that does not extend. Talk is not *le pont d'Avignon*, which stops in the middle of the Rhône. Teachers do not leave students there, peering into the water. Using student talk as an aid, they enable students to cross the bridge, to make a link between where they were and where the demands of the school want them to be. But if there is no bridge at all, students are just gazing at a distant territory with which they have no connection.

The report's list of conclusions and recommendations includes the following:

Children learn as certainly by talking and writing as by listening and reading.

(*ibid.*: 37)

Exploratory talk by the pupils has an important function in the process of learning.

(*ibid.*: 108)

A child's accent should be accepted and attempts should not be made to suppress it. The aim should be to provide him with awareness and flexibility.

(*ibid.*: 109)

Children should be helped to as wide as possible a range of language uses so that they can speak appropriately in different situations and use standard forms when they are needed.

(*ibid.*: 110)

A stimulating classroom environment will not necessarily of itself develop the children's ability to use language as an instrument for learning. The teacher has a vital part to play and his role should be one of planned intervention.

(*ibid.*: 112)

Oral work should take place in both large and small group situations, with an emphasis on the latter.

(*ibid.*: 113)

As part of their professional knowledge teachers should have:

- *an explicit understanding of the processes at work in classroom discourse;*
- *the ability to appraise their pupils' spoken language and to plan the means of extending it.*

(*ibid.*: 118)

To put the bridge metaphor in other terms, if there is no relation between school knowledge and the learner's experience, there is an alienation between the learner and the school. The young person becomes a 'reluctant learner', with only a grudging sense that what the school has to offer her or him is of any interest or value. In some cases, he or she develops an actual antagonism to the school's mission and tries to disrupt it.

Without wishing to deny the authority of the teacher, and while recognising that teachers in many cases do know 'the right answer', or at least 'a right answer', the Bullock Report argues that much contemporary classroom practice was denying learners the opportunity to develop a vital human and intellectual competence: that of the genuine enquirer. It concludes that properly managed pupil talk is one way in which young people can *be* genuine enquirers.

The potential of collaborative talk and of good teaching

'What children can do with the assistance of others'

One of the clearest accounts of the value of collaboration in learning is Lev Vygotsky's 'Interaction between Learning and Development', written in the early 1930s and published in English in 1978. Vygotsky understands a child's mental capacity in terms of its potential rather than its actual achievement. He is writing at a time when the testing of individual children and the assignment to them of a 'mental age' was commonplace, especially in the realm of educational psychology and research. But, he says, this is an inadequate, a static way of describing what a child can do:

> We give children a battery of tests or a variety of tasks of varying degrees of difficulty, and we judge the extent of their mental development on the basis of how they solve them and at what degree of difficulty. On the other hand, if we offer leading questions or show how the problem is to be solved and the child then solves it, or if the teacher initiates the solution and the child completes it or solves it in collaboration with other children – in short, if the child barely misses an independent solution of the problem – the solution is not regarded as indicative of his mental development. This 'truth' was familiar and reinforced by common sense. Over a decade even the profoundest thinkers never questioned the assumption; they never entertained the notion *that* what children can do with the assistance of others might in some sense be more indicative of their mental development than what they can do alone.
> (Vygotsky, 1978a: 85, my emphasis)

The zone of potential development

Vygotsky proposes that what children are capable of at any point in their development, but have not yet achieved, be called the 'zone of proximal [or potential] development'.[1]

Good teaching and the use of collaborative learning are both ways in which learners' incomplete grasp of an idea or a concept or a piece of knowledge may be helped towards completion, in which the zone of potential development may be explored. The zone is:

> the distance between the actual developmental level as determined by independent problem solving and the level of potential development as determined through problem solving under adult guidance or in collaboration with more capable peers.
>
> (*ibid*.: 86, original emphasis)

These insights of Vygotsky's have been quoted many times by writers on talk; and rightly so. It should not be forgotten, however, that Vygotsky attaches equal importance to the role of the teacher in helping learners to push at the boundaries of their potential understanding and competence.

A model of the process of learning through talk

Having harvested a little of the wisdom of the past, we could summarise it in terms of a working theory of the role of talk in learning.

The materials for learning

We start with the raw material – the learner. He or she has a certain quantity and kind of pre-existent knowledge and experience, a certain degree of linguistic power, and a certain set of social habits and attitudes which will influence the working relationship with the other learners with whom he or she will be asked to collaborate. To her or his pre-existent knowledge and experience, the teacher brings new material in the form of external knowledge, provided either directly by the teacher or indirectly through resources (for example, books, films, the internet) which he or she makes available to the learner, or shows the learner how to access.

The task

We then move to the task. The skill of the teacher, to return to the slightly extended quotation from Andrew Wilkinson included earlier, is 'to provide situations which call forth increasing powers of utterance [and of comprehension]'. The teacher does this by setting tasks which operate, in Vygotsky's terms, in the learners' zone of potential development. There will always be a degree of approximation in the judgement as to where this zone is, because it will not be exactly the same even for the participants in a discussion involving two people, let alone in a discussion involving the whole class. But judge the teacher must, and the more skilful and experienced he or she is, the likelier it is that the task will be pitched at a level which makes challenging demands on the learners, while maintaining the probability that, through collaboration and mutual support, they will achieve at least a considerable measure of success in finding the answer, solving the problem, discussing the issue, understanding the poem, making the argument: whatever is the nature of the task set.

The outcome

Finally, there is the outcome. The argument on which this chapter's case rests is that, as long as the learners are equipped with or have available adequate sources of knowledge and/or experience to bring to the task (an essential proviso), there is something in the acts of dialogue that occur in the course of doing the oral task that enhances, deepens and earths the new knowledge, skill or understanding that the teacher wishes the learners to acquire, and which reinforces existing but uncertain knowledge, skill or understanding.

Analysis of the outcome

Teachers don't have the time or the need to analyse the outcome of every oral task they set in any detail; but occasionally such analysis could bring a clearer sense of learners' progress in speaking and listening. If we ask of a particular oral task 'What has been gained?', we might be asking what has been gained cognitively, linguistically or socially, or in all of these respects.

Cognitively: what is being learned in the course of the talk, by whom, how does that learning come about, and can we see examples of learning which probably needed to happen in this specific context if they were to happen at all?

Linguistically: what types and degrees of facility with language do the talkers display, and is their facility affected by the topic or the mood of the discussion, or by the role or stance they adopt in it? Is there development or change in any of these areas during the course of the talk?

Socially: who dominates, who follows, who is anxious for consensus, who likes to strike postures of disagreement, how ready – if at all – are individuals to modify or abandon previous positions? Is there development or change in any of these areas during the course of the talk?

Recording development

These questions could be discussed while studying a tape and/or transcript of one particular oral activity. That kind of study is a cut across time. It is equally important to have some means of recording what progress is being made in learners' oral competence *through* time. The categories we might use in such a developing record don't have to be complex. For example, they could be framed in questions as simple as:

- *What are the natural qualities of this talker/listener as seen in class?*
- *How constructive is the part he or she takes in whole-class or large-group activities (for example involving exploration, exposition, argument, presentation, role-play, performance, debate)?*
- *How constructive is the part he or she takes in small-group or paired activities (for example involving exploration, research, examination of evidence, argument, response to and discussion of reading, preparation for writing)?*
- *In a supportive context, can he or she present, maintain, support, develop or modify ideas (and respond to others in doing so)?*
- *How much progress in terms of eloquence, coherence, span of attention, quality of attention, self-discipline in small-group and whole-class work has he or she shown since the last progress report on the student's oral work?*

(Adapted from 'Record-keeping: One model', in Richmond, 2012c: 92)

(These questions draw on part of a record-keeping system which was devised by the English department at Aylwin School in the London Borough of Southwark, whose work is acknowledged with thanks.)

We could express the attempt to describe the process of learning through talk more briefly in the form of a model (Figure 1.1).

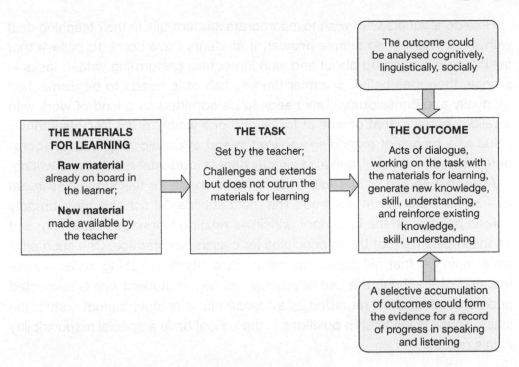

Figure 1.1 The process of learning through talk.

A note of warning

While enthusiastically acknowledging the role of talk in learning, I simultaneously acknowledge the practical difficulties which can confront teachers in
introducing student talk in the classroom.

These difficulties may lie in the discouraging attitudes to talk which some
teachers communicate to their students. Let us not be dewy-eyed. There are a
few teachers in the profession, with plenty of years of service behind them, for
whom the continuing and overriding priority in classroom management is that
they should retain a monopoly of control over every event in the room. In these
classrooms, there is a failure to discriminate between disruptive chatter which
slows or halts learning, and constructive talk which advances it. Here, classroom culture and routines have never been established in such a way that
learners recognise talk as a valid form of work. The desire to keep a monopoly
of control may come from a teacher's fear of what might happen if even a little
autonomy in learning were granted to students; or the ease with which a lazy
pedagogic habit can be repeated lesson after lesson, year after year.

How do teachers who wish to incorporate student talk in their teaching deal with this? There is no simple answer. If students have come to believe that talking equals messing about and working equals performing written tasks in silence, then their belief, or rather the first half of it, needs to be dismantled gradually and consciously. Talk needs to be admitted as a kind of work with a validity equal to that of written tasks, and one which, apart from its intrinsic value as a means of extending knowledge and of developing language competence and social skill, can also directly benefit students' reading and writing.

A teacher should not be expected to make space for talk in the classroom as a solitary pioneer in a school. The most successful schools have broadly agreed policies on the important principles relating language to learning, and on the implications of those principles for classroom practice. One such principle must be that, whatever the actual diversity of teaching styles across the staff of a school, the use of properly managed student talk is respected and admired, and not regarded as evidence that a teacher cannot control the class. Those in leadership positions in the school have a special responsibility in this respect.

The present situation in England

Then and now

The programme of study for talk in the original National Curriculum for English (Department of Education and Science and the Welsh Office, 1990) was entitled 'Speaking and Listening', and there was much debate at the time about the different connotations of the words 'speak' and 'talk'. Some supporters of talk felt that 'speaking' implied too formal, too presentational an understanding of the spoken language. It does tend in that direction; and this was a tendency the government of the day approved of. However, the title of a programme of study matters less than its contents; and the contents did allow for a diversity of kinds of talk. There was a continuum in the original programmes of study from the more tentative, exploratory and collaborative kinds of talk to the more finished, assertive and individualistic: from discussions to debates, from conversations to oral presentations.

In the years since 1990, many teachers have maintained their belief in the value of talk in learning, and have developed their practical skill in its implementation, through all the revisions and re-revisions that the National Curriculum has seen.

We zoom through time and come to the present day, to look at the new curriculum orders for speaking and listening in English at Key Stages 3 and 4, statutory as from September 2014 or September 2015, and the subject content for spoken language at GCSE English Language, statutory as from September 2015.

Key Stage 3

In comparing the statutory requirements on spoken language at Key Stage 3 which were statutory until August 2014 with those which have been statutory since September of that year or a year later, we can see a clear attempt to sideline exploratory, collaborative talk for learning and to replace it with talk seen almost entirely as formal performance. Here are the previous Key Stage 3 orders (Qualifications and Curriculum Authority, 2007):

Key processes

Pupils should be able to:

(a) *present information and points of view clearly and appropriately in different contexts, adapting talk for a range of purposes and audiences, including the more formal;*

(b) *use a range of ways to structure and organise their speech to support their purposes and guide the listener;*

(c) *vary vocabulary, structures and grammar to convey meaning, including speaking standard English fluently;*

(d) *engage an audience, using a range of techniques to explore, enrich and explain their ideas;*

(e) *listen and respond constructively to others, taking different views into account and modifying their own views in the light of what others say;*

(f) *understand explicit and implicit meanings;*

(g) *make different kinds of relevant contributions in groups, responding appropriately to others, proposing ideas and asking questions;*

(h) *take different roles in organising, planning and sustaining talk in groups;*

(i) *sift, summarise and use the most important points;*

(j) *use different dramatic approaches to explore ideas, texts and issues;*

(k) *use different dramatic techniques to convey action, character, atmosphere and tension;*

(l) *explore the ways that words, actions, sound and staging combine to create dramatic moments.*

Range and content

The range of speaking and listening activities should include:

(a) *prepared, formal presentations and debates;*
(b) *informal group or pair discussions;*
(c) *individual and group improvisation and performance;*
(d) *devising, scripting and performing plays.*

The range of purposes for speaking and listening should include:

(e) *describing, instructing, narrating, explaining, justifying, persuading, enter-taining, hypothesising; and exploring, shaping and expressing ideas, feelings and opinions.*

This is a perfectly acceptable set of demands. There is no reason why very good teaching could not take place within these constraints. In particular, the list of purposes for speaking and listening is excellent. No attempt at categorisation is ever going to be perfect, but teachers could do a lot worse than take that list, personalise it and keep it in mind as a repertoire of purposes for talk which students should encounter as a term and a year goes by.

By contrast, here are the new orders for spoken English at Key Stage 3 (Department for Education, 2014a):

Pupils should be taught to:

– *speak confidently and effectively, including through:*

• *using Standard English confidently in a range of formal and informal contexts, including classroom discussion;*
• *giving short speeches and presentations, expressing their own ideas and keeping to the point;*
• *participating in formal debates and structured discussions, summarising and/or building on what has been said;*
• *improvising, rehearsing and performing play scripts and poetry in order to generate language and discuss language use and meaning, using role, intonation, tone, volume, mood, silence, stillness and action to add impact.*

(ibid.: 85)

There you have it: admittedly there is one reference to 'informal contexts, including classroom discussion', but, apart from that, the use of the spoken language at Key Stage 3, so far as the government is concerned, should be dominated by formality and performance.

The more formal, more performance-based uses of the spoken language – debates, talks, speeches, presented or dramatic readings of poetry – should certainly be part of the spoken language curriculum. But it is perfectly clear that the government's vision of the use of the spoken language in state schools, at least at Key Stage 3, is that of a junior version of the Oxford Union. There is no sense here of the range of kinds of talk, from the most exploratory, collaborative and tentative through to the most finished, individualistic and assertive, that teachers should admit in their classrooms.

Key Stage 4 and GCSE

It might be expected that the new orders for the spoken language at Key Stage 4 would push teachers and students even more firmly in the direction of formality and performance. Surprisingly, there is a sort of about-turn, or at least half-turn, back towards a better balance.

Spoken English

Pupils should be taught to:

– speak confidently, audibly and effectively, including through:

- *using Standard English when the context and audience require it;*
- *working effectively in groups of different sizes and taking on required roles, including leading and managing discussions, involving others productively, reviewing and summarising, and contributing to meeting goals/deadlines;*
- *listening to and building on the contributions of others, asking questions to clarify and inform, and challenging courteously when necessary;*
- *planning for different purposes and audiences, including selecting and organising information and ideas effectively and persuasively for formal spoken presentations and debates;*
- *listening and responding in a variety of different contexts, both formal and informal, and evaluating content, viewpoints, evidence and aspects of presentation;*

- *improvising, rehearsing and performing play scripts and poetry in order to generate language and discuss language use and meaning, using role, intonation, tone, volume, mood, silence, stillness and action to add impact.*

(ibid.: 88)

Unlike the Key Stage 3 orders, this list does not actively prevent teachers from teaching well. It demonstrates, however, a lack of coherence in government policy on the teaching of spoken language as between Key Stage 3 and Key Stage 4.

Unfortunately, the statutory subject content for GCSE English Language (Department for Education, 2013a), for syllabuses taught from September 2015, is completely at variance with the Key Stage 4 orders and is only concerned with formal presentations:

presenting information and ideas: selecting and organising information and ideas effectively and persuasively for prepared spoken presentations; planning effectively for different purposes and audiences; making presentations and speeches;

responding to spoken language: listening to and responding appropriately to any questions and feedback;

spoken Standard English: expressing ideas using Standard English whenever and wherever appropriate.

(ibid.: 5)

This variance is either unintended – the result of a failure of coordination between those drafting different documents – or it is an exercise in saying something moderately enlightened about the Key Stage 4 curriculum, while knowing that most teachers are obliged to focus on the GCSE requirements and will therefore be under pressure to neglect the more exploratory and collaborative aspects of talk. Whatever the truth of the matter, many teachers at Key Stage 4 will feel obliged to yield to that pressure.

On top of this, the government's true estimation of the value of the spoken language is to be seen in the fact that, as from summer 2014, GCSE candidates' performance in the spoken language has no longer contributed to their final grade in the examination.

An alternative

In Chapter 9, readers will find an alternative curriculum for the spoken language 11 to 16, offering a better balance between more presentational, individual and more exploratory, collaborative uses of talk at Key Stages 3 and 4. In Chapter 10, they will find a proposal to restore to the spoken language the recognition it should receive at GCSE.

To conclude . . .

Schools and teachers should see the development of learners' confidence and capability in the use of the spoken language as one of their principal responsibilities.

To allow any measure of autonomy to learners in their use of talk means that a teacher must thereby relinquish complete, detailed control of classroom interactions. This relinquishing brings risk. The way to ensure that risk brings rewards is to structure the talk so that learners are operating within constraints (for example of time, or of purpose, or of format for their talk) which they can handle.

There are no set rules for what the constraints on learners' talk should be, but there is one developmental principle: the better established are the classroom culture and routines allowing for talk, and the more familiar are students with the idea that talk is a kind of work with equal validity to other kinds of work, the likelier it is that the constraints can be light, the task more open-ended, without discipline breaking down and the talk degenerating into aimless or destructive chatter.

All forms of, contexts for and groupings for talk have equal potential worth. Forms may range from exploratory discussion to oral performance. Contexts may range from conducting a piece of factual research (where there *are* right answers) to debating a moral issue (where there may not be). Groupings may range from pairs to the whole class.

Development in effectiveness as a speaker and sensitivity and responsiveness as a listener come when the teacher offers learners appropriately engaging and challenging oral tasks.

Despite the widespread agreement on the value of talk for learning which this chapter has summarised, and despite the wonderful work involving the spoken language which many teachers are doing, the achievement of a state of affairs where, in all schools in England, talk is seen as a normal part of the work of an effective and well-disciplined classroom is still some way off. In several respects, recent government legislation will impede progress in the direction which all serious authorities on language and learning would support.

Note

1 Robin Alexander, in his pamphlet *Towards Dialogic Teaching*, quotes Joan Simon (1987), 'a pioneering translator of the work of Vygotsky', who writes that '"Zone of potential [or next] development" is a more appropriate translation from the Russian than the more usual "proximal"' (Alexander, 2005: 11).

2 Reading 11 to 16

Peter Traves

Summary of main points

The ability to read well is vital in our society. It brings with it huge benefits in terms of pleasure, personal enrichment, practical value and power.

The demands on and expectations of readers are increasing. These need to be reflected in the absolute priority given to reading as part of the curriculum 11 to 16 and in the resources allocated to support it.

The teaching of reading requires an understanding of the different purposes for which we read, the complexity of the task of reading and the range of reading skills needed to support learning. The varied purposes and types of text, and the different means through which text is now carried, call for different skills on the part of the reader. These skills should be taught systematically, but not mechanically.

Effective reading is needed for success in all subjects and should be encouraged, taught and reinforced across the curriculum. This calls for a coherent whole-school approach to literacy. One feature of this approach is that productive use of the school library is at the heart of the school's life. Another is that teachers and other adults in school show students that they read too.

Reading is inextricably linked to the other modes of language: writing, speaking and listening. These links should be recognised in students' experiences of reading across the curriculum.

Pleasure in reading is the key. Research confirms a direct link between the commitment to reading for pleasure and wider educational success.

The interests and experiences learners bring to the classroom are one starting point for the encouragement of reading. But teachers have a responsibility to make sure that young people become ambitious readers, able to take on a wider range of texts outside their own immediate experience and at increasing levels of complexity and demand.

Reading for information is a basic tool across the curriculum and in life. Students need frequent, wide and deliberate experience of it and the demonstration, instruction and encouragement to take on ever more challenging tasks and material.

Students should be shown how literature and other texts achieve their effects. They also need opportunities to explore how their own perspectives, values and assumptions compare with those in the texts they encounter.

All learners can experience the pleasure and satisfaction that reading can bring. Those who initially fail to gain the benefits or those whose interest in reading has faded need particular help, tailored to their different histories and characteristics. Underachievement in and underuse of reading by boys are by no means inevitable.

All these principles apply with equal force to learners of English as an additional language (about one in six students in the age group with which this book is concerned). However, students who have begun to read and write in another language and are learning to write in English are additionally engaged in the complex process of making comparisons between writing systems. Appropriate books in the first language and in bilingual editions can help the comparison of the writing systems of English and the other language(s), in addition to the other benefits they bring. More advanced bilingual learners can derive especial benefit from paying attention to the structures and styles of the more academic forms of writing with which their previous reading in English has not made them familiar.

The coverage of reading for students aged 11 to 16 in the current National Curriculum for England is uneven. The alternative offered in Chapter 9 of this book is based on the consistent development of attitudes and skills across the curriculum and across the age range.

Reading – at large and in school

The ability to read and understand instructions and text is a basic require-ment of success in all school subjects. The importance of literacy skills does not, however, come to an end when children leave school. Such skills are key to all areas of education and beyond, facilitating participation in the wider context of lifelong learning and contributing to individuals' social integration and personal development.

(European Commission, 2001,
quoted in Kirsch *et al.*, *Reading for Change: Performance and Engagement Across Countries – Results from PISA 2000*, 2002: 15)

The most important job

If we are to achieve a coherent and systematic approach to the teaching of reading from 11 to 16, we should begin with an attempt to say what it is we are aiming for. We need to establish what we expect readers to be able to do in the world we live in now.

Our society assumes literacy and, as a result, greatly disadvantages those who lack reading skills. The fact that some people succeed despite low levels of literacy is a tribute to their resourcefulness and resilience, but such success stories are the exception rather than the rule. Those with low levels of competence as readers are more likely to be unemployed or insecurely employed and less likely to have good housing and health. Poor reading skills are not the only factors that contribute to these disadvantages, but the link is clear.

What reading is good for

Creating capable and keen readers is the most important job that schools can do. Here is one way of describing the high-value benefits that skilled independent reading can bring:

1 **Pleasure**: the pleasure of reading easy and entertaining material effortlessly, as well as the more strenuous pleasure which comes from understanding difficult material.
2 **Personal enrichment**: as a source of experience and of knowledge, reading extends your horizons, broadens your vision, enlarges your perspective.
3 **Practical value**: being able to put reading to use maximises your chances of benefiting from schooling and enables you to find out things from print, now and in the future.
4 **Power**: reading means access and enables you to find out things about your history and the society you live in which it's harder to discover in other ways; you can also discover things about other histories and societies which may surprise you.

(Raleigh, 'Independent Reading',
in *The English Magazine 10*, 1982; reprinted in *Where We've Been: Articles from The English & Media Magazine*, Simons [ed.], 1996: 118)

The vehicles of text

There is certainly no less demand for reading than in the past. There is probably more, as a 2006 survey of research for the National Literacy Trust remarked:

> *Adolescents entering the adult world in the 21st century will read and write more than at any other time in human history. They will need advanced levels of literacy to perform their jobs, run their households, act as citizens, and conduct their personal lives.*
>
> (*Reading for Pleasure:*
> *A Research Overview*, Clark and Rumbold, 2006: 5)

The vehicles by which text is carried have never been so varied, ubiquitous and powerful.

The digital revolution has sometimes been assumed to be reducing the extent and range of reading and to make reading more a matter of dealing with short and limited snippets of text. In practice, this does not seem to be the case. Instead, the digital carriage of text appears to have stepped up the volume and widened the range of the reading that is done for social, cultural and work purposes. It has increased the availability of previously rare material, factual and otherwise, giving us much easier access to, for example, historical records, old and new literature, and specialist information. It has transformed research as well as communication. It has also affected styles of reading, putting ever more of a premium on processes such as scanning and skimming, finding routes through sets of material, interpreting graphics, understanding and sometimes challenging the reliability of sources. Because so much more material is available to read than before, the skills of locating, digesting and evaluating information and ideas are in greater demand than ever.

What all good readers can do

The following list is an attempt to describe what all good readers – of any age – can do. It draws on a helpful set of materials produced by the English and Media Centre (*Spotlight on Literacy: Creative Interventions in English and*

Across the Curriculum, Bleiman *et al.*, 2013: 209) and on guidance from the School Library Association (*SLA Guidelines: Creating Readers: A Reflective Guide for School Librarians and Teachers*, Goodwin, 2013: 10).

Good readers:

- show versatility, reading different kinds of material in different ways (and sometimes the same material in different ways);
- develop and refine their own preferences for what to read while being open to new possibilities;
- find ways to cope with unfamiliar and challenging material;
- identify and follow the plot of a piece of writing (whether fiction or otherwise), inferring what is happening and speculating about where it may go next;
- interpret ideas, themes and patterns and form questions and comments as they go along;
- skim, scan, select and record in order to locate and log what they are after;
- appreciate multiple meanings, ambiguities and other twists and turns of language;
- connect what they read to their prior knowledge and experience;
- cross-refer, combine and compare information from a variety of sources, as well as connecting what they read with their prior knowledge and experience;
- make and articulate considered judgements about texts and how they are written;
- reflect on the ways in which they go about their reading.

Any or all of the abilities listed above can be applied to virtually any kind of text, whether literary or otherwise, long or short, highly imaginative or deeply routine. Neither is there any hierarchy of importance as between these abilities. Development in reading is not a matter of lockstep progress up through any such hierarchy. Apprentice readers have both the potential and the need to behave like more mature readers, and so can and should use the full range of abilities from the outset.

One last point about what many good readers do: they communicate and collaborate with others. Reading is not necessarily a solitary activity, though the satisfaction of 'getting lost in a book' is well understood. Discussion of reading with others is also a way of making reading come alive.

What teachers of reading can do

Teachers and librarians are key to developing students' enthusiasm for reading and for making reading prominent and talked about in the school. There is evidence that too many teachers have limited knowledge of literature for young people, factual and imaginative. It has often been inadequately covered in their training, and they are not able confidently to recommend books and authors.

One source of such evidence is the United Kingdom Literacy Association Teachers as Readers: Building Communities of Readers project, conducted in 2007 and 2008. The core goal of the project was to 'improve teachers' knowledge and use of literature in order to help them increase children's motivation and enthusiasm for reading, especially those less successful in literacy' (Cremin *et al.*, 2008). It did this by working with 40 teachers in five local authorities in England.

Here are the project's central findings:

As teachers in the project enriched their subject knowledge of children's literature and other texts, they took risks in their choices and responded more aesthetically. Many transformed their conceptions of reading and readers and recognised their professional responsibility to sustain their enhanced subject knowledge. Personally and professionally, the teachers took considerably more pleasure in reading.

The teachers' increased subject knowledge, combined with personal reflection and support, enabled them to create a more inclusive reading for pleasure pedagogy. This encompassed marked improvements in reading environments, read aloud programmes, book talk and book recommendations and the provision of quality time for independent reading. As teachers became more confident, autonomous and flexible in using their enriched subject knowledge, they began to articulate an informed and strategic rationale for selecting and using texts to support children's reading for pleasure.

Teachers came to appreciate the significance of the wider range of reading which children experience in their homes and communities. They recognised the importance of extending definitions of reading and providing a more satisfying and challenging reading curriculum.

Some teachers developed as 'Reading Teachers' and became increasingly aware of their [own] reading preferences, habits, behaviours and strategies and explored connections between their own reading practices and those of the children. As a result, these professionals sought to build reciprocal reading communities, which focused on readers' rights and identities and fostered learner autonomy. As potent role models, they markedly influenced the children's commitment to reading.

Shared understandings were established between teachers, children and families about the changing nature of reading and everyday reading practices. These supported children reading for pleasure and generated new kinds of talk about reading, both with and amongst children. Where relationships with local libraries were fostered, there was evidence of significant impact on individual children's lives.

(*ibid.*)

In brief, teachers of reading should be familiar with and enthusiastic about the range of factual and imaginative literature available to the learners for whom they are responsible. Equally important is the continuing development of teachers' own experience of reading, at their level. The project's definition of 'Reading Teachers' is 'teachers who read and readers who teach'. When teachers are enthusiastic and wide-ranging readers themselves, they are better teachers of reading.

No end to it . . .

The message of this section is that achievement in reading does not end with the acquisition of fluency in decoding words; neither does it come about simply from exposure to more text. Reading needs deliberate and continual development if our young readers are to match and surpass the demands made on them, now and in the future.

PISA (the Programme for International Student Assessment) makes regular international comparisons of educational performance. The section began with a quotation from the 2000 PISA Report on reading. It ends with another:

Literacy is no longer considered an ability only acquired in childhood during the early years of schooling. Instead, it is viewed as an expanding set of knowledge, skills and strategies which individuals build on throughout life in various situations and through interaction with their peers and with the larger communities in which they participate.

(Kirsch *et al.*, 2002: 24)

One snapshot from the past

The Bullock Report

Chapter 1 records the circumstances in which the Bullock Committee was set up more than 40 years ago. We are frequently in a state of crisis about reading standards. The Bullock Report was only one of a series of reports commissioned over the past century in response to a perceived decline in standards of reading. On each occasion, government and the media have expected confirmation of the alleged decline, followed by simple recommendations that would solve the problem. On most occasions, the reporting group has come up with a more nuanced response to the question it had been asked.

A Language for Life, published in 1975, went far beyond its original, narrow brief, to examine the contemporary state of literacy teaching and to describe the kinds of teaching which would provide learners with the abilities in language and literacy that would sustain them for life.

> *We have also suggested that a wider and more demanding definition of literacy should be adopted. The existing criterion is determined by the reading standards of seven and nine year old children of many years ago on tests whose limitations are acknowledged. It should be replaced by a criterion capable of showing whether the reading and writing abilities of children are adequate to the demands made upon them in school and likely to face them in adult life.*
>
> (The Bullock Committee, 1975: paragraph 3.3)

The report recommended that the teaching of reading should be based on an analysis of the demands made on the mature reader. It argued for a coherent approach encompassing the full range of reading abilities. Crucially, it did not believe that learners should be introduced to the wider range of abilities only when they had mastered the basic skills of decoding. Rather, it advocated a reading curriculum in which the broad range of abilities is introduced from the start and is built on at increasing levels of sophistication as the learner develops.

The report offered an elegant definition, still relevant today, of the demands on a student's literacy:

> *What are these demands? This question is best answered in terms of three basic objectives, simple enough on paper but far from simple in the execution:*

(i) the pupil needs to be able to cope with the reading required in each area
of the curriculum

(ii) he should acquire a level of competence which will enable him to meet
his needs as an adult in society when he leaves school

(iii) he should regard reading as a source of pleasure and personal development which will continue to be a rewarding activity throughout life.

(*ibid*.: paragraph 8.2)

Implications for teaching

The report went on to explore the implications of these demands for the teaching of reading. For example:

*The first of the three objectives is rarely recognised in schools as something
that calls for explicit instruction. Specialist teachers generally believe that
pupils need only to be fluent readers to cope with the reading demands of
their subjects. We shall argue, however, that there are specific reading techniques which pupils can acquire to improve the efficiency of their learning, and
that the subject teacher should help to develop these. We also believe that
he should know something about levels of reading difficulty in the material he
uses and about the capacity of individual pupils to cope with a particular book.*

(*ibid*.: paragraph 8.4)

This is an argument for a coherent and systematic approach to the teaching
of reading that takes account of the varied demands on readers across the
curriculum. One of the report's most celebrated sentences was a key driver of
the language across the curriculum movement.

*Since reading is a major strategy for learning in virtually every aspect of
education we believe it is the responsibility of every teacher to develop it.*

(*ibid*.: paragraph 8.9)

Bullock was received with considerable excitement by many in the educational
community, and it spurred many schools to produce policies for language
across the curriculum. Sadly, too often these policies existed only as written documents, and the process of translation into effective provision rarely
happened on the scale required to realise the report's ambitions. Sustained
attempts to build on the report's research and proposals have been rare over
subsequent decades. Indeed, there has been a trend towards the kinds of
definition of reading which the report explicitly rejected:

> *We believe that an improvement in the teaching of reading will not come from the acceptance of simplistic statements about phonics or any other single aspect of reading, but from a comprehensive study of all the factors at work and the influence that can be exerted upon them.*
>
> (*ibid*.: paragraph 6.3)

Although this book is directed to teachers of young people from the age of 11, I will briefly comment on the government's current policy with regard to early reading. This policy is based on a belief that systematic instruction in synthetic phonics is the only effective means by which young children learn to read, thus missing the point that learning to read is a broader, more complex task than could be achieved by any single 'method'. To challenge the policy is not in any crude sense to take an 'anti-phonics' position. There *are* many grapho-phonic correspondences in the English writing system, and it is sensible for teachers to take advantage of this convenient fact. But very many English written words, and especially many of the commonest ones – those that beginning readers will encounter most frequently – do not demonstrate straightforward grapho-phonic correspondences. They have to be learned by means in which phonics can play no part.

Furthermore, an excessive zealotry for phonics ignores one fundamental truth about reading, a truth that Bullock elegantly stated: that reading is essentially to do with the construction of meaning in the reader's mind, on the basis of the evidence provided by marks on a page or a screen.

> *It should be established from the beginning in the mind of the child that reading is primarily a thinking process, not simply an exercise in identifying shapes and sounds.*
>
> (*ibid*.: recommendation 73)

'Method', any method, is too narrow a term to do justice to the hypothesis-forming, rule-testing, rule-adapting, memory-employing, meaning-making complex activity which is reading.

40 years on . . .

The achievement of a coherent understanding of the demands which reading makes on learners in different areas of the curriculum remains a key element of a successful school's approach to learning. For organisational reasons, this coherence is harder to achieve in secondary than in primary schools. The Bullock Committee was 'convinced that the benefits [of implementing a policy for language across the curriculum in every secondary school] would be out of all proportion to the effort it would demand' (*ibid*.: paragraph 12.12). The key word here is 'implementing'.

The task for teachers and schools, put in other words than those used in *A Language for Life* but based on the principles spelt out in that report, is to use all the encouragement, resources and support schools can employ so that all learners gain the fullest pleasure, personal development, knowledge and understanding that reading can bring.

This in turn means:

- every school leader giving the highest priority to enabling all learners, regardless of their circumstances and starting points, to extend their experience, skills and use of reading;
- every teacher making sure that reading plays a central part in developing breadth and depth of knowledge and understanding in learning across all subjects.

The rest of this chapter offers advice as to how to take up this cause. The next three sections cover the teaching of reading under three broad headings: reading for pleasure; reading for information; and reading imaginative literature. These categories correspond roughly to the way reading is often organised in schools, but they are of course by no means watertight. Pleasure is, or should be, a feature of reading both information and literary texts; information texts can be of the highest literary value; and imaginative literature can be mightily informative about all kinds of aspects of the real world.

Reading for pleasure

The active encouragement of reading for pleasure should be a core part of every child's curriculum entitlement because extensive reading and exposure to a wide range of texts make a huge contribution to students' educational achievement.

(All-Party Parliamentary Group for Education, *Report of the Inquiry into Overcoming the Barriers to Literacy,* 2011: 6)

How well do we do?

At the beginning of this century, the indications were that England was not doing well in promoting pleasure in reading. The 2003 National Report for England of the Progress in International Reading Literacy Study (PIRLS) (Twist *et al.*, 2003), which compared 10-year-olds from 35 countries on a variety of literacy-related measures, showed that primary-school children in England were less confident about their reading ability and enjoyed reading less. Worse, 13 per cent of students actually disliked reading, compared to an international average of 6 per cent. Similarly, when asked how confident they were about reading, only 30 per cent were highly confident about their ability, compared to an international average of 40 per cent (quoted in Clark and Rumbold, 2006: 10).

By the time of the 2011 PIRLS Report for England, things were somewhat better:

England's performance in PIRLS 2011 was well above the international average and significantly higher than that seen in 2006. There was a wide range of achievement in England: the best readers were among the best in the world but there was a greater proportion of weaker readers than in many other high achieving countries. The difference between the reading achievements of boys and girls was greater than that seen in many other countries.

In common with a number of other high achieving countries, pupils' attitudes to reading were less positive in England than the average internationally. The more able readers were more likely to enjoy reading and be motivated to read than the weaker readers. Compared to 2006, fewer pupils in 2011 reported never or almost never *reading for fun out of school. Over half of pupils in PIRLS 2011 reported reading for half an hour or more every day out of school.*

(Twist *et al.*, 2012)

In the same year, however, Ofsted, in its report *Moving English Forward*, expressed concern about the neglect of reading for pleasure in schools and pointed to what it saw as misconceptions in much current practice:

In recent years the view has developed, especially in secondary schools, that there is not enough curriculum time to focus on wider reading or reading for pleasure. Inspectors also noted the loss of once popular and effective strategies such as reading stories to younger children, listening to children read, and the sharing of complete novels with junior age pupils.

(Office for
Standards in Education, 2012: 29)

The report of a recent survey of reading habits commissioned by Booktrust (*Booktrust Reading Habits Survey 2013: A National Survey of Reading Habits and Attitudes to Books Amongst Adults in England*) indicates that there is a substantial gap in reading habits between the economically advantaged and disadvantaged groups in the UK. The survey makes strong claims for the personal and practical benefits of regular reading for pleasure. Its report concludes:

Overall, the research highlights four justifications for initiatives to encourage reading for pleasure from an early age, particularly among disadvantaged groups.

- *People who read books are significantly more likely to be happy and content with their life.*
- *Most people who read books feel this improves their life. It also makes them feel good.*
- *People who were read to and encouraged to read as children are significantly more likely to read as adults, both to themselves and to their own children.*
- *Those who never read books live in areas of greater deprivation and with more children in poverty.*

(Gleed, 2013: 4)

What schools can do

In the light of these findings, what can schools do at the level of the whole institution to promote reading for pleasure? Despite the difficulties and obstacles, very many schools regularly and routinely find ways to make reading for pleasure a key part of school life. Here is a set of guidelines for promoting reading across the school.

Nine things a school could do to promote reading

1 Do a **survey of reading habits** in the school in order to get precise information about what and how much is read and the sources that young people get books from; and set up a system for monitoring changes in the nature and extent of independent reading as students go up the school.

2 Establish **a shared approach between primary and secondary schools** about provision for independent reading and work out how useful information about new secondary students' reading might be made available by primary schools.

3 Hold discussions with parents about voluntary reading and set up a **home-reading scheme**.

4 Form an **active library committee** (including students) to work with the librarian to ensure that the school library is: adequately stocked with books that students want to read; a place where books are displayed to full advantage and in ways students understand; an attractive and comfortable area; open for general use before school, during breaks and after school.

5 Devise **lists of useful and accessible books** to support and extend curriculum work in a full range of subjects, with these books to be made available within subject classrooms as well as in the library, and the reading of them given the status of homework.

6 Organise **visits to local libraries and bookshops** in school time so that students know their way into and around them. Establish secure ways for students to **buy books online**.

7 Run **regular book events**, during which special timetabling allows for: talks and readings by writers; exhibitions and sales; book-related activities and competitions.

8 Provide **a book-box** for each class so that students have immediate access to a supply of books which is: sufficient in quantity and wide enough in range and type for readers to make a reasonable choice; efficiently managed and maintained so that the books remain available and are regularly added to or changed.

9 Make **independent reading a fixture on the timetable** so that students get a regular chance in school just to read – and with opportunities in this reading time for promotional activities and help for students who find reading on their own difficult.

(Adapted from Raleigh, 1982,
reprinted in Simons [ed.], 1996: 120–121)

Enjoy!

The last quotation in this section goes to the author Philip Pullman, who in a 2003 article in *The Guardian* attributed at least part of the blame for schools' lack of drive on reading for pleasure to the National Curriculum and official guidance on it:

> *I recently read through the sections on reading in Key Stages 1 to 3 of the National Literacy Strategy, and I was struck by something about the verbs. I wrote them all down. They included 'reinforce', 'predict', 'check', 'discuss' . . . and so on: 71 different verbs, by my count, for the activities that come under the heading of 'reading'. And the word 'enjoy' didn't appear once.*

> (Pullman, 2003, in Clark and Rumbold, 2006: 12)

Reading for information

The invention of reading

The origins of writing and therefore of reading appear to lie in the unromantic matter of tax records. Poetry, story and the narratives of history and religion could be carried perfectly well within an oral culture. As city states expanded in Mesopotamia, along the Nile and in India and China, the need for a record of what was grown and could therefore be taxed led to the development of written records. Reading for information has a long history. When we contemplate a tax form we can at least console ourselves that we are part of the longest tradition of reading in the world. Every day, we are likely to refer to either paper or electronic text to get access to facts, information or processes.

The benefits

What are the benefits gained by effective readers for information? The following answer to the question is from New South Wales.

> *People who use information successfully display the following characteristics:*
> - *they are able to add to their core knowledge and frequently do so;*
> - *they use a variety of information sources and the necessary technology;*

- *they are able to process the information which surrounds them;*
- *they are confident in their ability to use information effectively.*

(New South Wales Department of Education
and Training, *Information Skills in the School:
Engaging Learners in Constructing Knowledge*, 2007: 6)

Our ability to read for information efficiently has the capacity to make our daily lives easier and more enjoyable. All learners need to develop this ability; schools need to help them to do so.

Beyond the comprehension exercise

To be downbeat for a moment: in too many schools, for too long, reading for information has often been confined to what is in effect the old-style comprehension exercise. Students are presented with factual information, in the form of a piece of prose in a book or on a worksheet or on the whiteboard. They are then required to find and repeat small parts of that information by answering a series of closed questions.

It would be going too far to say that the old-style comprehension exercise is entirely without value. The retrieval of factual information is something that children and adults alike do all the time. However, if students' experience of reading for information is confined to the old-style comprehension exercise, and if – especially in secondary schools – such exercises proliferate in subject after subject, without the respective subject teachers being aware of their relentless frequency across the school day, it is likely that the learner will greet the task of taking on new information with diminishing enthusiasm.

Instead, students should be introduced to a range of different ways in which texts can be mined for their information, and become aware for themselves of what is common and what is different in the approaches the reader adopts. Three examples of ways of mining texts follow later in the chapter.

The effective use of reading

Important research and development work on reading for information was undertaken by Eric Lunzer and Keith Gardner in the course of two Schools

Council projects, both based at the University of Nottingham. The first was 'The Effective Use of Reading', which ran from 1973 to 1976. The second was 'Learning from the Written Word', which ran from 1979 to 1982. The books carrying the findings of these projects are Lunzer and Gardner's *The Effective Use of Reading* (1979) and *Learning from the Written Word* (1984).

The thrust of the projects' argument was that learners need support to understand how information texts work, how they are structured and how ideas are developed through them. Lunzer and Gardner developed a methodology to help learners gain from texts information that often seems hidden to the inexperienced reader. They named this methodology Directed Activities Related to Texts. Broadly speaking, the methodology has two stages.

The first is 'reconstruction'. Students work with texts that have been modified by the teacher. They use either completion or prediction to produce a finished text. This may involve the use of cloze exercises, diagram completion, ordering or sequencing the text, or predicting its next part.

The second is 'analysis' and involves the students working with the original information text. They undertake exercises that identify key structural elements in the text. They highlight key words and phrases, use labels to summarise sections of the text's argument, produce diagrammatic representations of the argument, and extract information from the text which they re-present in tabular form. These activities support their understanding of the way concepts are embedded and linked in the text.

Unsettling the text

The Lunzer and Gardner projects inspired inventive ways of making reading for information a rich and challenging experience, providing alternatives to the use of undemanding comprehension questions and textbook instructions to 'answer in your own words'. One account of such approaches is given in an article published in 1983 in *The English Magazine*. Changing the metaphor a little from mining, the article described ways of what it called 'unsettling the text', re-establishing it as open to question and thus 'loosening the ideas up in order to explore them, rework them, extend them, apply them and finally, most writer-like of all, to get them back into some new and possibly quite different form'. The article categorised the activities under four headings: completing; comparing; re-forming; disputing. An edited version of the summary of these activities is given below.

Four ways of unsettling the text

Complete it

These activities use a text which has been doctored (for example through deletion or fragmentation or re-ordering) so as to be incomplete in some way, with the students being asked to reconstruct the whole text from what they are given.

Compare it

In these activities extras (for example texts on the same subject or a flow diagram or a set of notes) are provided to go along with the text and the students are asked to compare and relate the text and the extras in some way.

Re-form it

In these activities students are encouraged to represent what they have learned from reading the text in ways which help them make it their own (for example, through underlining, labelling, devising an oral version to talk through with a partner, creating a visual representation or patterned notes, or rewriting for a different audience).

Dispute it

These activities involve students in interrogating the text and evaluating what it has to say (for example through setting their own questions on the text, responding to statements giving different views about it, or marking up issues and problems).

(Adapted from Moy and Raleigh,
'Reading for Information', *The English Magazine 11*,
1983; reprinted in Simons [ed.], 1996: 184–185)

Dealing with difficult texts

For many students, the problem is keeping pace with the increasing demands that the reading of authentic material across the curriculum makes as they move through school. Part of the solution to the problem is engaging the students in deliberate discussion about what makes texts difficult and introducing ways of coping with them. *Spotlight on Literacy*, the teaching resource from the English and Media Centre referred to earlier in the chapter, has a helpful section on getting to grips with difficult texts and helping students to become more independent and resilient readers. The sequence includes:

- *running a 'reading clinic', which involves students and teachers bringing examples of texts they find difficult and discussing the features that account for the difficulty;*
- *use of 'performed reading', using different strategies to highlight key points and messages;*
- *stepping back from the detail to establish the bigger picture of what the text is about;*
- *using simple grids to identify 'what I know already', 'what I want to know' and 'what I've learnt';*
- *using skimming and scanning to investigate and locate particular items of information;*
- *evaluating the usefulness of different pre-prepared summaries of information in a text;*
- *re-presenting a difficult text for a different audience in order to focus on making key points accessible;*
- *sub-editing a text by giving it headlines, sub-heads and pull-quotes;*
- *paying close attention to the grammar of selected sentences in order to pick through the meaning and the style of the piece;*
- *giving the students key words, fragments and prompts before they see the text as a whole;*
- *asking the students to summarise as they go along, to pose questions about what they have read so far and to speculate and predict what is coming next;*
- *providing a focus for independent reading by asking students to identify a key passage or to sum up the argument in a few words; and*
- *encouraging students to formulate, pool and then try to answer interesting questions about the material they have read.*

(Bleiman *et al.*, 2013: 283–288)

Many of these approaches, especially those involving visual organisers such as simple grids, skimming and scanning, explicit focus on grammatical form, and the use of key words and summaries, would be particularly effective with EAL learners. Weaker EAL learners benefit from more able readers' re-presenting of difficult texts. There is more discussion of the needs and achievements of EAL learners in Chapter 7.

Reading imaginative literature

whatever else the pupil takes away from his experience of literature in school he should have learned to see it as a source of pleasure, as something that will continue to be a part of his life. The power to bring this about lies with the teacher, but it cannot be pretended that the task is easy.

(The Bullock Committee, 1975: paragraph 9.28)

We come now to a central responsibility of the English teacher: the teaching of literature.

Key questions

The teaching of English literature has always been a controversial matter. Some of the controversy has taken place at an academic level, but it has also attracted strong political interest; hence the tendency of politicians to impose their preferences as to which texts should be taught in schools. Going back in time, the development of the study of English literature as an academic subject coincided with a fierce debate in the late nineteenth and early twentieth century about English identity.

One problem with the debate is that all too often it gets bogged down in arguments about which texts should be taught. This is an important question, but it is not the only one. Teachers need to think about the 'why' as well as the 'what': about the purposes of their teaching in terms of their students' developing capabilities.

We could categorise the reading and the teaching of literature in three ways. It is to do with:

- engaging the reader with the text;
- understanding the text's rhetoric;
- relating the reader's perspective to that of the text.

Engaging the reader with the text

The first of the three categories is closely related to reading for pleasure, as discussed in the previous section. Our first and most enduring response to a literary text is to engage with it. If we fail to engage with the text, unless it is one we are forced to read, for example as part of an examination syllabus, we are unlikely to persevere with it.

It is valuable to choose some texts that reflect and explore the experiences and cultures present in the classroom. Young people respond to seeing their own world reflected in fiction, drama and poetry. However, it is also vital to nourish ambition in young readers. English literature is produced by writers from many different cultures and countries. Of the three most recent Nobel laureate poets writing in English, one is from St Lucia, one is from the USA and the third was from Ireland. This cultural diversity and richness should be represented in the reading young people do in school, whether for wider pleasure or close textual study. By the age of 16, students should have a sense that there is a remarkable source of enjoyment and stimulation out there in literature, and that this source is being enriched all the time by writers from a diversity of cultural backgrounds.

Young people need the opportunity not only to read widely but in some depth. They should from time to time have the chance to read a number of texts by one author, in one genre or exploring one theme. They need to read or hear whole texts (see the next sub-section), an experience which need not always be followed by detailed discussion or writing.

Students right across the range of attainment should have the experience of reading or hearing high-quality, demanding literary texts. The fact that a reader may not be fluent does not mean that he or she cannot enjoy, with help, a complex work of literature. The aim is to ensure that all students have experienced writers of this quality and make informed choices about what they like; most important of all, that they are ambitious as readers and do not place artificial limitations on what might or might not interest them.

Whole-class reading

'Whole-class reading' means sessions where the teacher reads a complete literary text to the whole class. This practice has been under pressure in recent years. Given the demands on teaching time and the need for schools to demonstrate measurable progress in learning, it can appear a luxury. Its value should not be underestimated. It allows the developing reader to hear how good expressive reading aloud can enrich the experience of a text. Done skilfully, reading aloud accentuates the listener's excitement, suspense and pleasure. For some young people, it is an experience not replicated elsewhere.

A complete text is not necessarily a full-length novel. It could also be a short story or a narrative poem. Sometimes the teacher may invite students to read sections. Sometimes he or she may stop to ask questions and invite comment. But in this kind of reading the most important thing is impetus. The listeners need to feel that they are being engulfed, absorbed by the experience.

Understanding the text's rhetoric

It is a teacher's responsibility to help young readers come to understand how a text works. If they care what happens to a character – that is, if they are engaged – how has the author made them care? If they are saddened by a poem, how has the form, structure, language and content produced this feeling? This is the province of rhetoric, the ancient study of how language can achieve an emotional and intellectual impact on listeners and readers. What might it include?

Vocabulary

The study might include close attention to the choice of words, the vocabulary. Why *this* word, and what weight or implications might it have? It is sometimes hard to say. Teachers need to provide structure and support. One way of doing this is to allow students to choose alternative words and compare their responses to them. This activity might take the form of a cloze exercise where synonyms are available to fill the spaces. Another approach is to look at two or more translations of the same poem or passage, or two or more versions of a classical myth, to compare the ways in which different authors have chosen different English words and to discuss the effects of the different choices.

Grammatical structure

It is in the context of looking at texts to see how meaning is made, how particular readers' responses are elicited, that it makes best sense to introduce the study of grammatical structure. The study of the structures of simple, compound and complex sentences, for example, is best done by looking at how these structures contribute to the meaning and impact of a worthwhile and engaging text. Students might substitute simple sentences for compound or complex ones, or vice versa, and consider the differences. Or they might discuss the impact on the narrative of a shift in tense. Students can also use their own and each other's writing to consider the impact of different grammatical choices. (See Chapter 4 for a detailed discussion of effective grammar teaching.)

Narrative structure

Above the level of words and sentences, readers need to be introduced to the way in which the overall structure of a narrative supports the tension of a story, or its pathos or humour. This can be done from the simplest to the most complex of narratives. Most students can grasp the management of time in a story. They can understand the impact of a circular narrative. They can recognise the way in which episodic structure might enhance or detract from a story's suspense. They can be shown how the use of voice impacts on a narrative, by being introduced to the distinction between an author and a narrator. They can be offered activities that focus on the difference between a first-person and a third-person narrative.

Learners are able to appreciate narratives before they are able fully to analyse them. This implicit appreciation needs to be harnessed to the development of explicit understanding.

Terminology

In studying the rhetoric of texts, students' implicit appreciation of the effect of a text is being guided towards explicit understanding. Some appropriate critical terminology by which to describe how a text has made meaning, has achieved its impact on them as readers, will help them along the way. The terms 'topic', 'introduction', 'development', 'conclusion', 'argument', 'assertion', 'evidence', 'example', 'plot', 'character', 'climax', 'author', 'narrator', 'first-person', 'third-person' are all potentially appropriate examples, depending on the kind of writing being discussed and the age of the students.

Relating the reader's perspective to that of the text

The third aspect of the teaching of literary texts involves setting the reader's values and assumptions in relation to those of the text. It offers the potential to call into question the values and assumptions of even the greatest literary works. Equally, it offers an opportunity for the reader to question her or his own values. Writing in the late sixteenth century, Michel de Montaigne observed that 'A speech belongs half to the speaker, half to him who hears it' ('On Experience', in *Essays*, Penguin, 1993: 372). Meaning is constructed in dialogue. The speaker or writer may be able to control what he or she intends to mean but cannot control the meaning actually made by the hearer or reader.

We read texts from particular perspectives, from particular positions. We may do so consciously or unconsciously. The great Nigerian writer Chinua Achebe, for example, expressed his difficulty in reading Joseph Conrad's *Heart of Darkness*. Achebe read the text from the position of a twentieth-century anti-colonial black African, and found the portrayal of Africans and Africa one that he could not accept. He was quite conscious of his position as a reader. Conrad, he said, uses:

Africa as setting and backdrop which eliminates the African as human factor. Africa as a metaphysical battlefield devoid of all recognizable humanity, into which the wandering European enters at his peril. Can nobody see the preposterous and perverse arrogance in thus reducing Africa to the role of props for the break-up of one petty European mind?

(Achebe, 'An Image of Africa: Racism in Conrad's *Heart of Darkness*', *Massachusetts Review 18*, 1977)

More recently, Achebe's fellow Nigerian and fellow writer, Chimamanda Ngozi Adichie, has addressed the question of literature which denies the fullness and complexity of a people's identity in her TED talk 'The danger of a single story' (Adichie, 2009).

Debating with the text

Achebe knew why he found *Heart of Darkness* unpalatable. At times, however, reading a text from our own position, we may be made uncomfortable but not understand why. What we are reading somehow challenges or affronts our own beliefs. Sometimes this matters; at other times, it is simply a mild irritant. Whether conscious and deeply significant or subconscious and vaguely discomfiting, this experience is an important and valuable aspect of reading. It is part of what we hope we gain from reading literary texts, that we can see the world – for a time at least and even if only partially – through someone else's eyes, someone else's consciousness. It is also an aspect of students' developing competence as readers that teachers can nurture and develop, helping students to make conscious the previously unconscious, helping them debate with the text.

As with all aspects of the teaching of literature, this is not teaching to be reserved only for the fluent and sophisticated reader. All readers bring their own experience of the world to the stories they hear, the texts they have read to them and those they read for themselves. They respond to the narrative and to the characters with their own assumptions and values. When readers comment on and discuss the behaviour of characters, the relationships between them, the settings in which they appear, the conversations they have, there is the opportunity to reflect on these assumptions and values.

Teachers of course have a responsibility to protect young people from texts that are not appropriate to their age or are likely to cause real hurt or offence. However, students' reading should not be confined to texts that are unproblematic, that offer only those values that can be easily accepted. The reader should have opportunities to locate and interrogate the values and assumptions of a text: values and assumptions that may not be explicit, that may not even have been apparent to the writer. Once located, these values and assumptions can be set against those of the reader and debated.

Students should be given the confidence to question the values of a text, even one with a revered place in the literary canon. This can be a sensitive matter. It can engage readers in the exploration of issues that radically affect their own lives. Writing of his experience as a teacher in east London, John Yandell recalls:

> For the young women of Turkish and Kurdish heritage with whom I read Romeo and Juliet . . . Juliet's attempts to negotiate the contradictions in her relationships with her family and her lover were often all too recognisable, all too close to their own life worlds.
>
> (Yandell, 2014: 3)

The relationship between the text and the reader is a two-way street. While the reader may challenge the text, the text should be allowed to challenge the reader. Teachers should ensure that, over time, students are introduced to some texts that do that.

Designing a literature curriculum

The development of a literature curriculum should include all three of the elements discussed in this section. It should:

- engage learners and extend the range and ambition of their reading;
- equip them with the skills and language to understand and analyse how texts achieve their effects on readers;
- give them the knowledge and confidence to interrogate the values and assumptions of the text in an informed, open-minded and confident manner.

Such a curriculum will involve the selection of texts to suit the particular purpose of the learning. Such an approach takes us beyond decisions about which books an 11-year-old or a 16-year-old should read (necessary as those decisions will be) to more dynamic questions such as:

- Which texts will engage this group of readers and extend their reading horizons?
- Which texts will best illustrate structural and linguistic features which this group of readers can usefully study?
- Which texts will provide this group of readers with the best opportunities for discussing the writer's and their own perspective?

The school library

The school library is the heart of the school which itself has learning at its core; and good libraries can empower the learner. The resources in a library can allow our imaginations to run free, introduce us to new experiences and promote access to knowledge and enjoyment.

(Department for Education and Skills, *School Libraries: Making a Difference*, 2004, quoted in Office for Standards in Education, *Good School Libraries: Making a Difference to Learning*, 2006: 4)

What's become of it?

School libraries make a vital contribution to the promotion and development of reading. The factors that make for good libraries were described in simple terms in an HMI survey published in 1989:

Better libraries:

- *are easy to get to and pleasant to be in;*
- *provide what readers want to read;*
- *are well matched to what learners have to learn;*
- *are well equipped to help the learning process;*
- *have skilled, enthusiastic staff who know how libraries work and have the time to see that learners' needs are met;*
- *develop and use pupils' skills as librarians;*
- *are funded to take sensible heed of costs and replacement needs;*
- *attractively present well-chosen stock which relates to learners' ages, abilities and interests;*
- *make good use of the expertise and stock of Schools Library Services;*
- *look regularly at what they have and how it is being used;*
- *are rooted in the active belief of all staff, clearly stated, that the library is essential to the healthy growth of learning and that the library and its use are the responsibility of all teachers and of all others concerned with promoting learning.*

(Department of Education and Science,
Better Libraries: Good Practice in Schools – A survey by H.M. Inspectorate, 1989: 6, original emphasis)

The 2006 Office for Standards in Education survey which carried the quotation at the beginning of this section found that:

Funding for libraries varied markedly, even across the schools with good libraries. The survey found a direct link between well-funded libraries and effectiveness. However, gaps in resourcing were less significant overall than under-use or poor management.

(Office for Standards in Education, 2006: 2)

A 2010 report from a commission on school libraries set up by the National Literacy Trust and the Museums, Libraries and Archives Council was scathing in its comments on the current national picture:

> *School libraries are an underutilised resource, often perceived by head-teachers to be a low priority. What should be a vital ingredient of our schools system is marginalised and seems not to be connected with the acknowledged educational priorities of literacy and information skills supporting knowledge acquisition, which are their core business.*
>
> (National Literacy Trust and Museums, Libraries and Archives Council, *School Libraries: A Plan for Improvement*, 2010: 5)

> *The research showed that, while some headteachers and governing bodies saw the school library as an essential element of their school development plan, many others had given little thought to the part it could be playing in the life of the school. In the consultation groups, headteachers who did not currently regard the library as a priority did not do so out of hostility but simply because they had not thought of it as a strategically useful resource.*
>
> (*ibid.*: 8)

The unevenness of both the extent and the quality of provision is a matter of major concern. Inequality of access to books and other resources as between schools is a fundamental failing.

Staffing

Crucial to the quality of school libraries is the question of staffing. The International Federation of Library Associations and Institutions guidelines for school libraries state:

> *Research has shown that the most critical condition for an effective school library program is access to a qualified school library professional.*
>
> (International Federation of Library Associations and Institutions, 2015: 18)

The School Library Commission (National Literacy Trust and Museums, Libraries and Archives Council, 2010) and various advocacy organisations for libraries have repeatedly made the point that without dedicated staffing, too many school libraries are underused and waste resources and potential. The School Library Association offers extensive advice to schools (School Library Association, 2015). It has established the School Librarian of the Year Award to recognise and highlight best practice.

However the staffing is achieved, the librarian is enormously influential in promoting books and other resources to staff and students, both individually and as classes, as well as being part of any programme teaching about how to read for information.

What's to be done?

Good School Libraries: Making a Difference to Learning made a series of recommendations about how the current situation could be improved. The first five of these relate directly to schools, and the last to the role of local authorities and other bodies providing support.

Schools need to:

- *improve evaluation of their library, taking account of the full range of evidence to assess its impact on pupils' learning, and requiring librarians to report formally;*
- *develop the quality and coherence of programmes for teaching information literacy to provide better continuity, challenge and progression in pupils' learning;*
- *extend use of the library by teachers and pupils throughout the day, but especially by primary pupils at lunch time;*
- *improve use of the library by Key Stage 4 pupils;*
- *consider ways to promote pupils' independent study by more effective use of the library.*

Those responsible for advising and supporting schools in developing their libraries need to:

- *work with headteachers and senior managers, as well as librarians, in order to develop provision and integrate developments with other whole-school priorities.*

(Office for Standards in Education, 2006: 3)

However, the report was clear about the single most significant factor in determining the quality and effectiveness of school libraries: 'the commitment and support of effective headteachers' (*ibid.*: 2).

Supporting readers who fail or fade

The problem

How is it that, in a notional mixed-gender and mixed-ability group of, say, 14-year-olds, some 40 per cent may end up not really reading very much at all, whether at school or at home?

Failing or reluctant readers have different histories. Some never seem to catch on, failing to achieve fluency by the end of Key Stage 1 and then struggling in this way into Key Stage 3 and beyond. Some succeed early on but fade later. Whatever their trajectory, readers who can't or don't read easily are a source of much anxiety to those who teach them. Their problems with reading impact ever more severely on their general progress as learners, eroding their confidence and sometimes leading to a belief on their part that their failure as a reader is part of a wider intellectual weakness. Poor reading skills become a source of shame. All of this makes the challenge greater. Students who go into Key Stage 3 with low levels of reading fluency will have had six years of seeing themselves fall behind and fail. That history is corrosive.

One of the articles in *The English Magazine* quoted earlier tracks the negative factors causing a notional child, later young person, to become a failing reader during his career in primary and secondary school:

- *You are a boy.*
- *There isn't much book-reading at home or among relatives and friends.*
- *You were initiated into reading by methods which highlighted the techniques rather than the functions of reading and which communicated to you a narrow sense of what reading is and what it's good for.*
- *At your primary school there was a heavy emphasis on reading aloud to the teacher from 'scheme books' (perhaps taking up to a term to finish one book in this way) and little opportunity for extended silent reading from self-chosen material.*
- *You tended to be slow with your other work in class and so missed most of the opportunities that there were for silent reading 'after you've finished'.*
- *You haven't talked much about books in school or elsewhere. You don't own any books yourself.*

- *You don't belong to a public library.*
- *The secondary school you go to doesn't have a decent library, or, if it has one, doesn't encourage you to use it.*
- *The school doesn't have adequate class library provision.*
- *Subject teaching in your school makes limited use of texts (i.e. limited as to type of text and kind of use); where it happens, reading is closely guided and frequently interrupted; the teaching stresses the demonstration of competence (literary or otherwise) over the development of interest and purpose in reading.*
- *You've been offered a series of inappropriate books by adults who are keen that you should do some reading.*
- *You see a considerable gap between the kinds of books legitimised in school and the kinds of books you might choose to read yourself if you could find them.*
- *You haven't developed your own reliable criteria for choosing a book and so have made a series of bad choices yourself.*
- *You don't think you're much good at reading.*

(Raleigh, 1982, in Simons [ed.], 1996: 119)

The National Union of Teachers' advice on school policy on reading for pleasure puts its diagnosis this way:

Many studies show that when such children select texts for themselves, this enhances their motivation and self-determination, since interested and determined readers will often persist with a demanding text, simply because of their desire to know, to understand and to make sense of it. Yet Ofsted reports that struggling readers are given less autonomy and choice in their reading and are exposed to less text and have fewer and more limited opportunities to practise than more skilled peers. As a consequence they may be slower to become fluent readers, are less likely to find reading rewarding and may seek to avoid reading activities, perpetuating their sense of failure.

(National Union of Teachers, 2015)

And the solution?

The answer is neither singular nor magical. There are useful intensive-support programmes for failing readers of the Reading Recovery kind. There is also some evidence that computer-based support, including talking books and computer programs for older students which promote and monitor independent reading, can encourage struggling readers in particular. However, the research evidence would caution us against optimistic over-reliance on any one system.

More privileged access

We are talking about learners who have often failed to respond to a dominant single methodology or set of materials and who may well not respond to a regime which is simply more of the same. These learners need additional support and resources, without doubt. But what is crucial is that they have *more privileged access* to the same range of experiences of written language as successful readers have had. These are experiences in which the high gears are at work, in which the affective, the cognitive and the linguistic areas of the mind are in interactive and mutually supportive operation, engaging with real language and getting the rewards – small to begin with, perhaps, but felt and accumulating – which encounters with real language bring. In short, what a failing reader needs is a personalised and intensive version of what the other students are getting, not something completely different.

The present situation in England

The new National Curriculum for English has the following overall aims for reading at all Key Stages. Pupils should:

- *read easily, fluently and with good understanding;*
- *develop the habit of reading widely and often, for both pleasure and information;*
- *acquire a wide vocabulary, an understanding of grammar and knowledge of linguistic conventions for reading, writing and spoken language;*
- *appreciate our rich and varied literary heritage.*

(Department for Education, 2014a: 14)

These intentions are unarguable.

Key Stage 3

In the reading orders for Key Stages 1 and 2, an unhelpful distinction is introduced between 'Word Reading' and 'Comprehension'. At Key Stage 3, this distinction has disappeared. There is one set of orders, simply called 'Reading'. This is welcome, as it avoids the divorcing of comprehension from the recognition and study of individual words.

On the other hand, it might be thought odd that word-based teaching has largely disappeared from the Key Stage 3 orders. The study of morphology is given great importance at Key Stage 2. It receives much less attention at Key Stage 3, although there is a requirement that pupils should read critically through 'knowing how language, including figurative language, vocabulary choice, grammar, text structure and organisational features, presents meaning' (*ibid.*: 83). It is also true that in the Key Stage 3 writing orders there is a separate section on grammar and vocabulary, under which morphology could presumably be studied. But there is no mention of etymology, again apparently so important at Key Stage 2, either in the reading or the writing orders.

As John Richmond argues in Chapter 4, the secondary years are the time when the analytic study of language should receive greater attention, whether this study is concerned with word classes, word structure (which would include morphology), sentence grammar, text grammar, the history of change in English (including etymology) or other aspects of knowledge about language. A principal failing of the new National Curriculum orders for English is that they are preoccupied with analysis at Key Stages 1 and 2 (and particularly at Key Stage 1) and much less concerned with analysis, at least in any detail, at Key Stages 3 and 4. Competence comes before analysis in learning; the orders have the relationship between the two precisely the wrong way round in the relative emphasis given to them in the primary and secondary years.

These criticisms notwithstanding, there is nothing in the Key Stage 3 reading orders which prevents teachers from teaching well. There is range and diversity in the requirements as to what students should read:

– *the range will include high-quality works from:*

- *English literature, both pre-1914 and contemporary, including prose, poetry and drama;*
- *Shakespeare (two plays);*
- *seminal world literature.*

(*ibid.*: 83)

. . . and in the requirements as to *how* they should read. For example, they should be taught to:

– understand increasingly challenging texts through:

- *learning new vocabulary, relating it explicitly to known vocabulary and understanding it with the help of context and dictionaries;*
- *making inferences and referring to evidence in the text;*
- *knowing the purpose, audience for and context of the writing and drawing on this knowledge to support comprehension;*
- *checking their understanding to make sure that what they have read makes sense.*

(ibid.: 83)

A notable omission, however: there is no mention of reading as an experience which can and very often does take place by digital and electronic means.

Key Stage 4

The orders for reading at Key Stage 4 have broadly the same good qualities as those noted at Key Stage 3. Once again, it will be perfectly possible for teachers to teach well within them.

There is, however, one oddity. Pupils should be taught to:

read and appreciate the depth and power of the English literary heritage through:

- *reading a wide range of high-quality, challenging, classic literature and extended literary non-fiction, such as essays, reviews and journalism. This writing should include whole texts. The range will include:*

  - *at least one play by Shakespeare;*
  - *works from the 19th, 20th and 21st centuries;*
  - *poetry since 1789, including representative Romantic poetry.*

- *re-reading literature and other writing as a basis for making comparisons;*
- *choosing and reading books independently for challenge, interest and enjoyment.*

(ibid.: 86)

The oddity is 'representative Romantic poetry'. Without in any way undervaluing the poetry of the Romantic movement, if the purpose is to insist on some great pre-1914 poetry, why not admit the Elizabethans or the metaphysicals or Blake or the Victorians as equally worthy candidates? In short, the requirement would be better as 'major lyric and narrative poetry written before 1914'.

The notable omission of digital and electronic media for reading persists into Key Stage 4. As far as the programme of study is concerned, teachers who see the urgency of showing their students something of the possibilities of reading on computers and other electronic devices, and of discussing how new media affect the experience of reading, will have do so without official support.

GCSE English Language and English Literature

For a full discussion of the reading requirements at GCSE English Language and English Literature, see Chapter 10. As John Richmond writes there, the reference to online texts at GCSE to some extent makes good the absence of any mention of them in the Key Stage 4 programme of study, while highlighting the anomaly of that absence.

An alternative

In Chapter 9, readers will find an alternative curriculum for reading 11 to 16, which retains the features of the statutory orders which can be welcomed, while addressing the shortcomings which have been discussed in this chapter.

To conclude . . .

As the Bullock Report puts it:

> *we have been anxious to establish the principle that young children should acquire from the beginning the skills that are employed in mature reading. These skills will obviously be used for more elaborate and demanding purposes as the child grows older, but the pattern is one that can be established early . . . The development of reading skills is a progressive one, and there are no staging points to which one can attach any particular ages.*
> (The Bullock Committee, 1975: paragraph 8.1)

The teaching and the uses of reading for learning need to be set in the broader context of what is now known about the development of language. Reading is from its earliest stages a complex and holistic intellectual and imaginative activity. This central truth needs to be reflected in the way it is taught. 'Learning to read' is not an activity to be divorced from 'reading to learn'. Rather, 'learning to read' and 'reading to learn' are processes which should enhance each other.

Schools and teachers need to consider the full range of purposes for which and approaches by which students should be asked to read in school. A curriculum which represents these purposes and approaches will develop in students the capacity to enjoy literature and to read for information in an efficient and productive manner. It will nurture in them the priceless habit of reading for pleasure. If a school is to offer such a curriculum in practice, it needs to adopt a whole-school strategy, fully supported, resourced and monitored by the school's senior leaders.

Effective teachers of literature ensure that students are engaged in their reading; they equip students with the analytical skills to understand how texts achieve their emotional and intellectual impact; and they help students to interrogate both the assumptions of the texts and the assumptions that they, the readers, bring to those texts.

A well-resourced, properly staffed, constantly used school library is essential to a school's effectiveness as a reading-promoting place.

The principles summarised here, if enacted, represent an agenda by which schools could enable their students to achieve satisfying success as readers: an achievement which will massively enhance the quality of their later lives.

3 Writing 11 to 16

John Richmond

Summary of main points

The purpose of the teaching of writing is to develop in young people a confident control of the medium and a sense of the pleasure that writing can bring.

The teaching of writing requires an understanding of all the characteristics and needs of a writer at work, and of the multiple demands that teachers make on learners when they ask them to write.

Competence in writing – at whatever level – precedes analysis of writing, not the other way round. This is true of language generally. Analysis of or specific attention to conventions of the writing system should take place in the context of the examination of whole, meaningful texts, whether these are texts produced by the student as a writer or those encountered by the student as a reader.

Learners' developing competence and confidence in handling forms of and purposes for writing will come about as a result of copious reading of high-quality texts – factual, instructional, persuasive and imaginative – which teachers should provide.

Preparation for writing should often involve oral work in various forms: paired, group and whole-class talk; role-play, improvisation and drama. Oral work in any of these forms can also be an outcome of writing.

Writers should have opportunities to write for a range of different purposes and in a range of different formats, sometimes individually and sometimes in collaboration with other writers.

Writers should be familiar with the process of redrafting in order to bring about a better and more satisfying final product.

Writers should write for readerships which, while including the teacher as the most important reader, are not confined to the teacher.

Teachers should show learners that they write too.

The modelling of writing, including the study of how other writers have made successful and pleasure-giving texts, should be a feature of the teaching of writing.

Recent, fast-moving advances in digital technology have transformed and will continue to transform the possibilities for the production and exchange of writing, and for the combination of writing with other modes, for example images and sound.

Teachers' interventions in students' writing should be concerned, first, with what the student has written in terms of the content and the overall structure of a piece.

Teachers' interventions in students' writing should be concerned, next, with the degree of correctness shown in the writer's handling of the writing system: with spelling, punctuation, layout and the grammatical order and forms of words in sentences.

There is always pattern in error. Teachers' attention to error in students' writing should have the principal aim of developing in writers the self-critical awareness which will enable them increasingly to attend to error themselves. That is, writers should be shown how to make their implicit knowledge of the writing system active in the critical examination of their writing.

Those few students who have not by the age of 11 developed a clear, relaxed handwriting style should be helped to do so. All students should learn keyboard skills so that they can type on a computer at least as fast as they can handwrite.

All these principles apply with equal force to learners of English as an additional language (about one in six students in the age group with which this book is concerned). However, students who have begun to read and write in another language and are learning to write in English are additionally engaged in the complex process of making comparisons between writing systems. There is likely to be a conscious transfer of knowledge and skill from one written form to another, and sometimes features originating in the first language will appear in EAL learners' English writing. Appropriate books in the first language and in bilingual editions can help the comparison of the writing systems of English and the other language(s), in addition to the other benefits they bring.

Writing – at large and in school

This chapter considers the progress of young people who are travelling in a direction which should lead them to full competence as writers. What are the waymarks along the journey? What is the best advice and help teachers can offer them as they go?

Writing at large . . .

There is no evidence that writing is on the wane in our society. Books, magazines, newspapers, journals and booklets continue to pour forth in immense
quantity. If it was true 300 years ago that someone with a good library and the
leisure and money to use it and add regularly to it could know more or less
everything that there was to know, it is now true that to keep up with developments even in one sub-branch of the total output of writing, whether it be
sociolinguistics or cookery books or detective fiction, is beyond most of us.

The arrival and explosive growth of digital technology in recent decades
relies very heavily on the written word in its websites, blogs, wikis and
social media exchanges, often in conjunction with images (still or moving),
spoken language and music, and in the millions of emails and texts written
and received every day. Every computer and mobile telephone and most
portable digital appliances have some kind of device (physical or electronically displayed typewriter console, alphanumeric keyboard . . .) to enable
the user to write.

. . . and in school

The production of writing remains, and seems likely to remain, a hugely important and immensely time-consuming part of a young person's schooling. There
are negative as well as positive reasons for this. Negatively, there is no doubt
that a close relationship exists between writing and control in classrooms.
Many teachers – perhaps all – have sometimes used writing as a means of
controlling or calming a group of noisy or difficult students. If that occasional
and understandable expedient becomes a regular practice, and writing comes
to be associated in learners' minds as a dreary duty or a mild form of punish-
ment, then something is badly wrong.

On the other hand, teachers also know that writing, although not without
its pains and frustrations, can be a deeply pleasurable and fulfilling activity;
and teachers who enjoy writing and write seriously for various purposes want
their students to experience the pleasure and fulfilment that writing offers.
In successful classrooms, learners regularly experience such pleasure and
fulfilment.

Correctness versus creativity?

In the 1970s, there was a debate amongst teachers, and amongst teachers of English in particular, about how best to help their students to write better. At its worst, the debate was sterile, with two sharply divided groups each claiming a monopoly of truth for its position. One group insisted that there had been a loss of nerve at some unidentified point in the 1960s, leading to a dereliction of duty on the part of the other group, and that a return to the basic groundwork of grammar drills, spelling and punctuation exercises and (in primary schools) handwriting practice was urgently needed. Writing should once more be stringently marked and graded, and every error pointed out to the writer; if teachers failed to do these things, how would the students learn?

The other group was sure that the methods of the first group had been tried and found wanting, and that the important priority was to provide an environment in which children and young people were stimulated and encouraged to write, drawing especially on their own experience. The one group was doggedly pessimistic, the other determinedly optimistic: students' writing would develop and improve, said the optimistic group, given the right learning environment.

There is a degree of parody in this account, but it contains enough truth to be worth the recalling. Later, a more mature and more useful position began to develop, based on the realisation that the written language has characteristics which require an understanding which is broader and more eclectic than the orthodoxy of either group.

Writing: profoundly creative . . .

Like the spoken language, the written language is a profoundly creative affair. People every day compose and write down sentences, paragraphs, whole texts which have never been written down before. Written language is creative too in the sense that it enables us to fix in the world, to make concrete ideas, feelings and opinions which we were uncertain of, or didn't even know we had, until we wrote them down. In *Aspects of the Novel* (2005 [1927]), E. M. Forster summed up the capacity of writing to do these things in his rhetorical question: 'How can I tell what I think till I see what I say?'

In these circumstances, any attempt to reduce the teaching of writing to the learning in advance of a set of rules or formulae which can then be permutated to produce the real thing is bound to fail. If anything, the opposite would be truer: young writers have an overall intention to write something, whether of their own free will or because the teacher has told them to, and in the course of fulfilling that overall intention they encounter the thousand details and demands of actually making marks sensibly on paper or on a screen.

Once young children have mastered the physical act of writing, their further development as writers requires that they have opportunities to write in meaningful contexts which make sense to them and which bring them a sense of achievement, with the help of constant exposure to other people's writing in the form of reading.

. . . and profoundly structured

But it is equally true that the written language is a profoundly structured affair.

If a reader is suddenly confronted with an abandonment of structure and convention – if rools the and structre's the of language writen decide we brake to – he or she is going to have difficulty understanding what the writer means. And beyond the level of the sentence, the reader does not expect a leading article in *The Times* to be written in the style of a teenage music magazine, or a report on a football match suddenly to turn into a general lament about the ills of contemporary society.

Language may be creative, but it's not anarchic, and it depends on an enormous amount of consensus between writer and reader about conventions of form and meaning. Teachers who understand both the profoundly structured nature of writing *and* its rolling, unpredictable creativity are in a good position to help their students with it.

Craft and art

Writing is a craft as well as an art. The difference between a craft and an art is that the good craftsperson always knows what he or she is doing, whereas the good artist frequently does not.

In reality, most constructive activities have both craft and art about them: makers are working confidently, pleasurably within themselves, using known and trusted skills; they are also daring, pushing open doors to as yet unexplored rooms, frightening the first time, less frightening the next. In writing, craft and art are tangled together in the process, and writers make both sorts of decision – those that are calculations and those that are gambles – all the time.

Just as it is important not to see calculation and gamble, craft and art, as unfriendly opposites, so it is important not to see them as hierarchically related either, with craft the poor relation and art the exalted muse. At the most accomplished level, the poet takes no less pleasure in the formal qualities of a poem than in its meaning, or mood, or intensity of feeling. At the level with which teachers are frequently concerned, students who see that they have learned to punctuate, or to handle a complex sentence or simply to write a page which looks nice, may gain as much from that sense of achievement as from the pleasure of having authentically expressed a strong personal feeling or articulated a complex idea on paper.

In other words, when young people develop as writers, their development happens most effectively on a broad front, in several areas at once, and development in one area is often supportive of development in another. On the other hand, young writers sometimes identify priorities for themselves for the time being, which become temporarily more important than anything else. The priority in question may be anything from neat handwriting to managing a balanced argument in a piece of discursive prose.

Teachers also, and often, set priorities for their students. The priorities that teachers set should reflect, over time, the broad front of competences and skills a writer needs. Effective teachers are not narrowly preoccupied with only one set of competences and skills: those of correctness.

The demands made on student writers

What do teachers need to know and do in order to teach writing effectively?

None of the answers to this question offered in this and the following four sections will be discrete or watertight. The content of one will sometimes leak back or forward into the content of another. This may not make for theoretical elegance, but a consolation will be that the answers, overlapping and cross-referring as they will sometimes do, are like the activity of writing itself, which is neither learned nor most effectively practised as a result of being chopped up into categories in advance, but can be helped by the discussion of those categories, and the terminology associated with the categories, along the way.

Many of the following ideas originated in work I did, in collaboration with colleagues, when I worked on the National Writing Project, which ran from 1985 to 1990 and was funded by the School Curriculum Development Committee. The aim of the project was to improve the quality of the teaching of writing in all curriculum subjects in primary and secondary schools in England and Wales.

In the years since 1990, the digital technological revolution which was beginning during the 1980s has gathered extraordinary pace. Young people make familiar use of a multiplicity of digital electronic devices and media in ways which would have bewildered most teachers 30 years ago and continue to challenge many today. Everything in this and the next four sections is intended to apply equally to writing employing digital technologies as to writing employing traditional, physical equipment and means of publication.

The first of the answers to the question 'What do teachers need to know and do in order to teach writing effectively?' is that teachers should *recognise the complexity of what they ask students to do when they ask them to write.*

Imagine that it is an ordinary day at school, and that the class has been set a writing task. At the end of the lesson, the teacher receives 30 pieces of writing. He or she reads them. In reading, the teacher might consider any of the aspects of writing represented in the diagram on page 72 (Figure 3.1), and consider some of issues raised there.

The categories contained within those boxes are not chronological in order of acquisition, or hierarchical in order of importance. Eight-year-olds may be learning to write fairy stories. They have accumulated a sufficient stock of fairy stories and fables, have understood some of the conventions of the genre sufficiently well, to attempt to write one. It may be that the 8-year-olds' sentences are simple rather than complex, that the piece contains several spelling errors, and that there are some errors the 8-year-olds do not make because they have not even got to the stage of attempting the constructions within which errors might be made. But the young writers are still writing fairy stories, and as such are attempting to handle that difficult quality called genre.

So it is not a case of building blocks of words going to make sentences, going to make paragraphs, going to make whole texts, and the process happening sequentially over time. Neither is this the case when 11-year-olds write up the report of a science experiment or 16-year-olds discuss a scene from *Romeo and Juliet*. The categories that we might isolate in order to see more clearly – and to help writers to see more clearly – what is happening in a piece of writing are not the categories that the writers perceive in doing a piece of writing.

A Piece of Writing

THE TASK

Is the piece carried through and finished?
Did it require more than one draft?
How consistent is it from beginning to end in terms of the requirements
of all the other boxes?

AWARENESS OF THE READER

Who is the writer writing for? Does the writing implicitly or explicitly show an awareness of its potential readership?

HANDWRITING OR KEYBOARD SKILLS

If the piece was handwritten, is the handwriting easily legible?
If the piece was word-processed, how advanced are the writer's skills?

WHO IS 'SPEAKING' THROUGH THE WRITING?

Is the piece personal or impersonal? Does it operate in the third person, in the first person with the writer speaking as herself or himself, or is the narrator not the writer but 'speaking' in role? How skilfully and consistently does the writer handle one of these options, or a different option?

LAYOUT, PRESENTATION AND MEDIA

How firm is the writer's grasp of the conventions and possibilities of layout and presentation in this piece?

VOCABULARY

What evidence of variety, aptness, accuracy or power in the writer's choice of vocabulary?

OVERALL IMPACT

What is the piece – factual, imaginative or a hybrid – saying to the reader? How effectively is it doing its job of communicating information, ideas, a point of view, emotional power?

CONTROL WITHIN A SENTENCE

Errors, miscues and confusions: how many and what sort?†
What variety of sentence introductions?
What variety of sentence lengths?
What variety of sentence structures?
How well are these handled?

THE FORM OF THE WHOLE TEXT

How firm is the grasp of the overall structure of the piece being attempted (whether it be a story, playscript, poem, factual description, discursive essay, text for a speech, diary or blog, letter, report of science experiment, set of instructions . . .)?
Is the writer able to manipulate mood in imaginative writing, showing a feeling for the poetic, the startling, the rhetorical? Does the writer present argument, opinion or polemic logically and persuasively? Is the writer accurate and clear in reports and instructional writing?

CONTROL BETWEEN SENTENCES

What are the relationships between sentences? Are they: *temporal/sequential* ('Once upon a time . . . The next day . . . Many years later . . .'); *causal* ('She would not speak to him. This made him very unhappy.'); *concessive* ('Some people say there are too many immigrants coming to this country. But I think . . .'); *rhetorical* ('His heart began to beat faster. The palms of his hands were damp. His fingers twitched.'); or of some other kind?
How well does the writer handle them?

Figure 3.1 Aspects of writing considered by the teacher.

† See the list of errors, miscues and confusions on page 156.

With that qualification in mind, let us look at the boxes in the diagram. When a teacher asks a student to do a piece of writing, the request is to: manipulate a pen, pencil or computer keyboard; order words in groups so that they make grammatical sense; observe the conventions of the English spelling and punctuation systems; maintain cohesion within a piece of writing, so that it holds together as a vehicle of meaning rather than being merely a sequence of discrete and unconnected sentences; be aware of conventions of genre while also remembering that those conventions are open to challenge and change; keep in mind the person or people for whom the piece is being written; and maintain the necessary stamina to see the job through. That is quite a list of demands, which must be met simultaneously.

Readers are invited to improve on the effort opposite; it is there as a prototype. (The note at the bottom of the diagram, referring to a list on pages 89 and 90, is an early signal of something to be discussed in more detail later: the fact that there is always pattern in error.)

The 'personality' of the writer

Below is a simple model (Figure 3.2) of the 'personality' of the writer. It works for student writers throughout their schooling and extends to the most sophisticated writing adults do.

Composer: Writing is almost never the simple transcribing onto paper of language already formed in the head. In the act of writing, writers discover what they mean; they formulate understanding in a way not available to them before they began to write.

Communicator: Most of the time, writers write in the expectation of having an effect on someone else. (Sometimes, admittedly, writers write solely for

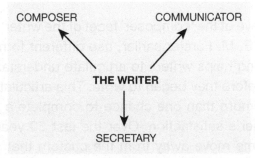

Figure 3.2 A simple model of the 'personality' of the writer.

themselves. Often, writing is both for themselves and for other people.) All writers need regularly to know – whether their readership is a single person or an unknown number of readers, whether their purpose is ephemeral or long-term – that their writing has been noticed and has made a difference.

Secretary: Writers work within the writing system of the language they are using. The system has evolved over hundreds of years (and continues to change) for a host of reasons: for example, the influence of other languages; the practices of scribes; the rise of print; the efforts of some groups to reform spelling.

Reconciling the three facets of the writer's 'personality'

'Composer', 'communicator' and 'secretary' are equally important facets of the 'personality' of the writer. Effective teachers, of which thank goodness the English-speaking world has many thousands, understand the need to nurture all three facets of the writer's 'personality'. Each must be respected and given the chance to flourish. Each interpenetrates with the others. There will be times when one or other of the three is uppermost in the mind of the writer. Draft observational notes on a science experiment, jotted down prior to writing a report, belong principally to the writer's characteristic as composer. A letter written to a children's author about a book that the class has just read belongs principally to the writer's characteristic as communicator. A lesson in which the teacher uses a piece of prose to show how commas are used in complex sentences belongs principally to the writer's characteristic as secretary. But it can easily be seen how the 'lesser' characteristics in each of these three examples still have their part to play.

Redrafting

The description above of the 'composer' facet of the writer's 'personality', and the quotation from E. M. Forster earlier, use different forms of words to say that the act of writing helps writers to articulate understanding in a way not available to them before they began to write. This articulation is often helped when writers have more than one chance to complete a piece of writing to their and the teacher's satisfaction. Over the last 30 years, there has been a major and welcome move away from the custom that students only ever had one go at a piece of writing, which was then judged by the teacher and forgotten about by the time the teacher issued an instruction to do another piece of writing.

This is a big step forward. Adults who write seriously for any purpose in their lives (a group which includes but is not confined to professional writers) work on a piece of writing until they're more or less satisfied with it. Students who are enabled to work on a piece of writing until they are more or less satisfied with it derive a similar satisfaction, generating a similar motivation to go on and write again, write better. They may in the process produce less quantity in total. The benefit in terms of quality far outweighs the disadvantage of a reduction in quantity. One of the reasons why many adults in the world do as little writing as possible is that their memory of the experience at school is of one-off attempts, abandoned rather than properly finished, few if any of which yielded satisfaction.

However, any good idea can become an arid orthodoxy if implemented too rigidly. To encourage the redrafting of handwritten or word-processed writing is not the same as to require endless complete longhand or on-screen rewrites. Not every piece has to go through a number of drafts. The right kind of flexibility in this regard is similar to the flexibility adults who write seriously offer themselves: some pieces need more reworking; some arrive at a satisfactory state more quickly.

To restate the positive: the process of distance-taking from their work, of becoming good critical readers of their writing – in which the drafting process plays a crucial part – is an essential trait of the 'personality' of mature and maturing writers.

A community of readers and writers

The section 'The demands made on student writers' concentrated on a piece of writing. The section 'The "personality" of the writer' concentrated on the writer. This section concentrates on the classroom. On page 76, again presented diagrammatically (Figure 3.3), is a model of what a writing classroom can and should be.

A range of audiences and means of publication

The teacher remains an immensely important audience for students' writing: probably the most important for most students. But the teacher should not

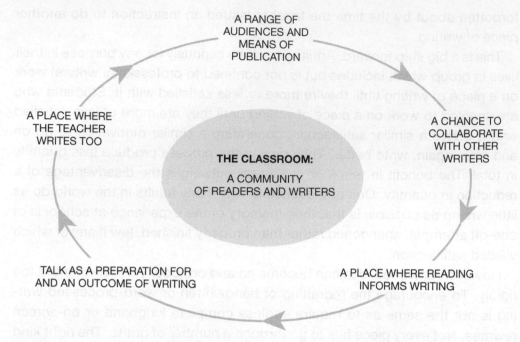

THE CLASSROOM:

A COMMUNITY
OF READERS AND WRITERS

A RANGE OF
AUDIENCES AND
MEANS OF
PUBLICATION

A CHANCE TO
COLLABORATE
WITH OTHER
WRITERS

A PLACE WHERE READING
INFORMS WRITING

TALK AS A PREPARATION FOR
AND AN OUTCOME OF WRITING

A PLACE WHERE
THE TEACHER
WRITES TOO

Figure 3.3 What a writing classroom can and should be.

be the students' only audience. Beyond the teacher, the readily available, day-to-day audience for students' writing is the other people in the classroom. Those who have gone beyond the classroom have found great benefits in, for example: students writing for younger children; students writing for a specific readership in the local community; letter, email and audio-visual exchanges with other schools (including schools in other countries).

Means of publication include: reading out loud, wall displays, a class folder with transparent loose-leaf holders containing recent writing from everyone in the class, word-processed and duplicated booklets of illustrated writing. To these long-established means we must add more recent electronic ones: e-books, websites and blogs, wikis, podcasts and other audio-visual presentations – on whiteboards, tablets and other appliances – in which writing is combined with sounds and images.

The means of publication – oral, handwritten, printed or electronic – will sometimes be ambitious; the audience will sometimes be beyond the classroom. But most of the time, the means of publication and the audience for writing should be straightforward for the teacher to organise with the community of readers and writers immediately available.

A chance to collaborate with other writers

Collaboration with other writers does not usually mean a group of students writing the same one piece by committee. It is true that writers often need peace and quiet and the chance to get on with something by themselves. But equally, students who write only and ever as a solitary effort, never as a contribution to a collective endeavour, fail to experience the way in which much writing in the real world comes into being. Scientific and educational books and papers very often have two or more authors. Newspapers and magazines combine the efforts of many contributors. When a group of teachers produces a policy statement of some kind at their school, it is a collaborative effort.

Quite often, students should similarly be undertaking group tasks involving writing, with individuals contributing different parts to an eventual whole. The eventual whole could be a display of research, a brochure about the school, an anthology of poetry, a collection of argument pieces on a topic of controversy: any activity which involves planning, allocation of tasks, mutual support and criticism, leading to a product where individuals can see their own contributions within a larger finished product. This collective and collaborative approach to writing may be realised in paper- and print-based or electronic means of publication.

A place where reading informs writing

The next section discusses the range of kinds of writing students should encounter and try out for themselves. It touches on the importance of models in giving students examples of how different kinds of writing have been achieved. Here, we cite one piece of research which looked in detail at how students' reading of one kind of writing, literary texts, influenced their own writing of literary texts.

The Reader in the Writer (Barrs and Cork, 2001) is the report of a year-long research project, organised by the Centre for Literacy in Primary Education, which studied the writing of Year 5 and 6 children in five primary schools. The project aimed to discover whether exposure to high-quality literary texts affected those children's own writing of literary texts. If it did affect the children's writing, did it improve it? If it did improve it, in what ways was the improvement demonstrated?

The research found that exposure to high-quality literary texts did significantly improve the children's literary writing. In particular, to quote or paraphrase some of the project's conclusions:

- *Children's reading of literary texts encouraged them to write differently, moving out of what might be termed their 'home style' into new areas of language.*
- *Children's experience of writing in first person, but not as themselves, helped them to assume different voices and enter areas of language that they did not normally use.*
- *Teachers in the project classrooms believed strongly in the value of continuing to read aloud to older children and regarded this as an important way in which they could bring texts alive for them and engage them with literature.*
- *Discussion around a text helped children to articulate aesthetic responses to the writing.*
- *Drama work led to strongly imagined writing in role.*
- *The most effective teachers helped children to plan their writing by offering 'open structures' which were supportive but not overly formulaic.*
- *Effective teachers put a great deal of emphasis on encouraging children to work on their writing together, for instance through the use of response partners or writing partners.*
- *Texts with strong clear narrative structures, such as traditional or folk tales, were helpful to all children, and especially to children for whom English was an additional language.*
- *Emotionally powerful texts, several of which were introduced to children in the course of the year, helped writers to adopt other points of view, and to explore the inner states of characters, more readily.*

(Barrs and Cork, 2001: 210–216)[1]

This work is confined to the use of literary texts with children in two upper-primary years. However, the lessons from the work are clear, and generalisable to secondary schools and to genres of writing other than the literary. As a result of reading or listening to high-quality texts, and aided by opportunities for engaging with texts through talk and drama, students' confidence and competence in writing texts of this kind themselves, and their sense of the options available to them in doing so, are greatly enhanced.

Talk as a preparation for and an outcome of writing

Oral work in all its forms – paired, group and whole-class talk; role-play, improvisation and drama – are very often essential preparations for effective writing. It's also true that the spoken language in these and other forms – for example, spoken presentations of various kinds to the class and to wider audiences – can be outcomes of writing, satisfying to the writer/reader/speaker and to the readers/listeners/spectators too.

A place where the teacher writes too

Teachers of writing should write too. Some of their writing should be shared with the students; from time to time, teachers should actually write in the classroom so that the students can see that they do it; on occasion, teachers should write 'in public', using an easel with large paper or an interactive whiteboard, inviting the collaboration of the class.

The benefits are various. The intention is not, of course, to say to students 'If only you could write like me, how lucky you would be'. There is the general truth that teachers teach by example as much as by instruction. If students see teachers writing, they are more likely to conclude that writing is worth the time and effort. They may even be interested in teachers' experiences and opinions, as teachers should be interested in theirs. If students see teachers engaging with the process, struggling with the difficulties, glad of the rewards, that example will support them when they find writing hard. When teachers show students that writers have the right to change their minds, they are teaching an important lesson. Teachers have a more advanced control of writing and the writing system than students do, from which the latter can learn. Finally, teachers' recent experience of writing themselves is bound to inform the quality of their teaching it.

A broad and varied repertoire for writing

The fourth answer to the question 'What do teachers need to know and do in order to teach writing effectively?' concentrates on the repertoire of kinds of writing which students should have the opportunity to experience. There is no correct number of kinds of writing which students should encounter. There are many different ways of naming and grouping kinds of writing.

Purposes, forms and media

We could list kinds of writing in terms of the *purposes* they serve, in terms of the *forms* they take, and in terms of the *media* by which they are communicated to a readership.

Purposes for writing could include: to recount (a series of events); to re-present (information gleaned from a variety of sources); to explain (the workings of a piece of technology); to instruct (the reader in making a cake); to advocate (a cause); to discuss (a controversial issue, with things to be said for and against a proposition); to narrate (a fictional or factual story, or one which mixes fact and fiction); to distil (a thought or idea in concise terms); to respond (to an aesthetic experience of some kind); to remember (facts or experiences which would be forgotten if they were not written down).

There are ten purposes in this list. The number is deliberately round and arbitrary; the reader will wish to add to or subtract from the list. The names given to the purposes here are negotiable: does the reader prefer 'debate' to 'discuss', 'report' to 're-present', 'argue' to 'advocate'? Improvements and amendments are welcome.

Let the list of forms also number ten. Forms of writing could include: chronological account, factual description, discursive essay, poem, prose story, playscript, diary, letter, speech (as in 'a speech'), set of instructions. The same flexibility applies here as to purposes; the reader should feel free to add or subtract and to rename.

The purposes for writing could be fulfilled in many of the forms. The forms of writing could achieve many of the purposes.

The media by which purposes for and forms of writing can communicate with a readership (media which will profoundly affect both purposes and forms) include: handwritten script on paper, word-processing on screen, physical book-making, wall display, poster campaign, blog, mobile phone text, email, staged presentation of script, filmed presentation of script.

Here are another ten possibilities in a third dimension of the universe of writing. There are now 1,000 theoretical combinations of purpose, form and medium (though some combinations are implausible or impractical). Students should encounter and attempt a sample of the possible combinations.

We could present the interaction of purposes, forms and media in a Venn diagram (Figure 3.4).

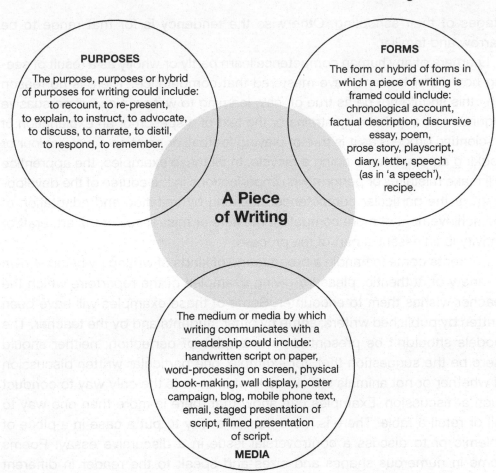

PURPOSES

The purpose, purposes or hybrid
of purposes for writing could include:
to recount, to re-present,
to explain, to instruct, to advocate,
to discuss, to narrate, to distil,
to respond, to remember.

FORMS

The form or hybrid of forms in
which a piece of writing is
framed could include:
chronological account,
factual description, discursive
essay, poem,
prose story, playscript,
diary, letter, speech
(as in 'a speech'),
recipe.

**A Piece
of Writing**

The medium or media by which
writing communicates with a
readership could include:
handwritten script on paper,
word-processing on screen, physical
book-making, wall display, poster
campaign, blog, mobile phone text,
email, staged presentation of
script, filmed presentation
of script.

MEDIA

Figure 3.4 The interaction of purposes, forms and media.

The teacher's constituency

The teacher's job in designing schemes or sequences of work is not, first, to make a list of purposes, forms and media and then to find excuses for employing them. The job is to decide, first, on the activities and topics which will constitute that work, and then to think imaginatively about how writing, in the fullness of its variety of purposes, forms and media, may play a part in it.

That said, teachers do have a constituency. They should be able to describe the range of kinds of writing which students should encounter at different stages of their schooling. Otherwise the tendency is for that range to be narrow and familiar.

Learners of any human competence learn partly or wholly as a result of seeing how other humans have mastered that competence. There is no reason why this should not be as true of, say, learning to write a piece of persuasive argument or a ballad in quatrains or the text of a speech or an explanation of a scientific process as it is true of playing football or painting a watercolour or cooking an omelette or riding a bicycle. In all these examples, the apprentice will make mistakes or perform with imperfections in the course of the development of the particular competence. Learning by imitation and adaptation of the achievement of more competent masters or mistresses of the art, craft or activity is an essential part of the process.

Students come to handle a broad range of kinds of writing by being shown a variety of authentic, pleasure-giving examples of the repertoire which the teacher wishes them to encounter. Some of these examples will have been written by published writers; some by other students and by the teacher. The models shouldn't be presented as examples of perfection; neither should there be the suggestion that, for example, one particular written discussion of whether or not animals should be kept in zoos is the only way to conduct such a discussion. Examples can show that there is more than one way to tell or retell a fable. There is more than one way to put a case in a piece of polemic or to discuss a controversial issue in a discursive essay. Poems come in numerous shapes and sizes and speak to the reader in different tones of voice.

Once students have been shown examples of a form of writing, they can try their hand at it themselves. It is then useful for the teacher to lead a discussion about some of the students' efforts. An approach which says, in effect, 'See how so-and-so has done this; let's look at the structure of the piece, the way it introduces the topic, develops its argument (or its plot or its description), comes to its conclusion. Does it work well? Are there other and better ways of doing it?' has a good chance of success.

In the course of these discussions of whole texts, students' and other people's, it is legitimate and desirable for the teacher to introduce appropriate metalanguage. The words 'topic', 'introduction', 'development', 'conclusion', 'argument', 'assertion', 'evidence', 'example', 'plot', 'character', 'climax' are all potential metalinguistic terms. Any of them could be called upon in a discussion, depending on the kind of writing being discussed and the age of the students.

Effective and ineffective structural analysis

Structural analysis of the kind described in the previous sub-section is useful, just as grammatical analysis, or attention to spelling patterns or conventions of punctuation, is useful in the context of the study of the students' or other writers' texts. However, the attempt to teach students to write across a range of genres by offering them theoretical terminology in advance of actual writing will fail. Such an approach doesn't work developmentally from the point of view of the learner. It makes the same mistake at the level of the study of whole texts as the imposition of synthetic phonics or of long lists of spelling rules or of heavy loads of decontextualised grammatical terminology makes in those fields of learning. Andrews and Smith (2011) point elegantly to the shortcomings of this approach.

> *The approach that builds on text-based genre theory has led to simplified worksheets which characterize genres by formulae. For example, an essay is seen to have an introduction, followed by points for the argument, points against, followed by a summing up or conclusion, stating the point of view of the writer. And yet we know from classical rhetoric that Aristotle, Cicero and Quintilian suggested at least seven variations on structural form between them, with Quintilian concluding that the number of parts must be determined by the function of the piece. Another variation of such a formula is the American 'five-paragraph essay' consisting of introduction, three supporting paragraphs and a conclusion. This happens to be one of the many variations of form suggested by classical rhetoricians, reduced to a packaged formula for pedagogic use. An over-emphasis on form and structure tends to drain energy from the writing process, which involves motivation to write, engagement with the audience, the formation of ideas or elements to be included and then a concentration on form.*
>
> (Andrews and Smith, 2011: 17)

It is tempting for those with an adult and analytical understanding of a field of learning to suppose that the understanding they have is also the way in which a learner comes to apprehend that field. It is not. Apprentice writers need to find their way towards full control of the characteristics of a particular kind of writing by trial and error. Transitional efforts at factual genres such as advocacy, discussion, instruction or report may include, for example, awkward mixtures of the personal and impersonal, switchings between present and past tense, and comings and goings of the active and passive voice. Only by allowing these awkward mixtures to present themselves and to be commented on will students move towards consistent control of the characteristics of a particular factual genre.

There should be no worry, initially at least, about students' 'lack of originality', about their imitation of style or structure in the writing of others, including that of established writers. Originality originates in imitation, as the classical rhetoricians knew. Masters and mistresses, present in the classroom or introduced from outside, teach apprentices, who come to develop their own style, their own way of handling structure, their own 'signature'.

Transgressing generic boundaries: two examples

Kinds of writing, whether expressed in terms of purposes, forms or media, are not watertight categories, each with a set of separate characteristics. Kinds merge into and intersect with each other. The dividing lines are smudgy, not sharp. To lighten the tone of what might have seemed a heavy section so far, here are two examples of merging and intersection.

Tony Harrison's wonderful poem 'Dark Times', about a kind of moth which has changed colour in a biologically astonishingly short period of time, mixes historical information, scientific information and speculation about the future.

> *That the* Peppered Moth *was white and now is dark 's
> a lesson in survival for Mankind.*
>
> *Around the time Charles Darwin had declined
> the dedication of* Das Kapital *by Marx
> its predators could spot it on the soot,
> but Industrial Revolution and Evolution taught
> the moth to black its wings and not get caught
> where all of Nature perished, or all but.*
>
> *When lichens lighten some old smoke-grimed trees
> and such as Yorkshire's millstacks now don't burn
> and fish nose waters stagnant centuries,
> can* Biston Carbonaria *relearn,*

if Man's awakened consciousness succeeds
in turning all these tides of blackness back
and diminishing the need for looking black,

to flutter white again above new Leeds?

(Harrison, 2013)

Factual reports can contain passages of lyrical description illuminating the facts. Here is an extract from Gilbert White's 1789 *The Natural History of Selborne*, about the felling of some oak trees:

> On the Blackmoor estate there is a small wood called Losel's, of a few acres, that was lately furnished with a set of oaks of a peculiar growth and great value; they were tall and tapering like firs, but standing near together had very small heads, only a little brush without any large limbs. About twenty years ago the bridge at the Toy, near Hampton-court, being much decayed, some trees were wanted for the repairs that were fifty feet long without bough, and would measure twelve inches diameter at the little end. Twenty such trees did a purveyor find in this little wood, with this advantage, that many of them answered the description at sixty feet. These trees were sold for twenty pounds apiece.
>
> In the centre of this grove there stood an oak, which, though shapely and tall on the whole, bulged out into a large excrescence about the middle of the stem. On this a pair of ravens had fixed their residence for such a series of years, that the oak was distinguished by the title of the Raven-tree. Many were the attempts of the neighbouring youths to get at this eyry: the difficulty whetted their inclinations, and each was ambitious of surmounting the arduous task. But, when they arrived at the swelling, it jutted out so in their way, and was so far beyond their grasp, that the most daring lads were awed, and acknowledged the undertaking to be too hazardous. So the ravens built on, nest upon nest, in perfect security, till the fatal day arrived in which the wood was to be levelled. It was in the month of February, when those birds usually sit. The saw was applied to the butt, the wedges were inserted into the opening, the woods echoed to the heavy blows of the beetle or mallet, the tree nodded to its fall; but still the dam sat on. At last, when it gave way, the bird was flung from her nest; and, though her parental affection deserved a better fate, was whipped down by the twigs, which brought her dead to the ground.

(White, 2004 [1789]: Letter 2)

As we see from these two examples – the one a poem which amongst other things tells us something we probably did not know about a speeded-up case of Darwinian adaptation, the other an account of tree-felling which captures our admiration by the deft economy of its description and which touches our emotions at the fate of the mother raven – it is dangerous to become over-specific about the necessary characteristics of a certain type of writing.

Digital makes transgression easier

These examples are from 'old' technology. Digital technology makes the crossing of generic boundaries easier, more 'normal'.

> *the habitual meta-genres of the conventional written mode – narrative, argument, description – are challenged by digital composition, where boundaries are crossed, hybrid genres are more common, and 'originality' takes the form of compositional originality rather than more purely expressive originality in a (seemingly) single mode.*

(Andrews and Smith, 2011: 124)

Groups of students in a Year 8 class in a London school recently produced four-page online newspapers containing reportage, opinion articles, letters, poetry, a short story, a quiz, photographs and a short film including commentary and music. The purposes of each piece of writing intersected with its form. The letter contained autobiographical information as well as an argued point of view. The poem was polemical. The short story was an allegory about a current environmental concern in the area the school serves. The newspapers were displayed on the class whiteboard, admired and discussed. This is an activity which a few years ago would have tested the ingenuity, organisational powers and technical competence of all but a few teachers. It is much easier to contemplate now. The old boundaries are weakened; they invite transgression.

An effective understanding of instruction

The great majority of developing writers' learning comes from experience: of talking, listening, reading – and writing. It is also true that beginning writers

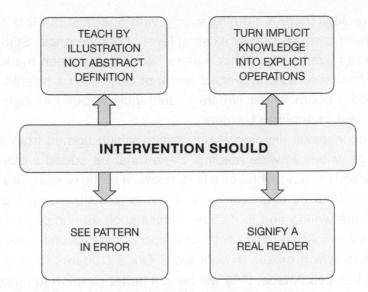

Figure 3.5 Teachers' interventions in students' writing.

engage in much conscious activity, for example to do with the forming of letters. As children move beyond the Early Years, and as their experience of
speech and of the written language (through reading and writing) broadens
and diversifies, the learning that they take from this experience is continuous,
very powerful and mainly unconscious. No child can learn to write without
such experience. It works from the little – where to put commas in sentences –
to the large – what are the structural characteristics of a successful piece of
factual explanation, or narrative or argument.

But for most students, learning to write is not only a matter of experience.
Teachers also have an essential job of instruction to do. The fifth answer to
the question 'What do teachers need to know and do in order to teach writing
effectively?' is concerned with the nature of that instruction: with the quality of
teachers' interventions in students' writing (see Figure 3.5).

Teach by illustration not abstract definition

This principle was asserted in the previous section in the context of the discussion of the structural analysis of whole texts. Students do not learn how
to control an element of writing by being given definitions and rules in isolation from the act of writing. Definitions and rules are abstractions, attempts

to analyse reality. There is nothing wrong with analysis; but it is only effective when there is some already existing level of competence. Students learn by seeing examples of how other writers have used speech marks or paragraphs, or discussed a controversial issue, or described a scientific process or composed a poem. Other writers should include other students and the teacher, as well as published writers.

To the unconscious learning about writing which comes from seeing the work of other writers in wide reading, there must be added a closer kind of reading in which the teacher takes a text, shows it to the whole class and leads a discussion about its characteristics. What is it in the content and overall structure of the writing and in its finer details such as choice of vocabulary, complexity (or simplicity) of its sentences, appropriate (or unconventional) use of punctuation which makes it work well? Once students have understood how a thing has been made, they will be in a better position to make a similar thing themselves. As acknowledged earlier, a 'similar thing' to the style and structure of a model is not to be criticised on grounds of lack of originality; close imitation is often a staging-point on the way to an individual 'signature'.

Turn implicit knowledge into explicit operations

Students know more about writing than they know that they know. Their implicit understanding of an element of writing – the understanding they have from all their other experiences of language – is in advance of their ability regularly and reliably to control that element under the pressure of production. The teacher should appeal to that implicit understanding in asking the learner to perform a conscious operation on the text; to be a critic or a detective. 'We've got a bit of a problem with the marking of sentences – with full stops and capital letters. There are about six places on this page where you haven't marked the sentences right. Can you find them?' Most students can find most of them.

See pattern in error

There is no such person as a writer, however unsuccessful, whose writing is just a mass of ignorance and confusion. There are always a few things – maybe no more than two or three – which are causing the major difficulties.

The teacher's skill is in looking past the superficial symptoms, seeing the pattern in the error, and attending with the writer to the two or three things which matter most at this particular moment in the writer's development.

'Progress in Pat's Writing' (Richmond, 2012b) is a study I made of the development of a 15-year-old girl's writing over a period of 12 months. The study revealed a hierarchy of frequency of error in Pat's writing, with a small number of categories accounting for the overwhelming majority of individual cases. It was immediately clear that if I could attend with Pat to this small number of categories, which in her case were to do with the incorrect marking of sentences, the misspellings of certain words, the incorrect use of speech marks, the occasional omissions of words, and the uncertain use of commas, Pat would make rapid progress, which she did. Still more important was my realisation that Pat's implicit knowledge of the conventions of the writing system was far in advance of her ability regularly and reliably to observe those conventions as she wrote. She certainly knew more about writing than she knew that she knew.

So once I formed the habit of, as it were, turning Pat into an error detective on her own work, using the kinds of prompts suggested in the previous subsection, Pat soon became an efficient sub-editor of her writing. Of course, there were also occasions when I simply taught; these went hand in hand with the occasions when Pat, having been shown how to be self-critical, taught herself.

Later, when I was working on the National Writing Project, I studied the writing of pupils in primary schools in three local authorities to see if my discoveries with Pat also applied to younger writers. I found that they did. I drew up the following list of categories of common error, miscue and confusion. The list of these features is ordered by frequency in the work of the writers with whom I worked.

1 incorrect marking of sentences;
2 misspellings;
3 uncertain control of tense;
4 grammatical derailment – the sentence doesn't hold together grammatically;
5 incorrect marking of speech in a narrative;
6 omission or duplication of words or phrases;
7 omission or redundant use of commas;
8 omission or redundant use of apostrophes;
9 omission of capitals or their redundant use in mid-sentence;

10 omission of question marks;

11 splitting a word: 'neighbour hood'; or shunting together a phrase: 'afterall';

12 confusion over similar- or identical-sounding very common words: 'there'/ 'their', 'when'/'went', 'were'/'where';

13 uncertainty about singular/plural, particularly when a word has an irregular plural form: 'woman'/'women'.

The insight that students can apply their implicit understanding of the conventions of writing in explicit self-critical interventions in their work is of central importance in moving practice away from the model of the teacher as the only assessor and examiner of writing.

Signify a real reader

When students are engaged in writing for a purpose they understand and for an audience they care about, they are usually determined to get the conventions right too. The single most important principle of intervention is that teachers should behave as real readers; their first response should be to what writing is saying.

Instruction as applied to spelling, punctuation and layout, handwriting and typing, and grammar

It should be clear by now that this chapter advocates a holistic approach to the teaching of writing: one that holds together attention to content, structure and system. However, it will be useful to say something specific here about some aspects of writing commonly lumped together as features of the writing system, while pointing out straight away how unhelpful is that lumping together.

Spelling, punctuation and layout are indeed specific to the writing system. Handwriting and typing are motor skills required for the visible realisation of writing. Grammar underlies all language, spoken and written. In all these cases – even with beginning writers, for whom a higher degree of conscious learning is required than is the case for beginning talkers or readers – the heavy load of learning is carried by experience of language; the lighter but still significant load is carried by instruction in language.

Spelling

Students come to have a secure grasp of spelling by recognising and remembering the way words are spelt in the context of meaningful sentences and texts. 'Meaningful sentences and texts' should not be taken to mean only the writer's own sentences and texts. The phrase means all the meaningful sentences and texts which students encounter as readers and produce as writers (before, in the latter case, encountering them as readers of their own writing).

So, most important of all, effective teachers ensure that their students read copiously all manner of worthwhile and pleasure-giving texts.

There *are* spelling patterns, grapho-phonic correspondences, in the English writing system, and teachers can make use of this convenient fact in those cases where the correspondences apply. But they also need to be careful not to make excessive claims for these correspondences. If they claim that spelling patterns are always or even nearly always regular in English words, they are misleading the students.

It can be helpful to display on the classroom walls lists of words, included in meaningful sentences, which – to use language appropriate to an 11-year-old student:

- look like each other and sound like each other;
- look like each other but do not sound like each other;
- sound like each other but do not look like each other.

It is important for teachers to be aware of accent variation across the country. The examples in each of the three lists will vary depending on where the school is. For example, 'blood' and 'book' sound different in the south of England, the same in some parts of the north of England and different again in others. Some EAL learners make no difference in pronunciation between certain words – for example 'ship' and 'sheep' – when most first-language English speakers do.

Words with unusual spellings which commonly give difficulty can be displayed on the classroom walls in the context of meaningful sentences.

Students should be shown the use of dictionaries, printed and electronic, appropriate for their age group.

It can be helpful for students to have their own spelling books, physical or electronic, in which they accumulate spellings which they have needed in the course of their writing.

Students should be shown what to do when they're not sure of a spelling (for example, they could go to a word bank or dictionary, classroom-made or published; they could ask a friend; they could write out the word in different ways before looking it up or asking an adult). Once new correct spellings are in the spelling book, students can practise them using the Look–Say–Cover–Write–Check routine:

> **Look** at the word carefully and mark any parts of it which are causing you problems. **Say** the word to yourself. **Cover** the word and close your eyes; remember the word by trying to see it in your head; say it slowly in a way that helps you remember how to spell it. **Write** the word down, keeping the word you looked at covered. **Check** the spelling to see if you have got it right. If you haven't, try again or try working with your spelling partner.
>
> (O'Sullivan and Thomas, 2000: 81)

When students write on computers, they can use the spellchecker and note down in their spelling books the words which the spellchecker corrected. (But they should be warned that spellcheckers are not infallible; they cannot detect homonyms or homophones.)

Before a class is to undertake a writing task, the teacher can ask for, contribute and display a collection of words that will be useful in the task.

When the teacher writes publicly for and with the students, using paper-based or electronic equipment, he or she can draw them into discussion of how to spell particular words that they and the teacher suggest.

To repeat an earlier recommendation, students should be encouraged to become their own and each other's 'spelling detectives'. If they are told that there are a certain number of spelling errors in a piece of writing, and asked to try to identify and correct them, they will be able to do so in many cases. If their independent efforts or the help of their friends fail to produce a correct spelling, the teacher will provide it.

Punctuation and layout

As with the teaching of spelling, conscious teaching of punctuation is best done in the context of the study of meaningful sentences and texts. Once again, these sentences and texts include but are not confined to the learner's own writing.

Often, in the course of the whole-class study of a piece of writing, the teacher can point out a writer's correct and effective use of punctuation, and draw attention to its value in making clear the writer's meaning. Punctuation is best understood as an aid to meaning. It can be an indicator of grammatical choices.

Sometimes, a student's writing can be shared (with the writer's agreement) with the whole class. The writing will contain some errors of punctuation (and perhaps of spelling too). After a discussion of the qualities of the content of the writing, the teacher can invite the class to help the writer to identify and correct the errors.

Examples of the use of features of punctuation (for example, capital letters to begin a sentence or as the first letter of a proper noun; apostrophes to indicate possession or abbreviation; commas to separate items in lists or to isolate phrases or clauses; semi-colons to separate phrases or clauses in long sentences) can be displayed around the classroom, always as features of meaningful phrases, clauses or sentences.

Print and the internet have so rich a diversity of presentation and layout that it is easy to show students models of how texts can be organised, presented and enhanced as appropriate by the use of boxes, different fonts and colours, diagrams and illustrations.

Handwriting, typing and word-processing

Most students will have developed a relaxed, clear and individual handwriting style long before they arrive at secondary school. But a few will not. And there is evidence (for example, in the Office for Standards in Education's *Moving English Forward*, 2012) that many children at Year 3 and beyond, and especially boys, still need frequent opportunities to practise their handwriting.

It is often helpful for those students who still need practice in handwriting to copy texts appropriate for their age and maturity, so that they are concentrating purely on the physical formation of letters and words, without the pressure of composition. There will in these cases be a need for the teacher to reinforce this basic competence and to help the student to hold a pen or pencil more firmly and naturally.

The most effective way to encourage good handwriting is to show students the importance of attractive final copy for some of their writing (see the remarks in the section 'The "personality" of the writer' about redrafting). The desire to 'look good in public', whether the public is an audience in the student's class or beyond, unites the physical act of writing with the wider sense that writing is *for* someone, for a readership whom the writer wishes and needs to impress.

It is a curiosity of officialdom's nervousness and uncertainty about the digital revolution which has profoundly affected all of us – teachers and students alike – that there is no acknowledgement of the existence of the digital world in the new National Curriculum orders for writing (see the critique of this failing in the new orders later in the chapter).

Students should be helped to develop keyboard skills. The intention is not to produce touch typists with record-breaking speeds, but to enable students to write on a computer at least as quickly as they can handwrite. A desirable stage in the development of handwriting is 'automaticity' – a level of fluency which means that the physical act of forming letters and linking them in words is operating at a largely unconscious level, so that the writer's brain can be occupied with other important matters such as composition. Equivalently, if students writing on computers are stuck at the 'hunt and peck' stage of typing letters, they will not be engaging with larger tasks such as wrangling with a text's overall structure or thinking about the needs of their audience. So students should have some instruction in typing and word-processing, whose aim should be that they can compose at the keyboard at least as fast as they can handwrite.

Grammar

Chapter 4 contains a detailed discussion of the place of grammar teaching within the English curriculum, and of the relationship between grammar teaching and students' achievement in writing. This sub-section considers grammar only in the context of teachers' interventions in students' writing to correct grammatical errors.

In the list on pages 89 and 90, the third and fourth categories of error, miscue and confusion which I found in working with students relate to grammar: 'uncertain control of tense' and 'grammatical derailment – the sentence doesn't hold together grammatically'.

The most effective teaching of grammar, as it relates to errors in students' writing, is – with the help of appropriate terminology such as 'present tense', 'continuous present (the "-ing" form)', 'past tense', 'first-person verb ending', 'third-person verb ending' – to point out the error, and to appeal to the students' underlying grammatical understanding as speakers of English.

The usual reason why a writer has made a grammatical error is that, in composing a part of a text, the need to compose has made too heavy a demand on the process of transcription, causing the writer to produce a word-form or an arrangement of words which he or she would never have produced in speech. By appealing to the writer's profound understanding of the grammar of her or his spoken language, the teacher turns the writer into a critical reader of the text.

Students who are learning English as an additional language, and students who have access to a non-standard variety of English in their speech repertoire, will sometimes produce grammatical forms in their writing which owe their existence to the grammar of a first language or of a non-standard variety of English. There is more on this in Chapters 7 and 8.

Writers experiencing difficulty

This section has dwelt at some length on aspects of difficulty in writing. Readers looking for separate and different advice on teaching writing to reluctant or failing writers will not find it here. A student who is having difficulty with writing is likely to need a more explicit, more individual, more closely guided version of one or more of the interventions just recommended. However, three general principles apply to reluctant or failing writers:

1 The greater the difficulty, the more urgently the writer needs to be shown the *possibility* of what he or she can achieve.
2 The frailer the confidence, the higher should be the quotient of *encouragement* in the teacher's mix of encouragement and criticism.
3 The further a writer still has to go before attaining anything like the competence which we would expect from most writers of her or his age, the more he or she is likely to need *models* rather than *analysis*.

A working theory of the teaching of writing

The last five sections have offered answers to the question 'What do teachers need to know and do in order to teach writing effectively?' Between them, the answers amount to the statement of a working theory for the teaching of writing. In short, effective teachers:

- hold in their minds the complexity of the task which confronts students when they are asked to write;
- are concerned for content as a first priority, allowing a concern for correctness and control to emerge as a consequence of that concern;
- provide a broad and diverse range of contexts for writing in which students write in a range of forms, for a variety of purposes, making use of a diversity of media, intended for a variety of audiences (including, of course, the teacher) within and beyond the classroom;
- make full use of the possibilities offered to writers by digital technologies;
- teach about aspects of the writing system principally by showing examples of how writers have handled those aspects successfully;
- manage the writing classroom as an environment which replicates as closely as possible the conditions in which writers operate well.

The present situation in England

This section examines the extent to which the government's new National Curriculum orders for writing at Key Stages 3 and 4 represent an understanding of writers and the writing process likely to encourage the kind of teaching which will bring students to a confident maturity in writing by age 16.

Overall

Paragraph 6.3 of the new National Curriculum orders for English at Key Stages 1 to 4 (Department for Education, 2014a) has this to say in general about writing:

> *Pupils should develop the stamina and skills to write at length, with accurate spelling and punctuation. They should be taught the correct use of grammar. They should build on what they have been taught to expand the range of their writing and the variety of the grammar they use. The writing they do should include narratives, explanations, descriptions, comparisons, summaries and evaluations: such writing supports them in rehearsing, understanding and consolidating what they have heard or read.*
>
> *(ibid.: 11)*

We can isolate the key lexical words from the first three of these sentences: 'stamina', 'skills', 'spelling', 'punctuation', 'grammar', 'writing', 'grammar'. The current government's essential vision of the effective teaching of writing resides clearly in these words. In the fourth sentence, and well down the pecking order, we see that students must also write across a certain rather narrow and arbitrary range of forms. There is no mention of the possibilities which digital technologies offer student writers. This statement of priorities, and the balance of teaching approaches it envisages and commands, are a world away from the understanding of writers and the writing process advanced in this chapter.

Key Stage 3

The orders for writing at Key Stages 1 and 2 are a striking example of excessive micro-management. They are full of long lists of spelling rules and grammatical terminology. These adult-speaking-down-to-child analytical and deductive obsessions are transformed, however, into a simple and trusting brevity at Key Stage 3.

The Key Stage 3 writing orders cover just over half a page. They pay some attention to *what* students should write ('well-structured formal expository and narrative essays; stories, scripts, poetry and other imaginative writing; notes and polished scripts for talks and presentations; a range of other narrative and non-narrative texts, including arguments, and personal and formal letters' [Department for Education, 2014a: 84]); and they mention planning, editing and proofreading.

With regard to spelling, teachers are referred to Appendix 1 on spelling, as provided for Key Stages 1 and 2. It is presumed, wrongly, that all the essentials to do with spelling will have been covered by Year 6. The requirement at Key Stage 3 is merely that students should '[apply] the spelling patterns and rules set out in English Appendix 1 to the Key Stage 1 and 2 programmes of study for English' (*ibid*.: 84). This simple and trusting brevity over spelling is wrongly balanced in terms of the requirements made of students of different ages. There should be *more* conscious, analytical attention to spelling in the secondary phase, including the study of spelling patterns, and *less* in the primary phase.

Grammar and vocabulary at Key Stage 3

Whereas 'vocabulary, grammar and punctuation' were regarded as part of writing at Key Stages 1 and 2, at Key Stage 3 'grammar and vocabulary' are given separate status, along with 'reading', 'writing' and 'spoken English'. Grammar should indeed be treated independently of writing, because it so obviously applies to all the modes of language. There is detailed discussion of the requirements for grammar at Key Stage 3 in the next chapter.

The orders for grammar at this Key Stage simply refer teachers to the grammatical knowledge which children are supposed to have acquired during the primary years, and require that they should extend and apply that knowledge in order 'to analyse more challenging texts' and by 'studying the effectiveness and impact of the grammatical features of the texts they read' (*ibid*.: 84). Exactly as with the requirements for spelling, this requirement runs contrary to everything which experienced educators know about how learners' powers of analysis develop on the basis of existing competence. The government has declined to be specific about grammar teaching at Key Stages 3 and 4 in favour of being ultra-specific about it in the primary phase: precisely the wrong way round.

There is confusion in the intended meaning of 'vocabulary'. The word seems to mean 'lexis' – the conscious use of words in texts – in one place: 'drawing on new vocabulary and grammatical constructions from their reading and listening, and using these consciously in their writing and speech to achieve particular effects'; and 'terminology' in another: 'discussing reading, writing and spoken language with precise and confident use of linguistic and literary terminology' (*ibid*.: 85).

There are two good requirements to do with knowledge about language and Standard English. They concern:

- *knowing and understanding the differences between spoken and written language, including differences associated with formal and informal registers, and between Standard English and other varieties of English;*
- *using Standard English confidently in [pupils'] own writing and speech.*

(*ibid*.: 84)

Key Stage 4 and GCSE

The Writing and Grammar and vocabulary orders for this Key Stage are so brief that they may be stated in full.

Writing

Pupils should be taught to:

– write accurately, fluently, effectively and at length for pleasure and information through:

- adapting their writing for a wide range of purposes and audiences: to describe, narrate, explain, instruct, give and respond to information, and argue;
- selecting and organising ideas, facts and key points, and citing evidence, details and quotation effectively and pertinently for support and emphasis;
- selecting, and using judiciously, vocabulary, grammar, form, and structural and organisational features, including rhetorical devices, to reflect audience, purpose and context, and using Standard English where appropriate.

– make notes, draft and write, including using information provided by others [e.g. writing a letter from key points provided; drawing on and using information from a presentation]
– revise, edit and proof-read through:

- reflecting on whether their draft achieves the intended impact;
- restructuring their writing, and amending its grammar and vocabulary to improve coherence, consistency, clarity and overall effectiveness;
- paying attention to the accuracy and effectiveness of grammar, punctuation and spelling.

(*ibid.*: 86–87)

Grammar and vocabulary

Pupils should be taught to:

– consolidate and build on their knowledge of grammar and vocabulary through:

- studying their effectiveness and impact in the texts they read;
- drawing on new vocabulary and grammatical constructions from their reading and listening, and using these consciously in their writing and speech to achieve particular effects;

- *analysing some of the differences between spoken and written language, including differences associated with formal and informal registers, and between Standard English and other varieties of English;*
- *using linguistic and literary terminology accurately and confidently in discussing reading, writing and spoken language.*

(*ibid.*: 87)

The government's statutory *English Language GCSE Subject Content and Assessment Objectives* (Department for Education, 2013a), which apply to courses beginning in September 2015, are similarly brief:

Writing

- *producing clear and coherent text: writing effectively for different purposes and audiences: to describe, narrate, explain, instruct, give and respond to information, and argue; selecting vocabulary, grammar, form, and structural and organisational features judiciously to reflect audience, purpose and context; using language imaginatively and creatively; using information provided by others to write in different forms; maintaining a consistent point of view; maintaining coherence and consistency across a text;*
- *writing for impact: selecting, organising and emphasising facts, ideas and key points; citing evidence and quotation effectively and pertinently to support views; creating emotional impact; using language creatively, imaginatively and persuasively, including rhetorical devices (such as rhetorical questions, antithesis, parenthesis).*

(*ibid.*: 5)

With regard to writing, the orders for Key Stages 3 and 4 and the requirements for GCSE English Language do not actually prevent or impede good and imaginative teaching. The orders for Key Stage 4 and the objectives for GCSE, taken together and within their limitations, are perfectly acceptable. There is something there about range, something about the composition process, something about purposes and audiences.

However, the orders are in denial about one of the fundamental characteristics of the social reality in which students live and move, in and out of school: that of the use of digital technologies and media to compose, receive and respond to writing. There is nothing about writing enterprises which involve collaboration. Nothing about the combining of writing with other modes such as sound and image. In this respect, the new National Curriculum orders for writing greet the present and the future by firmly turning their back on both.

To conclude . . .

Writing is a mode of communication best understood in terms of wholes rather than parts. A single text is evidence of the effort of the writer to say something, to marshal thought, to communicate that marshalled thought to a reader, to draw on examples – consciously imitated or unconsciously internalised – which may offer help in the marshalling, to conform to the conventions of the writing system insofar as he or she has come to understand them, to sustain the physical effort of putting linked groups of words on paper or on the screen. That is what all writers, including student writers, do. Teachers can most effectively teach writing by recognising that wholeness.

The learning which student writers undertake is best understood as a journey in which equipment will be provided progressively along the way rather than all supplied in advance.

The universe of writing is a family of forms best understood in terms of nuances of difference rather than hard edges. The kinds of writing in the world, some of which students should encounter and try out for themselves in the course of their schooling, exist as part of a connected and interactive network, not as isolated, unique entities. Some of these kinds have been created or transformed by the digital revolution.

The new National Curriculum orders for writing are uneven, and inadequate in important respects. These shortcomings will one day need to be addressed by government and the profession.

In Chapter 9, readers will find an alternative curriculum for writing 11 to 16 which better represents what we know about how young people are best helped to competence and confidence as writers than do some features of the new orders for writing at Key Stages 3 and 4. The alternative nonetheless willingly acknowledges those features of the new orders which can be welcomed.

Note

1 Reproduced by permission of the Centre for Literacy in Primary Education, www. clpe.org.uk.

4 Grammar and knowledge about language

John Richmond

Summary of main points

Competence in language precedes analysis of language, not the other way round. Competence *in* language is implicit knowledge *of* language, brought about by a host of influences which affect the learner, consciously and unconsciously, and by a range of kinds of instruction and intervention by the teacher.

The teaching of grammar is a valuable and interesting activity, so long as it is pitched at an appropriate level of difficulty for the learners in a class, so long as it occurs in the context of the study of worthwhile texts, and so long as it engages learners actively in investigating language in use. Grammar teaching out of the context of students' broader language learning is useless.

The principal benefit of grammar teaching is on learners as readers and as people who discuss texts, including their own.

There is now some evidence that appropriately pitched grammar teaching, involving the study of worthwhile texts and engaging learners actively in investigating language in use, can have a beneficial influence on writers' developing competence (especially in the case of writers who are already more able), in that appropriately pitched reflection on language can feed back into competence.

The teaching of grammar sits best within the overall study of language as a phenomenon. To understand grammatical concepts and terminology is to understand one aspect of language as a system shared by its users. The knowledge about language which young people should acquire is broader than that, however, especially in the secondary years. This broader knowledge could be categorised in five ways, each of which interact with the others:

- variety in and between languages;
- history of languages;
- language and power in society;
- acquisition and development of language;
- language as a system shared by its users.

The government's new legal requirements on grammar teaching will at some point need to be changed to make their demands on primary-school pupils more modest and realistic, and to shift some of these demands to teaching post-11, where requirements should be greater and more explicit than they currently are in the new orders for Key Stages 3 and 4. Chapter 9 offers an alternative curriculum for the teaching of grammar and knowledge about language, which represents this shift of emphasis.

'The grammar question'

I come now to an argument about teaching which – along with the argument about how to teach early reading – has caused the most debate and controversy, provoked the most intense outpourings of outrage, of all the areas of English teaching and language education. It is the grammar question.

There is an argument for dealing with grammar as an element of writing. The argument runs that discussions about grammar nearly always arise in the course of discussions about writing, and that the new requirements of the National Curriculum for English with regard to grammar form part of the programmes of study for writing at Key Stages 1 and 2 (where they are the most problematical). There is reference to grammar in the new programmes of study for writing at Key Stages 3 and 4; but in both cases 'Grammar and vocabulary' are also given sections of their own.

Grammar – not simply to do with writing

My reason for addressing grammar in a separate chapter is simple. It is that grammar, as I also say in the chapter on writing, is not simply a province of the country of writing. It is often lumped together with spelling and punctuation, but grammar is a bigger and broader thing than either spelling or punctuation.

This is not to underestimate the importance of spelling and punctuation, which are key elements of the English writing system. Punctuation, it is true, can also be an indicator of grammatical choices, again as acknowledged in the chapter on writing. For example, in the sentence, 'Although the sun was shining brightly, I went to the cinema', the comma after 'brightly' indicates the end of the subordinate clause beginning 'Although . . .'. In the sentence, 'There wasn't a cloud in the sky; conditions were perfect', the semi-colon in the middle of the sentence indicates that there are two syntactically balancing and semantically interrelated main clauses on either side of it.

Grammar enables meaning

Grammar is nothing less than a fundamental language system within which words – spoken and written – are enabled to make sense, are imbued with meaning, as an outcome of the order in which they are arranged (syntax) or as an outcome of the way they change their form (morphology).

Grammar makes links

Furthermore, beyond the level of the written sentence or spoken utterance, writers and speakers make grammatical choices, and readers and listeners infer those grammatical choices, to give sense to or make sense of the structure of whole written texts or pieces of spoken discourse. For example, the reader of a chronologically narrated short story understands that the sentences and paragraphs which form the story proceed via linear time. The same reader, reading a piece of argumentative journalism in a newspaper, understands that the sentences and paragraphs which form the piece proceed via the writer's appeal to her or his sense of reason or logic. The grammatical linkages between sentences and paragraphs in the argumentative journalism will be different from those in the short story.

Grammar belongs to speech as much as to writing

Speech is not an imperfect version of writing. Typically, there is more informality and less explicitness in most forms of speech than in most forms of writing, but these are tendencies on a continuum. There are examples of more formal and more explicit speech (a political speech or an oral judgement in a court) and less formal and less explicit writing (an email exchange between friends).

Grammar teaching helps readers

Strange as it may seem, the principal direct benefit to a learner in conceptually grasping grammatical terms lies not in her or his future writing, but in her or his future encounters with texts: in her or his reading and discussion of that reading. This is another way of putting the argument for not discussing grammar merely as an aspect of writing: the principal direct benefit of teaching it is to be seen more in future acts of reading than in future acts of writing.

'But,' I hear my own reader saying, 'acts of reading are very often acts by which a reader reads her or his own writing; surely by this route explicit grammatical understandings can benefit the learner as a writer.' I shall come back to this good point in a moment.

The positive role of grammar teaching

Let me say something clear and positive about the role of grammar in the language education of young people. Grammatical analysis, taught at the right level of complexity for a particular stage of students' development, is interesting and useful.

Why is it useful? Because to be able to speak about language, to have a technical language with which to discuss and describe language, a metalanguage, is as useful as it is to have a technical language with which to speak about any other area of human endeavour. To have technical vocabulary at one's command brings a sense of mastery and clarity to the person so equipped.

Why is grammatical analysis interesting? Too obvious an answer, really: language is perhaps the most delicate and remarkable of human achievements, and to study some of its elements – including the way that words join together in groups and change their form so that they make sense – is therefore self-evidently worthwhile.

Halliday's three kinds of language learning

Marie Clay, in a chapter entitled 'Getting a Theory of Writing' in *Explorations in the Development of Writing* (Kroll and Wells [eds], 1983), elegantly summarises some earlier work by Michael Halliday:

> *Halliday (1975) has provided an argument for the interrelatedness of language processes . . . He described three aspects of language learning: (1) language learning or constructing the system we know as the child's*

mother tongue, (2) learning through language as the child constructs his/her picture of the world and using language as a social process to acquire and share meaning, and (3) learning about the nature of language itself. He saw all three processes as largely subconscious but brought to the level of consciousness in education so that they can be consolidated and expanded. Learning to read and write are major tasks in such expansion. According to Halliday the three language processes should be allowed to take place side by side because they reinforce each other, and they should take place as social processes shared between the child and significant others. These three processes of constructing symbol systems, using these to explore the world and experience, and exploring the symbols themselves may be, at another level of abstraction, what we understand by education itself, he says.

(Clay, 1983: 274–275)

Halliday proposes that his third aspect of language learning can reinforce the other two. So do I. I have already said that having a command of metalanguage helps the learner as he or she encounters texts, as long as it is appropriate to her or his stage of development. I should go a little further and happily acknowledge that the texts that the learner will read will include some that he or she has written. And here the interaction between the learner as writer and the learner as reader is complex and mysterious.

Good writers are generally careful and critical readers of their own writing. If I have acknowledged that it is useful for readers to have access to technical terms, including grammatical terms, surely a learner reading her or his own writing and using or thinking about grammatical terms, or having them pointed out by the teacher, will thereby benefit as a writer. Yes; this is a benefit arising from the writer's growing sense of mastery of the craft, of the precision in criticism which the appropriate use of grammatical and other technical terms supplies.

The myth of grammar teaching

There is the positive welcome for the idea that appropriately pitched teaching about grammar aids learners as people who read and discuss texts, including texts which they have produced themselves. Let us now flip this much-rubbed coin and put the other side of the argument. Here it is, bluntly expressed in pseudo-mathematical terms (Figure 4.1):

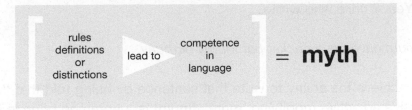

Figure 4.1 The myth of grammar teaching.

(This expression, and one more diagrammatic model which appears later in the chapter, are taken from my 'What Do We Mean by Knowledge about Language?' in *Knowledge about Language and the Curriculum: The LINC Reader* [1990], edited by Ronald Carter.)

This is the nub of it. A century has gone by, as we shall see shortly, and the problem has not been solved. There is no peace. Politicians, journalists, academic writers regretful at the loss of an imagined past of certainty and correctness, and enraged writers of letters to newspapers all insist, in effect, that the word at the right-hand end of the expression should be 'truth', not 'myth'.

Some of these people sincerely believe, with Samuel Johnson, that 'tongues, like governments, have a natural tendency to degeneration'; and, with him, resolve: 'we have long preserved our constitution, let us make some struggle for our language' (Preface to *Dictionary of the English Language*, 1975). They may also believe, in effect, that the teacher's role is 'to refine our language to grammatical purity', which is what Johnson claimed he had been doing for two years in his twice-weekly periodical *The Rambler* (*The Rambler 208*, 1752), and which was also one of his missions in compiling his dictionary. I respect these sincere believers, while disagreeing with them. Governments are *un*like tongues in their natural tendency to degenerate. There are those in power in our own day who make statements such as Johnson's because they can see the popular advantage of advancing them; whether or not they are truthful or reasonable is of secondary interest to them.

Competence precedes analysis

Here are three examples of writing which I've collected from classrooms in recent years. They are powerful evidence that competence in written language *precedes* analysis of written language, not the other way round.

The Year 2 child who wrote:

My mum gave me a cricket bat for my birthday.

did not achieve the ability to write that sentence by being told that 'My' is a possessive adjective modifying 'mum', 'mum' is a common noun in subject position, 'gave' is a past-tense verb which uses a 'strong' form rather than the 'weak' *-ed* ending used by other verbs, 'me' is an indirect object pronoun (though its form is identical to a direct object pronoun as in 'My mum hit me with a cricket bat.'), 'a' is the indefinite article, 'cricket', though usually a noun when referring to the game, is here an adjective modifying the common noun 'bat', the three-word phrase 'a cricket bat' is a direct object phrase governed by 'gave', 'for' is a preposition expressing purpose and governing 'my birthday', 'my' is once again a possessive adjective modifying the common noun 'birthday', and the three-word phrase 'for my birthday' is adverbial, modifying 'gave' in terms perhaps temporal, perhaps expressing purpose.

The A-level student who wrote an essay on *King Lear* which included the sentence:

Although Edmund's motive stems in part from the fact that he is illegitimate and proud of it, it does not explain the full horror of his actions.

was, in the handling of written sentences, a long way ahead of the child whose mother gave him a cricket bat for his birthday. Although our student may have been taught about subordinate clauses of concession (of which the last 12 words are another example), and although she may as a result have been able to identify that group of words *as* a subordinate clause of concession had she been called upon to do so (the last 30 words are yet another example), it could not have been analytic teaching which enabled her to write that clause. She could write that clause because of countless previous encounters with similar clauses in her reading and in her experience of the spoken language. I was not sitting inside her head when she wrote that sentence, but I am as sure as I can be that she did not approach it with the conscious thought, 'I shall need a subordinate clause of concession here'.

The writer of the sentence about the cricket bat was seven. The writer of the sentence about Edmund was 17. In between, here is an 11-year-old writer:

The school that I would like would be one where the teachers asked you what you wanted to learn that day.

Did our utopian Year 6 child learn to write that sentence as a result of receiving lessons in advance on the use of the conditional mood and modal verbs, as in 'would like would be'? Surely she could not have written 'one where the teachers asked you what you wanted to learn that day' without prior knowledge that that group of 13 words is a subject complement to 'The school that I would like', and that the group of 13 words includes a smaller group of 7 words – 'what you wanted to learn that day' – which is a noun clause in object position? Surely (to switch for a moment from grammar to rhetoric) I could not have written the previous sentence without being taught in advance that irony is the occupation of the space between an apparent and an underlying reality? Surely she could. Surely I could.

If grammatical analysis were prior to grammatical competence, our lives would not be long enough to achieve even the most elementary degree of competence in written or spoken language, because the grammatical conventions, rules, structures of language – even of apparently very simple written sentences or spoken utterances – turn out to be extraordinarily subtle, complex and sometimes ambiguous when analysed.

'She walked down the street.': pronoun, verb, preposition, article, noun.
'She put down the pen.': pronoun, verb, adverb, article, noun.

At first glance, here are two very simple and very similar sentences. The first, third and fourth words of each are identical. Quite young children could easily have written either sentence. We can equally easily see that the correct use of 'down' in the two sentences does not require an advance understanding that in the first case 'down' is a preposition and in the second an adverb within the phrasal verb 'put down'. Phrasal verbs are a category which may be tested by moving the adverb to another place in the sentence to see whether the sentence is still grammatical. 'She put the pen down' is equally grammatical to 'She put down the pen'. 'She walked the street down' is not equally grammatical to 'She walked down the street'. Users of language don't usually have the time for great swathes of this kind of prior analysis.

Snapshots from the past

Bullock on grammar

The Bullock Report, *A Language for Life* (The Bullock Committee, 1975), refers to another government report, published more than half a century previously:

> *The Newbolt Report* [The Teaching of English in England, *published in 1921]*
> *suggested that examinations should be tests of the power of 'communi-*
> *cation' in English rather than tests in grammar, analysis, and spelling. The*
> *only compulsory test it was prepared to recommend was one of the ability*
> *'to grasp the meaning of a piece of English of appropriate difficulty'. The*
> *Committee also recommended that 'oral examination should be resorted to*
> *more frequently' and urged that a reasonable standard of English should be*
> *required in all subjects of the curriculum. Two years earlier than the Newbolt*
> *Report the Secondary Schools Examination Council had recommended that*
> *there should be no separate test of formal grammar; awareness of grammar*
> *would be shown in candidates' writing. It also asked for more imaginative*
> *and fewer abstract essay subjects, but to no avail. The Council's recom-*
> *mendations, then and later, had no more effect than those produced by*
> *the Newbolt Committee. The Council had been set up in 1917 to carry out*
> *the Board of Education's new responsibility as a Co-ordinating Authority for*
> *Secondary School Examinations. Eight Examining Boards were approved,*
> *and the patterns of their papers were established by the early twenties; forty*
> *years later, in the early sixties, they had changed little. There was a précis,*
> *letter writing, paraphrase, analysis and other grammatical exercises, the cor-*
> *rection of incorrect sentences, the punctuation of depunctuated passages*
> *and, of course, an essay, the titles of which in 1961 were sometimes indis-*
> *tinguishable from those of 1921.*
>
> (The Bullock Committee, 1975: paragraph 11.32)

Bullock has much to say, on its own account, about the teaching of grammar. For example:

> *Since the beginning of this century a good deal of research has been*
> *devoted to [the question of whether exercises in themselves and by them-*
> *selves will improve the child's ability to write], and though many believe*
> *its results to be inconclusive some of the individual experiments have*

carried much conviction. One such study [by Harris, 1963] is particularly worth singling out for attention. One class in each of five schools was taught formal grammar over a period of two years, a corresponding class in each school having no grammar lessons during that time. The latter took instead what might be described as a 'composition course', consisting of practice in writing, revising, and editing, and an inductive approach to usage. At the end of the period both groups were given a writing test and a grammar test. In the writing test the 'non-grammar' classes gained significantly higher scores than the 'grammar' classes, and overall there was no effective correspondence between high scores in the grammar test and improvement in writing.

We do not conclude from this that a child should not be taught how to improve his use of language; quite the contrary. It has not been established by research that systematic attention to skill and technique has no beneficial effect on the handling of language. What has been shown is that the teaching of traditional analytic grammar does not appear to improve performance in writing. This is not to suggest that there is no place for any kind of exercises at any time and in any form. It may well be that a teacher will find this a valuable means of helping an individual child reinforce something he has learned. What is questionable is the practice of setting exercises for the whole class, irrespective of need, and assuming that this will improve every pupil's ability to handle English.

(*ibid*., paragraphs 11.18 and 11.19)

'[T]he teaching of traditional analytic grammar does not appear to improve performance in writing.' That broad truth remains valid today despite furious attempts by governments since it was written to deny it.

Katharine Perera on grammar

Katharine Perera's *Children's Writing and Reading: Analysing Classroom Language* (1984), already quoted in Chapter 1, is written by a linguist, for teachers. It contains a most detailed description of the grammar of English. It contains an equally detailed discussion of the development of grammatical competence in children before and during their school years. Perera believes that teachers should know these things. She is rightly concerned to correct the misunderstanding that, when children arrive at school, already having achieved a remarkable mastery of many of the grammatical structures of their language, the job is more or less done. As I say in Chapter 1, she shows, with evidence, that the job is very far from done, and that many more complex grammatical structures remain to be mastered.

But the striking thing is that this linguist, who also understands a great deal about learning, has this to say about the explicit teaching of grammar:

> *To suggest that a framework of grammatical knowledge can be of benefit to teachers is not to suggest that it should be formally taught to children. Since the beginning of the century, a body of research has accumulated that indicates that grammatical instruction, unrelated to pupils' other language work, does not lead to an improvement in the quality of their own writing or in the level of their comprehension. Furthermore, the majority of children under about fourteen seem to become confused by grammatical labels and descriptions . . .*
>
> *Although some teachers of older secondary pupils may want to introduce a systematic study of grammar, generally speaking, the 'planned intervention in the child's language development' [a quotation from the Bullock Report] that is advocated in this book can be implemented by means of demonstration and example, without the use of technical terminology or batteries of exercises.*
>
> (Perera, 1984: 12–13)

More reviews of 'the grammar question'

Two significant large-scale reviews of the available research on the question 'Does explicit grammar teaching make for better writers?' (Hillocks, 1986 and Andrews *et al.*, 2006) found no evidence that grammar teaching, *offered outside the context of the study of authentic texts*, makes for better writing.

Both these reviews, however, acknowledge that sentence-combining (a practice mainly confined to schools in the USA, in which students are offered sets of two separate sentences which could then be made into one in a variety of ways) does seem to improve students' handling of sentences, at least when the students were tested soon after the sentence-combining exercises had been offered.

Hillocks and Smith are rather blunt about the non-effect of grammar teaching on writing:

Why does grammar retain such glamour when research over the past 90 years reveals not only that students do not learn it and are hostile toward it, but that the study of grammar has no impact on writing quality? Many explanations have been adduced, some not so flattering: it is easy to teach by simply assigning page and exercise numbers; it is easy to grade; it provides security in having 'right' answers, a luxury not so readily available in teaching writing or literature . . .

the grammar sections of a textbook should be treated as a reference tool that might provide some insight into conventions of mechanics and usage. [Grammar] should not be treated as a course of study to improve the quality of writing.

(Hillocks and Smith, 1991: 600)

In the conclusion to their article, Andrews and his colleagues write:

On the basis of the results of [our] two in-depth reviews, we can say, first, that the teaching of syntax . . . appears to have no influence on either the accuracy or quality of written language development for 5- to 16-year-olds. This does not mean to say that there could be no such influence. It simply means that there have been no significant studies to date that have proved such an effect.

(Andrews *et al.*, 2006: 51)

Of sentence-combining, Andrews *et al.* (2006) write:

the teaching of sentence-combining appears to have a more positive effect on writing quality and accuracy.

(*ibid.* 51)

James Moffett, in *Teaching the Universe of Discourse*, published in 1968, has an interesting qualification to offer to the assertion, which he does not in principle dispute, that sentence-combining seems to generate in students the ability to write more complex sentences.

Intricacy of thought does not necessarily correspond to linguistic intricacy . . . Indeed, sometimes a single well chosen word can replace an entire clause, producing a far simpler and far better sentence (though any evaluation must depend on a writer's intent). Compare:

I don't like what is left in the cup after you finish drinking.
to
I don't like the dregs.
Unless the speaker wished to convey ignorance of vocabulary itself, the second sentence is better. But the first is considerably more complex.

(Moffett, 1968: 173–174)

Going back a few more years, we can also remind ourselves of Harris's 1963 study quoted in the Bullock Report, which showed that a 'composition course' led to better writing than did grammar lessons. Or we can quote from the government-commissioned Lockwood Report, *The Examining of English Language*, published in 1964:

Our eighth criticism is directed to that part of the present [examination] papers which consists of questions on grammatical and other minutiae. Some of the most eloquently critical replies we received from the schools were directed against these questions; we share the view that they are of doubtful utility in any examination of English language and that in their present form they do great harm . . . No examination is serving a useful purpose for schools, candidates, employers or the outside world generally if it encourages pupils to adopt a form of examination room English instead of seeking to express appropriately what they have to say.

(The Lockwood Committee, 1964: paragraph 51)

'The grammar question': government answers since 1984

English from 5 to 16

In 1984, Her Majesty's Inspectorate published a slim booklet called *English from 5 to 16*. Unexceptionably, the booklet proposed that teachers should be promoting pupils' development as speakers and listeners, readers and writers. It then said that teachers should:

teach pupils about language, so that they achieve a working knowledge of its structure and of the variety of ways in which meaning is made, so that they have a vocabulary for discussing it, so that they can use it with greater awareness and because it is interesting.

(Her Majesty's Inspectorate, 1984: 3)

From today's perspective, this proposal, quoted in isolation from the rest of the booklet, sounds eminently reasonable. Reading the booklet as a whole at the time, however, weighing up what its authors might really have in mind as the more important things to teach pupils about language, and putting these thoughts next to worries about other aspects of the booklet (the detail in its proposals for age-related objectives for pupils at 7, 11 and 16, and its narrow, muddled and often backward-looking collection of statements about what a language or English curriculum should contain), many teachers came to the conclusion that the booklet was once again proposing something which had been vigorously debated for the previous 20 years, and rejected: the tempting idea that learners, in order to get better at using an element of the language they are learning as mother tongue, need a set of rules, definitions and distinctions about that element in advance.

Decoded, the part of *English from 5 to 16* from which I have quoted was returning to a dispute over whether English teachers needed to reinstate old-fashioned grammar teaching as a major element of the curriculum. Overwhelmingly, those who wrote down their responses to the booklet and sent them in to HMI said 'No'. Their suspicion was that the distinction which, for example, Katharine Perera made in her book, published in the same year as *English 5 to 16*, between teachers' understanding of grammar and grammatical development and the use of grammatical categories in explicit teaching, was being blurred.

When HMI published *English from 5 to 16: The Responses to Curriculum Matters 1* in 1986, it acknowledged the degree of dissent from the original booklet on this and other topics. It suggested setting up an enquiry, 'with the ultimate object of drawing up recommendations as to what might be taught [about language] to intending teachers, to those in post and to pupils in schools' (Her Majesty's Inspectorate, 1986: 40).

The Kingman Report

The government accepted the idea of an enquiry and convened the Kingman Committee to discuss the matter. The Kingman Report was published in March 1988. On the particular question of grammar teaching, the report declared:

> *Nor do we see it as part of our task to plead for a return to old-fashioned grammar teaching and learning by rote. We have been impressed by the evidence we have received that this gave an inadequate account of the English*

language by treating it virtually as a branch of Latin, and constructing a rigid prescriptive code rather than a dynamic description of language in use. It was also ineffective as a means of developing a command of English in all its manifestations. Equally, at the other extreme, we reject the belief that any notion of correct or incorrect use of language is an affront to personal liberty. We also reject the belief that knowing how to use terminology in which to speak of language is undesirable.

(The Kingman Committee, 1988: paragraph 11)

This statement, quoted from Chapter 1 of the report, was greeted by a deep sigh of relief from the profession, although there was some puzzlement that the committee had apparently discovered groups of teachers who refused to accept that there was such a thing as an incorrect use of language and never used any terminology in their teaching, and had felt that this tendency was as dangerous as 'old-fashioned grammar teaching and learning by rote'.

The Cox Report

The government was less than delighted with the Kingman Report, because it had failed to provide what the government wanted, which was a ringing endorsement of the virtues of 'old-fashioned grammar teaching'. Persisting in its belief in these virtues, it produced the terms of reference for the Cox Committee, which was to propose the contents of a National Curriculum for English (to include students' knowledge about language). I quote:

The Kingman Committee . . . has made recommendations for attainment targets for knowledge about language at the ages of 7, 11 and 16. The Working Group [i.e. the Cox Committee] should build on these to recommend attainment targets covering the grammatical structure of the English language.

(The Cox Committee, 1989: Appendix 2, paragraph 3)

Precariously, the terms of reference tried to link grammar teaching with great literature, as follows:

The Working Group's recommendations on learning about language [for which, in the government dictionary, read grammar] and its use should draw upon the English literary heritage.

(*ibid*.: Appendix 2, paragraph 3)

The Cox Committee's proposals for the National Curriculum for English deftly declined the government's invitation to produce attainment targets on grammar, and gathered together a much broader set of concerns under the title 'knowledge about language': accent, dialect and Standard English; some of the forms and functions of speech; the nature of literary language; historical change in English; some of the forms and functions of writing; characteristic differences between speech and writing. The committee, in giving reasons for the list that it had chosen, explained that it did not want to overload teachers with too much that was unfamiliar; it believed that teachers' own knowledge about language was not complete or sure enough to justify further recommendations. The Cox Report optimistically says:

> *substantial programmes of teacher training are required if teachers are themselves to know enough to enable them to design with confidence programmes of study about language. Such training is now under way. It may be, when such training programmes have been followed for a few years, that it would be appropriate for knowledge about language to become a separate profile component.*

> (*ibid*: paragraph 6.3)

The first National Curriculum for English

There is much to admire in the original programmes of study for English (Department for Education and Science and the Welsh Office, 1990). As mentioned in the introduction to the book, they are over-detailed, and the attempt to corral the iterative nature of learning in English within ten attainment levels led to theoretical and pedagogical absurdities. But the vision of learning which the programmes of study embodied remains one which, a generation later, I broadly support.

However, as a result of Cox's concern about the limitations of teachers' knowledge about language, including grammar, the references to grammar in the original programmes of study are occasional and brief.

The orders for speaking and listening and for writing, spelling and handwriting variously require that pupils should come in time to have a firm grasp of Standard English, spoken and written; this requirement is properly tempered by another, that at Key Stages 2 to 4 'Pupils should be encouraged to respect their own language(s) and dialect(s) and those of others'. The orders for speaking and listening also require that at Key Stages 3 and 4 pupils should consider 'grammatical differences between the speech of the area and spoken Standard English'.

The orders for reading require that at Key Stages 3 and 4 pupils should be aware of 'some of the ways in which English is constantly changing between generations and over the centuries', and of 'grammatical features such as structural repetition' and of 'the use of grammatical deviance for special effect'.

The orders for writing, spelling and handwriting require that pupils should: 'be taught, in the context of discussion about their own writing, grammatical terms such as sentence, verb, tense, noun, pronoun' (at Key Stage 1); be taught about 'some common prefixes and suffixes' (at Key Stage 2); come to understand linguistic features such as the passive and subordination in the impersonal style of writing (at Key Stage 3); 'learn . . . how they can achieve different stylistic effects in their writing by a conscious control of grammatical structures and lexical choices' and 'be taught how to recognise and describe some of the lexical, grammatical and organisational characteristics of different types of written texts' (at Key Stage 4).

The Language in the National Curriculum Project

The training to which the Cox Report referred in 1989 was at the time beginning to be provided by the Language in the National Curriculum Project. This is not the place to recount in detail the history of the LINC Project and the political strife it caused. (Readers wishing to know the full story could consult my article 'The Knowledge about Language Debate 1984–1993' [Richmond, 2012a] or Alastair West's article 'How We Live Now: LINC, Politics and the Language Police in Toytown LEA', in *Where We've Been: Articles from the English and Media Magazine* [1996].)

Suffice to say that the government wished the project to conduct a top-down programme of training in grammar, which would eventually touch every secondary English teacher and every teacher in primary schools in England and Wales, and that those who led the project prepared a set of training materials which, while including attention to grammar, embodied a much broader understanding of knowledge about language, something closer to Halliday's third aspect mentioned above – 'learning about the nature of language itself' – and indeed very close to the list of topics to do with knowledge about language proposed in the Cox Report. The government eventually refused to publish the training materials. Neither would it waive Crown Copyright so that a commercial publisher might publish them. Despite this act of blatant censorship, tens of thousands of copies of the materials have since been distributed in unofficial form by the University of Nottingham, where Professor Ronald Carter, the project's director, was and is based.

Grammar in the National Literacy Strategy

As we speed over the revisions and re-revisions of the National Curriculum for English which have taken place since it was introduced, we see an increasing emphasis on explicit grammar teaching. Given what I have said towards the beginning of the chapter, about the value of appropriately pitched grammar teaching in helping students as readers and as talkers about texts, I can only welcome this.

However, it appears that policy-makers simply decided to ignore the research evidence then available to them on grammar teaching and competence in writing, some of which I have summarised. (I accept that the research by Andrews *et al.* [2006] is relatively recent.) Probably frustrated by the failure of the LINC Project to deliver the goods they had ordered, they resolved to push on with their conviction that explicit grammar teaching will make better writers. (Such a position also makes good copy in some quarters of the press.) While there was general agreement not to return to what Kingman called 'old-fashioned grammar teaching and learning by rote', the direct connection between explicit grammar teaching and the quality and correctness of students' writing was asserted as truth.

The National Literacy Strategy, part of the government's National Strategies which ran from 1997 to 2011, saw such teaching as essential in the effort to raise standards of literacy generally, and proposed a three-part framework for teaching grammar at word, sentence and text level. For example, the introduction to *Grammar for Writing* (2000), a document published by the National Literacy Strategy and directed to schools teaching pupils at Key Stage 2, begins thus:

> *We all use language to think and communicate. Language is systematically organised by its grammar which is inextricably linked to meaning and communication – we cannot make sense without shaping grammatical and linguistic structures. All pupils have extensive grammatical knowledge. Much of this is implicit, but they are able to generalise and improvise from this knowledge.*
>
> (Department for Children, Schools and Families, 2000: 7)

All perfectly true.

> *Teaching which focuses on grammar helps to make this knowledge explicit, extend children's range and develop more confident and versatile language use.*
>
> (ibid.: 7)

True, in the senses we have discussed so far; that is, as providing a meta-language for the discussion of language.

> *Some would argue that the study of grammar is worth teaching in its own right because it is intrinsically interesting – and so it is. This is not the primary aim here; our aim is to improve children's writing. Grammar is fundamental to this, as a means to an end, but a means which involves investigation, problem-solving, language play and a growing awareness of and interest in how language works. This book focuses on the teaching of sentence level objectives in the Literacy Hour but, throughout, the emphasis is on how children's growing understanding and use of grammar helps them to write more effectively.*
>
> (ibid.: 7)

'[I]nvestigation, problem-solving, language play and a growing awareness of and interest in how language works': all excellent things. But the idea that the study of grammar improves learners' writing in a direct sense, that the 'understanding and use of grammar', as a result of conscious analytical teaching, helps them to write more effectively, is here an article of faith, a piece of dogma, not a statement based on evidence. The article of faith continues:

> *It should be clear from this that the purpose of teaching grammar is not simply the naming of parts of speech, nor is it to provide arbitrary rules for 'correct' English. It is about making children aware of key grammatical principles and their effects, to increase the range of choices open to them when they write.*
>
> (ibid.: 7)

Not the naming of parts: good. Not arbitrary rules for correctness: good. But the sentence that follows betrays the same illusion, the same false idea of causality. To have a theoretical understanding of what an adjective is and does grammatically does not directly lead to more effective use of adjectives in writing. To be shown a range of adverbial phrases – of place, of time, of manner, of concession – does not directly lead to the more apt selection of an adverbial phrase next time a writer needs one.

The relationship between competence and reflection

Is there any escape from the sterility of the disagreement described in the chapter so far? Earlier, I offered a pseudo-mathematical expression of a negative kind. Here is a diagram of a positive kind to express my view of the proper relationship between developing competence in language and the ability to reflect on aspects of language (Figure 4.2).

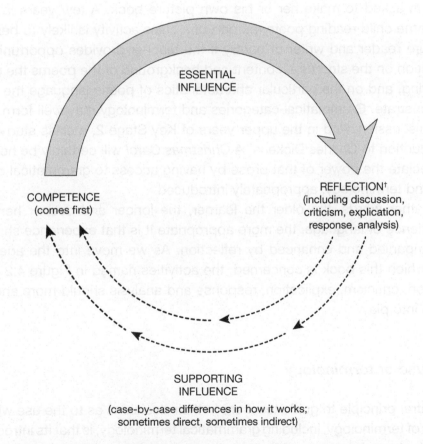

ESSENTIAL
INFLUENCE

COMPETENCE
(comes first)

REFLECTION†
(including discussion,
criticism, explication,
response, analysis)

SUPPORTING
INFLUENCE

(case-by-case differences in how it works;
sometimes direct, sometimes indirect)

†Reflection involves appropriate use of terminology; it might be described as 'turning round on your own (and others') practice'

Figure 4.2 The relationship between competence and reflection.

If we could get a right relationship between language competence and reflection on language (which will include analysis and the use of terminology), we would have solved our problem.

The 3-year-old child learning to talk is acquiring and demonstrating large amounts of implicit knowledge, but there would be no point in engaging the child in reflection on the psycholinguistic processes involved. To say to her or him 'Isn't it interesting that you were over-generalising from verbs with *–ed* endings in the simple past tense when you said "drived" just then?' would be absurd. There is an accumulation of competence which will much later feed into reflection, but there is no feedback from reflection to competence at this stage. The same child at five, however, reading a picture book, will enjoy the story in the book and also reflect on the arrangement of words and images there. There will be some feedback from reflection to competence when the child is asked to make her or his own picture book. A few years later still, the same child reading poetry as part of a class activity is likely to benefit as a future reader and writer of poetry if the teacher provides opportunities for reflection on the structure, content and background of the poems the class is studying, and on the particular characteristics of poetic language the poems demonstrate. Grammatical categories and terminology may well form part of that discussion. And in the upper years of Key Stage 2, a class studying the introduction to Charles Dickens' *A Christmas Carol* will certainly be helped to appreciate the power of that prose by having access to grammatical categories and terminology, appropriately introduced.

In other words, the older the learner, the longer and deeper her or his experience of language, the more appropriate it is that experience should be accompanied and enhanced by reflection. As we move into the age group with which this book is concerned, the activities named in Figure 4.2 as discussion, criticism, explication, response and analysis should more and more come into play.

The use of terminology

A central principle to guide teachers in their decisions as to the use with students of terminology, including grammatical terminology, is that its introduction must be based on some prior understanding of what the terminology refers to. At some point in their development children have to encounter and understand the word *word* (a metalinguistic term describing a particular category within language) and *sentence* (though for the teacher to use the term *sentence* in purposeful discussions with students is a very different thing from defining in an abstract way that thing which comes between a capital letter and a full stop) and *noun* and *verb* and *adjective* and *adverb* and *subject* and *object* and *connective*. As long as these terms are introduced at an appropriate stage in learners' development as users of language (and I am well aware that teachers teach whole classes, not isolated individuals, and will have to make judgements sometimes based on their sense of what the majority of learners in a class are able to understand), there is a good chance that many in the class will be able to make sense of the terms. If the use of grammatical terminology is offered to learners who have no prior, implicit, conceptual understanding of what the terminology refers to, the offer will be meaningless.

All areas of the language and English curriculum carry terminology, of course; terminology is not confined to grammar, nor to writing conventions, nor to literary terms. We could set the terms we have used so far within a potentially endless list: *speech mark*, *metaphor*, *text*, *pronoun*, *play*, *character*, *rhyme*, *alliteration*, *chapter*, *genre*, *paragraph*, *intonation*, *accent*, *alphabet*, *fiction*, *database*, *script*, *caption*, *camera angle*. Here is an assortment of terms, some little and some large, all of which signify important concepts or refer to potentially valid activities in the language and English curriculum. If teachers ask themselves, when in doubt, 'Will this piece of terminology serve meaning?', that will help them in the fine judgements they have to make.

Grammar teaching which can help writing

As we have seen, until recently no evidence had been found of a direct connection between explicit grammar teaching, outside the context of the study of real texts, and the quality and correctness of students' writing. However, there is now one large-scale piece of research which shows that such a connection can exist, as long as the teaching of grammar occurs *within* the context of the study of writing which is worthwhile for its own sake, which commands the learners' attention and gives pleasure.

In 'Re-thinking Grammar: The Impact of Embedded Grammar Teaching on Students' Writing and Students' Metalinguistic Awareness' (Myhill *et al.*, 2012) and in 'Grammar for Writing? An Investigation of the Effects of Contextualised Grammar Teaching on Students' Writing' (Jones *et al.*, 2012), Debra Myhill and her colleagues at Exeter University report on their study of '744 [Year 8] students in 31 schools in the south-west and Midlands of England' (Myhill *et al.*, 2012: Abstract). This was a scientifically rigorous survey, with the subjects divided into a 'comparison' and an 'intervention' group. Both groups studied narrative fiction, persuasive writing and poetry.

> *Both the intervention and comparison group were taught the three types of writing over the same period, addressing the same curriculum teaching objectives, and producing the same written outcomes . . . Both groups were given the same set of stimulus materials and resources, but only the intervention group had detailed teaching units, planned at lesson level, in which grammar was explicitly taught. Thus it is reasonable, as far as is possible within a naturalistic context, to conclude that any differences in writing performance are attributable to the intervention.*
>
> (Jones *et al.*, 2012: 1248)

> *The detailed teaching schemes for the intervention group were designed by the project team, and explicitly sought to introduce grammatical constructions and terminology at a point in the teaching sequence which was relevant to the genre being studied; for example, exploring how the use of first or third person can position the narrator differently or looking at how expanded noun phrases can build description in poetry.*
>
> (Myhill *et al.*, 2012: paragraph 3.1.2)

All the students undertook 'pre-test' and 'post-test' writing tasks. Both were 'first-person narrative, drawing on personal experience and written under controlled conditions'. The students' 'post-test' writing was compared with their 'pre-test' writing by a reputable body of external assessors, and marked according to three criteria: 'Sentence structure and punctuation', 'Text structure and organisation' and 'Composition and effect' (*ibid.*: paragraph 3.1.3).

The results may be summarised as follows:

> *The statistical results indicate a significant positive benefit for the intervention, but they also indicate that this benefit was experienced more strongly by the more able writers in the sample.*
>
> (Myhill *et al.*, 2012: Abstract)

> *more able writers in the intervention group improved significantly more than less able writers who received no significant benefit from the intervention.*
>
> (Jones *et al.*, 2012: 1254)

> *teacher LSK [linguistic subject knowledge] was a significant mediating factor in the success of the intervention. The qualitative data provide*

further evidence of the impact of teacher knowledge on how the intervention was implemented and on students' metalinguistic learning. It also reveals that teachers found the explicitness, the use of discussion and the emphasis on playful experimentation to be the most salient features of the intervention.

(Myhill *et al.*, 2012: Abstract)

So, explicit grammar teaching, offered to Year 8 students, especially when their teachers had good linguistic subject knowledge (LSK), offered in the context of worthwhile teaching resources using interesting texts, did have a clear positive effect on the writing of those students who were already abler writers.

The pedagogic principles which informed the design of the teaching schemes are important:

- *The grammatical metalanguage is used but it is always explained through examples and patterns.*
- *Links are always made between the feature introduced and how it might enhance the writing being tackled.*
- *The use of 'imitation': offering model patterns for students to play with and then use in their own writing.*
- *The inclusion of activities which encourage talking about language and effects.*
- *The use of authentic examples from authentic texts.*
- *The use of activities which support students in making choices and being designers of writing.*
- *The encouragement of language play, experimentation and games.*

(*ibid.*: paragraph 3.1.2)

The research which Myhill and her colleagues have done is, so far as I know, the only significant evidence yet produced of a positive link between grammar teaching of a certain kind (see the pedagogic principles above) and better writing. The research was done in secondary schools. The benefits were greatest with abler writers. There was 'no significant benefit' for less able writers. The teaching materials were excellent, according to some of the teachers interviewed in the research. When teachers had good LSK, this significantly benefited students' writing. On the other hand, when teachers lacked confidence in teaching about grammar, they made matters worse for students by offering:

advice to writers which either made no sense at all, or was insufficiently elab-orated or explained to be meaningful for students. One teacher told her students that 'if you use verbs, adverbs or nouns, you will be able to write a very powerful description', which is not helpful – it would be hard to write at all without using verbs, adverbs or nouns and, moreover, it is perfectly possible to write weak and ineffective descriptions using verbs, adverbs and nouns. Another set of less helpful comments related to the idea of sentence variety, which was a teaching focus of the schemes of work. Teachers regularly advocated the use of variety: 'variety is important'; 'make sure you have sentence variety'. However, there was rarely any explanation of why this variety was beneficial, implying that variety, of whatever quality, was a good thing.

(*ibid.*: paragraph 4.4.1)

Another pattern of response which links to lack of confidence in handling linguistic terminology was the strong tendency to give students semantic definitions for word classes, rather than linguistically precise descriptions. So verbs were regularly defined as 'doing' words, thus leading to student difficulties when they encountered verbs which do not appear to involve any action (e.g. are, will, wonder, consider) . . .

(*ibid.*: paragraph 4.4.2)

Myhill and her colleagues are clear about the reason for the apparent disparity between their findings and the findings of all major previous investigations into the supposed connection between grammar teaching and writing competence. They admit that 'Empirical studies investigating the efficacy of grammar teaching provide little evidence of any beneficial impact upon students' competence in writing' (Jones *et al.*, 2012: 1242). But these studies have been confined to the separate, abstract teaching of grammar, without relation to actual worthwhile texts. And 'none of the studies theorise an instructional relationship between grammar and writing, which might inform the design of an appropriate pedagogical approach' (*ibid.*: 1243). Myhill and her colleagues claim to be different; and indeed they are.

A theory of the relationship between grammar and writing

Myhill and her colleagues continue:

The theoretical approach adopted in this study builds on descriptivist views of grammar. Understanding and analysing how language works in different purposes and contexts makes connections for learners between language as an object of study and language in use, as realised in the act of writing. This is, in effect, a theory of grammar centred upon rhetorical understanding.

(*ibid.*: 1245)

This theory incorporates three principles:

Firstly, writing is a communicative act supporting writers in understanding the social purposes and audiences of texts and how language creates meanings and effects; secondly, grammar is a meaning-making resource: supporting writers in making appropriate linguistic choices which help them to shape and craft text to satisfy their rhetorical intentions; and finally, connectivity, supporting writers in making connections between their various language experiences as readers, writers and speakers, and in making connections between what they write and how they write it.

(*ibid.*: 1245)

How does this theory connect with our competence/reflection model?

Can we apply our positive welcome for Myhill's and her colleagues' research to our competence/reflection model? I think we can. With the qualifications I have listed taken into account, teaching of this kind is a good example of what I have called 'discussion, criticism, explication, response, analysis' in the model, likely to feed back as a 'supporting influence' on future writing.

I remain convinced, however – and nothing that Myhill and her colleagues say suggests that they would disagree – that the principal driver of competence in writing is enjoyable reading and discussion of a diversity of worthwhile texts, plenty of practice in writing across a range of genres and styles, and interventions by teachers which pay attention first and foremost to what the learner has written and then to the effectiveness and correctness, or otherwise, of the manner in which it has been expressed.

Teachers' linguistic subject knowledge

We saw a few paragraphs ago that, in the course of their research, Myhill and her colleagues met some teachers in the 31 schools which took part who did not know enough grammar to be able to teach it effectively. This lack of knowledge remains a major obstacle to giving grammar its proper place within the language and English curriculum.

One simple thing which the government or an agency commissioned by the government could do now would be to take the new non-statutory glossary of terms which accompanies the orders (Department for Education, 2014a: 89–107) and adapt and expand it, making it a more enjoyable read, with a more learner-friendly mode of organisation than the alphabetical, and with the grammatical categories accompanied by full examples, embedded in real and interesting texts, rather than by the thin and decontextualised examples used at present.

The present situation in England

The requirements for grammar teaching in the new English orders (Department for Education, 2014a) represent an unbalanced understanding of the relationship between competence and reflection, between use and analysis.

A digression into Key Stages 1 and 2

Although this book is addressed to teachers of students from age 11, a digression to look at the grammar orders for primary schools will be useful. Appendix 2 of the new National Curriculum orders for English, on vocabulary, grammar and punctuation, which is statutory and which applies principally to Key Stages 1 and 2, begins thus:

> *The grammar of our first language is learnt naturally and implicitly through interactions with other speakers and from reading.*

> (*ibid.*: 75)

Perfectly true.

> *Explicit knowledge of grammar is, however, very important, as it gives us more conscious control and choice in our language. Building this knowledge is best achieved through a focus on grammar within the teaching of reading, writing and speaking. Once pupils are familiar with a grammatical concept*

[for example 'modal verb'], they should be encouraged to apply and explore
this concept in the grammar of their own speech and writing and to note
where it is used by others.

(*ibid.*: 75)

This is much more dubious. In particular, it is not the case that, once learners have been taught about modal verbs as a category, they will make more
sophisticated and correct use of modals in their writing. Such an expectation demonstrates a simplistic view of how competence develops. To go back
to the competence/reflection model, this view wants to turn the arrow linking reflection back to competence into a straightforward road from cause to
effect. It may be that at the end of an effective, appropriately pitched lesson on
modal verbs, learners will be able to recognise and indeed generate examples
of properly positioned modals in sentences. It is going too far to say that in
the weeks and months to come they *will*, as a result of that lesson, also use
modals better in their writing. Perhaps there will be an influence; if there is, it
will be an aid to the major driver and developer of competence, which is positive experience of reading and writing.

Metalinguistic overload

In the new orders for Key Stages 1 and 2, there is an extraordinary overload of metalinguistic concepts and categories to be taught explicitly. At
Year 1, children must learn about plural noun suffixes and that the prefix
un- changes the meaning of verbs and adjectives. In Year 2, they must learn
subordination and noun phrases. In Year 3, as well as learning about con-
junctions, adverbs and prepositions, they must understand the use of the
present perfect tense and take their understanding of subordination as far
as the concept of the subordinate clause. Year 4 pupils must know about
fronted adverbials and determiners. Relative cla uses and cohesion are statutory for Year 5 pupils, while at Year 6 they must be introduced to the passive
voice and to ellipsis. The subjunctive makes an entry in the upper years of
Key Stage 2. In Appendix 2, it is there admittedly as a non-statutory example
of the statutory requirement to study the difference between structures characteristic of informal and of formal language. In the 'Writing – vocabulary,
grammar and punctuation' orders for Years 5 and 6, however, learning about
the subjunctive is statutory: pupils must be taught to '[recognise] vocabulary

and structures that are appropriate for formal speech and writing, including subjunctive forms'.

The above is a small selection from the statutory requirements for grammar; I say nothing here about punctuation or non-grammatical elements of vocabulary. This formidable set of new responsibilities for teachers is accompanied by the (non-statutory) glossary of terms (*ibid*.: 89–107) to which I referred in the previous section and which, taken as a whole, could usefully serve as part of the syllabus of an A-level course in language and linguistics. I hasten to say that it is desirable that teachers, *at their level*, should know about the grammatical categories and terms listed in the glossary. The glossary announces itself 'as an aid for teachers, not as the body of knowledge that should be learnt by pupils'. Nonetheless, the grammatical terms as defined there are offered as supports for the explicit teaching to primary-school pupils of many of the concepts and categories they represent.

This will not work. Most primary-school teachers will do their best to meet statutory requirements, as they always have done, but a price will be paid. Too much time will be given up to separate grammar teaching at an unrealistically advanced level, at the expense of time given to the teaching of writing, which – I hope I have made sufficiently clear in Chapter 3 – will include attention to all the aspects of convention and control which developing writers need: to the manner as well as the matter of what they write.

Key Stage 3

We emerge from this 'extraordinary overload of metalinguistic concepts and categories' into a relatively simple, 'trust-the-teacher' brevity in the new orders for Key Stage 3.

The Key Stage 3 writing orders cover just over half a page. (I discussed them in more detail in Chapter 3.) Grammar is mentioned three times. There is then a separate set of orders on grammar and vocabulary, with the same status as those on reading, writing and spoken English. (It may be remembered that at the beginning of this chapter I weighed the arguments for and against treating grammar in a chapter of its own.) After the unrealism of the demands at Key Stages 1 and 2, we might have expected that the new Key Stage 3 orders would make demands hitherto appropriate for first-year students on a degree course in linguistics. But, a surprise:

Pupils should be taught to:

- *consolidate and build on their knowledge of grammar and vocabulary through:*

• *extending and applying the grammatical knowledge set out in English Appendix 2 to the key stage 1 and 2 programmes of study to analyse more challenging texts.*

(Department for Education, 2014a: 84)

So the assumption is that the initial explicit work on grammar and vocabulary should have been completed by the time children leave primary school.

Key Stage 4 and GCSE English Language

I'll take together the references to grammar in the new statutory orders for Key Stage 4, and the subject content and assessment objectives for GCSE English Language syllabuses (Department for Education, 2013a).

As at Key Stage 3, grammar is mentioned three times in the Key Stage 4 writing orders, and 'Grammar and vocabulary' has its own section, which is only a little longer than that at Key Stage 3.

Grammar and vocabulary

Pupils should be taught to:

- *consolidate and build on their knowledge of grammar and vocabulary through:*

• *studying their effectiveness and impact in the texts they read;*
• *drawing on new vocabulary and grammatical constructions from their reading and listening, and using these consciously in their writing and speech to achieve particular effects;*
• *analysing some of the differences between spoken and written language, including differences associated with formal and informal registers, and between Standard English and other varieties of English;*
• *using linguistic and literary terminology accurately and confidently in discussing reading, writing and spoken language.*

(Department for Education, 2014a: 87)

Meanwhile, the subject content and assessment objectives for GCSE English Language syllabuses make rather modest demands with regard to grammar.

> *GCSE specifications in English language should enable students to:*
>
> - *read a wide range of texts, fluently and with good understanding;*
> - *read critically, and use knowledge gained from wide reading to inform and improve their own writing;*
> - *write effectively and coherently using Standard English appropriately;*
> - *use grammar correctly, punctuate and spell accurately;*
> - *acquire and apply a wide vocabulary, alongside a knowledge and understanding of grammatical terminology, and linguistic conventions for reading, writing and spoken language.*
>
> (Department for Education, 2013a: 3)

There are brief and appropriate references to grammar in the sub-sections on 'Critical reading and comprehension' and 'Writing' in the section on 'Scope of study' in the subject content and assessment objectives.

Grammar in primary and in secondary: the wrong way round

As I asserted earlier, if there is a time when knowledge about language should become more explicit, when the use of terminology should advance, when analysis of texts, including grammatical analysis, should occupy more of the teacher's and the students' time and attention, it is at the secondary-school stage. This is when students come much more to 'know what they know', to reflect on their knowledge, to engage in acts of what psychologists and psycholinguists call 'metacognition': learning about learning, reflecting on learning. Metalinguistic knowledge is a part of metacognition. And yet all the government's new, explicit, detailed, statutory demands about the learning of grammar apply to primary-school pupils. Secondary-school students are merely required, in a general way, to 'carry on the good work'.

This is the wrong way round. By all means let there be more grammar teaching in secondary schools, as long as it respects the principles I have repeatedly proposed. Let there be some but less grammar teaching at Key Stage 2. Let there be a little grammar teaching at Key Stage 1, but let those pupils be overwhelmingly preoccupied with the essential task of becoming confident users of language.

The topsy-turvy understanding of the relationship between competence and analysis, represented by the different requirements on teaching grammar at the four Key Stages, proceeds from a wrong conception of learning. 'Get the rules straight first,' says this conception, 'and competence will follow.' Wrong. A right conception of learning says 'Enable, encourage, support developing competence first, and awareness and application of the rules – and an active interest in those rules – will follow.'

Readers will find a more detailed, more demanding set of proposals for the teaching of grammar at Key Stages 3 and 4 in Chapter 9.

Grammar within knowledge about language

The teaching of grammar sits best within the overall study of language as a phenomenon (Halliday's third kind of language learning, as quoted in the section '"The grammar question"'). In the alternative curriculum in Chapter 9, I sketch the broad lines of a teaching programme for knowledge about language. Here I summarise the programme's five categories (which, as it happens, are quite close to the Cox Report's proposals for the teaching of knowledge about language [The Cox Committee, 1989], as described in the section '"The grammar question": government answers since 1984'). The categories are:

- variety in and between languages;
- history of languages;
- language and power in society;
- acquisition and development of language;
- language as a system shared by its users.

We can expand each of these five sub-divisions.

Variety in and between languages: between speech and writing; of accents and dialects; of functions, registers and genres in speech and writing, including those of literature; differences and similarities between languages, including comparisons of words and scripts.

History of languages: historical change in English, and in some of the world's other languages, ancient and contemporary; ephemeral as well as long-term change; the emergence of Standard English and its importance in today's society.

Language and power in society: speaker/listener, reader/writer relationships, for both interpersonal and mass uses of language, with a particular concern for the ways in which social power is constructed and challenged through language.

Acquisition and development of language: babies learning to talk; children learning to read and write; a potentially lifelong expansion of language repertoires.

Language as system: vocabulary – connotations, definitions and origins of words; grammar – the functions and forms of words in groups; phonology – the sound systems of spoken language; graphology – the systems of marks that give us written language (including spelling, punctuation, layout and handwriting); the structure of longer pieces of spoken and written text (for example conversations, sports commentaries, speeches, stories, arguments, descriptions, poems, reports, campaign posters, online diaries and blogs).

Whether in the course of other activities within the English curriculum or as specific investigations, students might look explicitly at language in ways which pay attention, variously or simultaneously, to some aspects of all five of these things. The individual topics are not, of course, offered as lesson keynotes; if we enter the explicit consideration of language through any one door, we are immediately walking about in a room which could have been entered through other doors. And we should remember that the magnificent, mysterious reality of language will always elude complete attempts at analysis: a warning which applies particularly aptly to the study of grammar.

To conclude . . .

At present, an agreement which would unite government and the profession on the teaching of grammar is a long way off. There are those in powerful positions who cling to the idea that students lack a grasp of 'proper grammar', a lack which, it is said, profoundly disadvantages them as writers, and that this has been the fault of teachers insufficiently concerned with correctness and over-indulgent of a loose and uncritical 'creativity' in the work of their students. Such people claim that large amounts of analytical grammar teaching early on will solve the problem.

This view is wrong; furthermore, it is often advanced for reasons of political advantage rather than as a result of sincere conviction arrived at after careful thought. However, grammar teaching, appropriately pitched and taught in the context of the study of actual, authentic, interesting texts, is to be welcomed. This chapter is not an 'anti-grammar' tract. It is 'pro-grammar', as long as the understanding of the place of grammar in the English curriculum as a whole is properly judged. There is a key difference between the teaching of grammar as a set of decontextualised drills and exercises and its teaching as part of the study of real, continuous, pleasure-giving texts. The first will fail, as has been shown by repeated research over many years; the second has a good chance of success.

The new orders on grammar teaching are unbalanced in terms of the excessive expectations they place on primary-school pupils and teachers, and the insufficiently demanding expectations they place on secondary-school students and teachers. Chapter 9 contains a more demanding, more detailed alternative curriculum for grammar at Key Stages 3 and 4.

The teaching of grammar is best done in the context of the wider study of language as a phenomenon.

Some teachers' own linguistic subject knowledge is inadequate to the task of teaching grammar in the way recommended in this chapter. The government, or an agency commissioned by the government, could help to meet this lack by adapting and expanding the existing non-statutory glossary of grammatical terms, accompanying the terms with full examples, embedded in real and interesting texts.

5 Drama

John Richmond

Summary of main points

Drama's potential contribution to learning and to the life of schools is diverse and enriching. It is a means of enhancing learning in a range of curriculum subjects and areas. It has the potential to develop qualities of empathy and respect for difference in children and young people. It enables active and collaborative learning.

Drama has close links with literature and with narrative generally, and therefore has a special significance within English teaching.

Drama is an art form.

Drama is a prominent feature of a school's extra-curricular cultural life.

Like all other forms of learning, drama is affected by and may be realised via digital and electronic technologies and media. These new technologies and media can extend the realistic possibilities of what may be achieved in the classroom and drama studio. For example, a few years ago, the idea that drama could be filmed, played back and instantly commented on would have seemed ambitious. Today, tablet computers and smartphones mean that such a practice is easily achievable.

There is a weakness at the heart of drama's official relationship with the statutory curriculum in England. This stems from the failure of the UK government, when the National Curriculum for England and Wales was introduced in 1989 and 1990, to grant drama the same status as was accorded to art and music: that of foundation subject. The situation today remains as it was then, despite strenuous efforts by organisations and individuals representing drama teaching to persuade successive governments to grant drama foundation-subject status.

Statutorily, drama sits within English. The references to drama within successive versions of the National Curriculum for English since 1989 have never amounted to a coherent and rigorous description of the subject. They offer no sense of progression and development. The references in the new National Curriculum for English are no more adequate than those in previous versions. Chapter 9 offers an alternative.

Educational drama has a long theoretical history. During the second half of the twentieth century, expert thinkers extended our understanding of drama as a mode of learning, and showed how this understanding can bear fruit in effective classroom work. A debate (and sometimes a dispute) developed between those who preferred to emphasise learning *through* drama and those who preferred to emphasise learning *about* drama. The former were less concerned with drama as product than with the multiple benefits of drama as process. The latter, while not denying the value of drama as process, wished to assert that drama is an art form which can be taught, and that drama activity will and should often have an outcome in performance. There is no need to decide in favour of drama as process or as product. It is both.

Theorists of drama teaching

This section owes a great debt to Nicholas McGuinn, the first half of whose *The English Teacher's Drama Handbook* (McGuinn, 2014) offers a superb selective summary of the evolution of an understanding of what drama in education is or could be. McGuinn's contribution to the section amounts to a form of co-authorship.

Rousseau and Froebel

Two famous figures from past centuries established the idea that a child's play is a centrally important element in her or his education: Jean-Jacques Rousseau, in *Émile* (Rousseau, 1979 [1762]), and Friedrich Froebel, in *The Education of Man* (Froebel, 2005 [1826]). Linked to this thought is another, equally profound: that the teacher and the learner should not be fixed in asymmetrical power relationships, with the learner always subservient to and dependent on the wisdom and benevolence of the teacher.

> *From a drama teacher's perspective, one of the most significant points on which Rousseau and Froebel are particularly united is their insistence that, from birth, children are actively engaged in the construction of meanings. A child's play, Froebel argues, 'is not trivial, it is highly serious and of deep significance' (Froebel, 2005: 55). If adults cannot understand this, it is because they do not know how to interpret what they see.*
>
> (McGuinn, 2014: 6)

It may easily be imagined how ideas of this kind did not chime with the utilitarian purpose of universal state education as introduced in the UK in 1870. Indeed, the conflict between those who see education as the taxpayer's investment in a future economically productive workforce, and those who – while recognising the necessity for young people to emerge from schooling literate and numerate – see education as a broader, more human process, as something to do with culture, is with us today.

Piaget and Vygotsky

Two great psychologists of the twentieth century also saw, in different ways, the central importance of play in the child's development, and were interested in the relationship between play and drama. They were Lev Vygotsky, some of whose thinking is touched on elsewhere in the book, and Jean Piaget.

> *Piaget acknowledges that there are similarities between drama and symbolic play . . . For [him], the key distinction between play and drama is that the participants in the latter . . . are consciously aware of and reflective upon the fiction with which they are engaged.*
>
> (Piaget, 1976 [1951]: 569, in McGuinn, 2014: 14)

> *Vygotsky sets particular store on the aesthetic qualities of drama. It is, he argues, the most 'syncretic [that is, the most combining] mode of creation', because it affords children access to so many of the arts . . . 'Drama, more than any other form of creation . . . is closely and directly linked to play . . . The staging of drama provides the pretext and material for the most diverse forms of creativity on the part of the children.'*
>
> (Vygotsky, 2004 [1967]: 71, in McGuinn, 2014: 15)

Three English pioneers

In summarising the work of the most influential twentieth-century writers on drama in education in an English context, McGuinn finds two unifying themes and one fault line. The unifying themes are inherited from the four writers I have just named: that the teacher is a co-learner along with the child, though one with particular rights, responsibilities and knowledge; and that drama is a development of play. The fault line is in the differing emphases given to process and product in drama, as between drama as a form of learning, engaged in for the benefit of the learners, and drama as performed art, engaged in for the benefit of performers and audience.

Three early twentieth-century writers on drama seem to straddle this fault line without difficulty. Harriet Finlay-Johnson (author of *The Dramatic Method of Teaching*, 1912), Henry Caldwell Cook (author of *The Play Way: An Essay in Educational Method*, 1917) and Marjorie Lovegrove Hourd (author of *The Education of the Poetic Spirit: A Study of Children's Expression in the English Lesson*, 1949) all share 'Froebel's enthusiasm for play as a powerful learning medium'; 'all three practitioners are implacably opposed to systems of rote-learning – and the examination systems that necessarily accompany them' (McGuinn, 2014: 17–18). Finlay-Johnson gives examples of her use of drama as a learning medium which still sound exciting, if perhaps a little imperialistic:

> inkwells are transformed into 'breathing holes' for seals in a geographical simulation of a voyage to Newfoundland . . . or a chalk pit outside the school is commandeered as the setting for a re-enactment of General Wolfe's scaling of the Heights of Abraham in 1759, or a 'roll-call' is improvised to lend poignancy to a reading of Tennyson's poem 'The Charge of the Light Brigade'.
>
> (Finlay-Johnson, 1912: 136, 118, in McGuinn, 2014: 23)

At the same time, the students of all three writers rehearse and perform plays, including those by Shakespeare.

Peter Slade

Peter Slade's book *Child Drama* was published in 1954. Slade became 'world-famous as a pioneer of drama therapy, as a champion of children's theatre and as an educator of drama teachers' (McGuinn, 2014: 28). He advocated and practised an extreme version of child-centredness in pedagogy.

> it is we who must learn. The Children [Slade always writes 'Child' or 'Children' with an initial capital] teach us . . . all that is wanted is a place where Children go to the Land [of Child Drama – capital D] with the help of an understanding adult.
>
> (Slade, 1954: 278, 296, in McGuinn, 2014: 28–29)

Slade's contribution is enormous.

> *He went far beyond his predecessors by boldly declaring . . . 'Child Drama is an Art in itself, and would stand by that alone as being of importance' . . . [He] took up the challenge of thinking through just what exactly the 'domain' . . . of Child Drama might contain . . . [He] attempts, in his first book, to create a conceptual map of what [child] development might look like in terms of a young person's staged, incremental encounter with drama . . . [He attempts] to provide a metalanguage for the domain of Child Drama . . . Where Finlay-Johnson and Caldwell Cook offer consistently enthusiastic but ultimately rather nebulous endorsements of [play's] qualities, Slade attempts a more sustained scrutiny of what he, just as much as his predecessors, believes 'may be the correct approach to all forms of education'.*
> (Slade, 1954: 105, 12, 75, 12–14, 42, in McGuinn, 2014: 34–35)

Slade was strongly opposed to the artifice of conventional theatre. He considered it a danger to children's well-being.

> *'the proscenium form of theatre has disastrous effects on the genuine Drama of the Child . . .' The 'showing off' encouraged by acting for an audience might be bad enough; but for a child to be a member of an audience is to signal something close to spiritual and moral capitulation: 'Nothing is more cruel than to force Children to sit as audience when others are playing. If they want to, then things have gone very far wrong – we have suppressed them.'*
> (Slade, 1954: 44, 58, in McGuinn, 2014: 31–32)

On the other hand, Slade was 'not averse to young people being taught theatre skills when they have reached the requisite stage of maturity and development' (McGuinn, 2014: 34–35).

Teachers who have taken children (lower-case c) to the theatre (proscenium or otherwise), and drawn pleasure and satisfaction from their enjoyment of the experience, may well find Slade's warnings about the dangers lurking there absurd. McGuinn, while paying due credit to Slade's contribution and influence, is aware of another contradiction in his legacy. His insistence that drama is an art form, and his romantic conception of the wisdom of the child, sit uncomfortably with his declaration that 'some of the best work with Children is done by experienced teachers *who really understand what they are doing* [original italics], and yet, strangely enough, have very little knowledge of

Drama' (Slade, 1954: 271, in McGuinn, 2014: 37). As McGuinn says, 'where does that leave the key elements of effective pedagogy: content knowledge and application, planned progression, differentiation, classroom management, formative and summative assessment?' (McGuinn, 2014: 37).

Brian Way

Brian Way's *Development through Drama* (1967) was a major advance, in that it linked theoretical understandings of drama's value with practical, detailed advice on how to bring that value to bear in the reality of classrooms which were often physically less than ideal for drama, and which contained 30 or more young people not all of whom were naturally wise or desperately keen to engage in dramatic activity.

(In 1974, having been appointed, as I thought, to teach English in a secondary school in south London, having a degree in English literature but no post-graduate training of any kind, I arrived to start work two days after my appointment. I was handed my timetable. It did indeed include two English classes which I would teach for five lessons a week. It also included nine drama classes which I would teach for one lesson a week each, in a small hall surrounded by rooms where academic subjects were being taught to students sitting quietly in rows. After a few days of something close to chaos, I found *Development through Drama* in Dillon's bookshop, and the quality of my teaching improved a notch or two.)

> *More than any specialist described so far, Way provides such detailed descriptions of drama exercises, improvisations and extended role plays that it would still be possible today for a teacher to deliver a lesson or sequence of lessons from the instructions provided in the book. In the section on Speaking, for example, Way offers forty scenarios for improvised dialogue . . . which, with a little updating, could still be employed to good effect in an English classroom focused on the language of persuasion and argument.*
>
> (McGuinn, 2014: 54)

> *Perhaps most innovative of all from an English perspective is Way's enthusiasm for media conventions and strategies . . . Arguing that students must learn to look 'with the selectivity of the lens of a sensitive camera' (Way, 1967: 59), he devotes a section of the book's chapter on Improvisation*

*to an exploration of potential links between drama and film – considering,
for example, how a photographic image might afford the starting point for
improvisation, or a freeze frame might be 'shot' from different camera angles;
or thinking about how a musical score might enhance mood and atmosphere.*

(McGuinn, 2014: 55)

Gavin Bolton and Dorothy Heathcote

Gavin Bolton and Dorothy Heathcote, two more hugely influential figures in the
evolution of teachers' understanding and practice of drama, share Brian Way's
more practical approach, recognising the great skill required of a teacher,
whether specialist in drama or not, if he or she is to bring about students'
successful and satisfying learning. Two of their most important publications
are *Drama as Education: An Argument for Placing Drama at the Centre of
the Curriculum* (Bolton, 1984) and *Drama for Learning: Dorothy Heathcote's
Mantle of the Expert Approach to Education* (Heathcote and Bolton, 1995).

Like Way, Bolton and Heathcote are scornful of lax, optimistic approaches
to drama teaching which assume that any kind of free expression must be
good. All three reject Slade's romantic idealisation of the child.

Two phrases in particular have come to be associated with Bolton's and
Heathcote's work: Heathcote's *mantle of the expert*; and the idea and practice
of *teacher in role*.

Mantle of the expert means that learners in a drama lesson, as long as in possession of or supplied with the necessary information, understanding or skill,
can exercise an authority role in the drama by deploying that power. Sometimes
a learner will already have the necessary information, understanding or skill.
Sometimes the teacher will need to provide it or show the learner how to get
hold of it. The benefits of the combination of the deployment of information,
understanding or skill with the realisation of the effect of that deployment on
others in the drama lie in the gaining of a profounder grasp of whichever area
of knowledge or experience is under consideration than could be achieved by
other means.

Teacher in role self-evidently means that the teacher no longer simply sets
up a drama, watches it unfold, and brings it to a conclusion or accepts the
conclusion which the learners offer. He or she intervenes in the drama, taking
a role of some kind. The role may range from one of fictional authority to one
of fictional subservience.

In giving the mantle of the expert to the learner, and/or in taking on a fictional role, the teacher casts off for fictional purposes a conventional authority role, of which in one sense the learners are nonetheless still aware, and provokes a dynamic in the drama lesson of trust and suspension of disbelief which is of rare value. The relationship between teacher and learners is, for the moment, changed.

Peter Abbs and David Hornbrook

Whatever differences there were between the approaches and beliefs of Slade, Way, Bolton and Heathcote, whatever the distance travelled over the years during which they worked, it would be fair to say that their principal concern is for drama as process and as an instrument of learning. They are proponents of learning *through* drama. Peter Abbs and David Hornbrook shift the emphasis from learning *through* drama to learning *about* drama. Their key books are *Living Powers: The Arts in Education* (Abbs [ed.], 1987a), which Abbs edited and to which he contributed the essay 'Towards a Coherent Arts Aesthetic' (Abbs, 1987b), Hornbrook's *Education and Dramatic Art* (Hornbrook, 1989) and his *On the Subject of Drama* (Hornbrook, 1998).

It is important, however, to stress the word 'emphasis' in the previous paragraph. Learning through and learning about drama are dualisms which, taken literally, could suggest that one group is only interested in, let us say, trust games or the empathetic taking of roles in the re-creation of historical events; and the other group is only interested in voice projection and stage lighting. These are parodies. Slade, despite his objection to proscenium theatre, believed, as we have seen, that young people could be taught theatre skills 'when they have reached the requisite stage of maturity and development'. Neither Abbs nor Hornbrook would say that the practices promoted by Way, Bolton and Heathcote are without value. Like these three figures, Abbs and Hornbrook are critical of loose, free-wheeling approaches to dramatic expression. They call for 'an appropriate balance between a knowledge of drama and the mastery of its practices' (Hornbrook, 1998: 9, in McGuinn, 2014: 68).

That said, the difference in emphasis between Abbs and Hornbrook and what went before is clear. Abbs and Hornbrook believe that there is a body of knowledge which can be identified as the territory of drama, and that it can be taught.

Abbs clearly sees drama's future within the arts. He proposes:

> *that drama shares with the performing arts a conceptual terrain that can be defined by four present participles: 'making', 'presenting', 'responding' and 'evaluating' (Abbs, 1987a: 63, 54) . . . Writing a decade later, Hornbrook endorses this position, though, in order to cement the relationship further, he conflates 'evaluating' with 'responding' (Hornbrook, 1998: 63).*
>
> (both quotations in McGuinn, 2014: 68)

Both writers wish to reinstate (or possibly establish for the first time) the teaching of conventions and techniques within drama. And there is an unmistakable shift in the direction of theatre in their work, however broadly that word may be defined. (It *is* broadly defined; Hornbrook's vision of theatrical culture worth teaching is global.) He writes:

> *Students will not simply intuit how to light a performance, any more than they are likely to perform well without being taught at least the rudiments of acting or direct without studying the way in which stage pictures are organised.*
>
> (Hornbrook, 1998: 56, in McGuinn, 2014: 69)

Hornbrook admires the master/apprentice relationship of the medieval guild or craft. This emphasis is different from that implied by the giving of the mantle of the expert to the learner, or by the taking of a fictional role by the teacher.

Process or product?

McGuinn sums up well the dilemma produced if the Abbs and Hornbrook position is regarded as the kind of alternative to the Bolton and Heathcote position which forces the practitioner to choose.

> *Introducing curriculum rigour in terms of content and critical method not only gives the lie to those who would regard drama as academically 'soft' and inextricably linked to the vagaries of 'self-expression'. It can also . . . empower learners with real expertise . . . Choosing this route, however, brings significant consequences for English pedagogy. First, it requires the construction of a coherent and progressive drama curriculum. Second, it implies, in some measure at least, that the dais be returned to the classroom [a reference to*

Frank Whitehead's famous publication, The Disappearing Dais: A Study of the Principles and Practice of English Teaching *(Whitehead, 1966)] and that the teacher move from co-learner to transmitter of knowledge – a drama-specific knowledge that might lie beyond the ambit of traditional training in English pedagogy. Third – and perhaps most important of all – it threatens to weaken the commitment to democracy, inclusivity and personal growth that makes drama so appealing to English teachers in the first place. If skills are to be taught and applied, then, inevitably, some students will learn to apply those skills more effectively than others . . . Subject-specific discourse might empower, but it might also intimidate and exclude. What drama might gain in terms of aesthetic crafting, it might lose in terms of 'spontaneity and camaraderie'.*

(McGuinn, 2014: 75–76)

So, as we survey the situation now, is there such a dilemma?

Jonothan Neelands

Jonothan Neelands' paper, 'Drama: The Subject that Dare Not Speak its Name' (2008), was written principally 'for student teachers of English in England . . . to introduce them to the main issues informing drama pedagogy in contemporary classrooms' (McGuinn, 2014: 77). The paper has reached far wider audiences since its publication. Its polemical title drops a heavy hint that the author knows that all is not well in drama's relationship with the official curriculum. The hint is confirmed in the text.

In theory [the current position of drama in the official curriculum] presents schools in the English system with the opportunity to design and implement their own ideas and values of what drama means in terms of curriculum, pedagogy and assessment. In practice, the lack of a national consensus about what drama is and where it might be best positioned, taught and assessed leads to a degree of professional insecurity amongst teachers employed as drama specialists and has also led to a long and sometimes fierce contest to define what is legitimate drama in schools.

(Neelands, 2008: 2)

Neelands is frank about the process/product debate, or division, which has preoccupied drama for so long.

In the literature of drama in schools in anglophone countries, battle lines are often drawn between so called 'product' and 'process' approaches to teaching drama . . . The product approach is often associated with 'theatre' as a subject of study and the 'process' approach with improvised forms of drama used as a method of teaching and learning across the curriculum. A 'product' approach tends to assume that drama is properly concerned with the study of the western traditions of playwriting and performance and focuses on the development of the performance skills needed to realise an 'established' canon of plays and authors and also the critical and cognitive skills and understandings needed to understand and appreciate drama in both its literary and dominant performance modes. This approach tends to be uncritical of the class and culturally restricted paradigm of theatre, which underpins it, a paradigm of theatre and theatrical production that closely reflects the history and tastes and preferences of the English middle class theatre audience.

(*ibid.*: 4–5)

If the latter part of this quotation is an oblique criticism of Abbs and Hornbrook, it is unfair in the sense that their understanding of theatre goes far beyond 'the western traditions of playwriting and performance' and 'the tastes and preferences of the English middle class theatre audience'. However, the first two sentences are crisp and accurate. Meanwhile:

In its extreme forms, process drama approaches may eschew any attempt to 'perform' or to engage students with the literary tradition of theatre. Instead, students are engaged in creating drama experiences through improvisation and spontaneous forms of role-play . . . Process drama is often considered to be a method or means of learning for use across the curriculum, rather than as a subject. It is often closely associated with 'liberal' or 'progressive' models of teaching and it claims to develop a wide range of social, personal, critical, cognitive, communication and imaginative/creative skills and understandings. At its heart is the idea that students learn through the direct experience of working within a fictional drama context, which is not observed by an audience.

(*ibid.*: 5)

Process or product: no need to choose

Neelands offers a table of genres of work in drama, ranging from those at the more theatrical, product-focused end of the continuum to those more focused on process and on students' learning (*ibid.*: 3–4). He says, clearly enough:

Increasingly, good drama practice at all levels is characterised by a more holistic approach that seeks to capture the strengths of both the process and the product traditions.

(ibid.: 6)

In other words, Neelands proposes that we should have our cake and eat it when it comes to the theory and practice of drama. There is no need to sign up to membership of the process or the product 'club'. All the approaches which have been proposed by the major theorists of drama have their validity. Only extremes are excluded: that is, the positions of those who would condemn performance as irrelevant to or even dangerous for learners' emotional and cognitive development and well-being; and of those on the other hand who would insist that 'an actor (or stage manager or director or lighting technician) prepares' is the only motto for educational drama worth bothering with.

The present situation in England

My understanding of educational drama follows Neelands' in seeking 'to capture the strengths of both the process and the product traditions'. Drama can be many things, drawing on both traditions and a mixture of them. And an enormous amount of excellent, diverse drama work is being done in schools.

However, the official status of drama in the statutory curriculum is a story of missed opportunities. The fact that drama *can* be many things does not mean that it *is* or *has been* all or – in some schools – any of those. The failure of legislators to make up their minds about where drama sits in the curriculum has led to long-term uncertainty about the subject and, in some schools, to a hopefulness that drama is being done somewhere and somehow, because the clear responsibility for doing it does not lie unequivocally with anyone.

An opportunity lost

The greatest loss of opportunity, in terms of drama's status in the school curriculum in England, occurred when those who legislated for the National Curriculum which took effect in 1989 and 1990 decided not to give drama the status of a foundation subject, along with art and music. English was given the guardianship of drama. Although in the first English orders for speaking and listening (Department of Education and Science and the Welsh Office, 1990) the occasional mention of imaginative play, improvised drama, role-play, simulations and group drama encouraged, indeed required, teachers in primary schools and secondary English teachers to use drama in their teaching, the lop-sided, half-in, half-out legal status of drama was taken as a signal that schools did not need to provide for it in the way that they needed to provide for art and music.

Mitigating the effects of the government's failure

Numerous worthwhile efforts have been made since 1989 to deal with the problem of drama's Cinderella status in the National Curriculum. The government itself, via its National Literacy Strategy (later National Strategy), published detailed advice on teaching and assessing drama (Department for Education and Employment, 1998; Department for Education and Skills, 2001, 2003). The Office for Standards in Education offered guidance to school inspectors and teaching staff on evaluating the quality of teaching and learning in drama (for example, Office for Standards in Education, 2002). There was much to commend in these publications. However, they could not overcome the structural problem which schools had inherited as a result of the failure described in the previous section.

Other organisations weighed in to help. For example:

> In 2003, the Arts Council published the second edition of Drama in Schools
> [Arts Council England, 2003] which was intended to fill the gap left by drama's
> exclusion from the National Curriculum as a subject in its own right. In the
> absence of any national agreement on drama, many schools [were] left without
> the levels of support and guidance offered in National Curriculum subjects.
> (Dickinson, Neelands and Shenton Primary School, 2006)

The document to which these authors refer is excellent. Amongst other things, it offers brief statements of what good drama looks like at Foundation Stage, at the four compulsory Key Stages, at post-16 and in special schools. Here is an extract from the statement for Key Stage 3:

> Good teaching at Key Stage 3 builds on that in primary schools. Pupils
> research, discuss and use drama techniques to explore character and situa-
> tions. They devise and present scripted and improvised dramas in response
> to a range of stimuli, demonstrating their ability to investigate ideas, situations

and events and an understanding of how theatre can communicate in innovative, challenging ways. They experiment with sound, voice, silence, movement, stillness, light and darkness to enhance dramatic action and use theatre technology creatively. They take part in scenes from plays by a range of dramatists and recognise the particular contributions that directors, designers and actors make to a production.

(Arts Council England, 2003: 16)

The statements are accompanied by case studies of successful drama lessons at each age group.

An important chapter in the book is 'Structuring Drama in Schools', which is a kind of manifesto for drama, proposing a framework within which it should be taught, practised and assessed.

Drama should be taught progressively through and across each key stage, building upon previous learning. The three interrelated activities of making, performing and responding provide a useful framework for identifying and assessing progression and achievement, and match similar categories in music: composing, performing and appraising, and in dance: creating, performing and evaluating. For the purposes of planning and assessment, making, performing and responding are treated separately, although they are frequently integrated in practice. Pupils improvising, for example, are simultaneously making, performing and responding. Similarly, the emphasis placed on each can change across the key stages. However, the principle of balance is important and teachers should aim to include aspects of each activity in their schemes of work.

Making encompasses the many processes and activities employed when exploring, devising, shaping and interpreting drama.

Performing covers the skills and knowledge displayed when enacting, presenting and producing dramas, including the use of theatre technology.

Responding incorporates reflecting on both emotional and intellectual reactions to the drama. This reflection is deepened as pupils gain a knowledge and understanding of how drama is created.

To ensure breadth of study during each key stage, pupils should be taught the skills, knowledge and understanding required to make, perform and respond to drama through:

- *a broad range of stimuli, including artefacts, literature, non-fiction and non-literary texts such as photographs and video clips;*
- *working in groups of varying size and as a class;*

- *performing to a range of audiences;*
- *a range of genres, styles and different media;*
- *seeing a variety of live and recorded performances from different times and cultures; and*
- *using ICT to explore and record ideas, research themes and enhance their production work.*

(*ibid*.: 29)

The making, performing (or presenting), responding trilogy is familiar now. The manifesto is followed by a detailed set of level descriptions for pupils' achievement in making, performing and responding at each level of the (now abandoned) National Curriculum eight-level scale plus 'exceptional performance'. I make use both of the trilogy and of the descriptions of achievement in the alternative curriculum for drama in Chapter 9.

Drama in the new National Curriculum

While other organisations and individuals have been trying to bring clarity to an unclear situation, successive governments since 1989 have been responsible for numerous revisions and re-revisions of the National Curriculum for English. None of these has significantly enhanced the value given to drama in official terms. It has continued to shelter awkwardly in English. We will skip over these superficial changes and come to the present day. In the new National Curriculum orders for English, the following requirement appears in an introductory general section on spoken language:

> *All pupils should be enabled to participate in and gain knowledge, skills and understanding associated with the artistic practice of drama. Pupils should be able to adopt, create and sustain a range of roles, responding appropriately to others in role. They should have opportunities to improvise, devise and script drama for one another and a range of audiences, as well as to rehearse, refine, share and respond thoughtfully to drama and theatre performances.*

(Department for Education, 2014a: 15)

Below is every reference in the new orders to drama at Key Stages 3 and 4 and to activities connected, however tangentially, with it.

Key Stage 3

The reading orders at Key Stage 3 include the requirement that pupils should:

> [read] a wide range of fiction and non-fiction, including in particular whole books, short stories, poems and plays with a wide coverage of genres, historical periods, forms and authors. The range will include high-quality works from English literature, both pre-1914 and contemporary, including prose, poetry and drama, Shakespeare (two plays), seminal world literature . . .
>
> (*ibid*.: 84)

Pupils should be taught to 'read critically through . . . understanding how the work of dramatists is communicated effectively through performance and how alternative staging allows for different interpretations of a play' (*ibid*.: 84).

The writing orders at this Key Stage include the requirement that pupils should be taught to produce 'writing for a wide range of purposes and audiences, including . . . stories, scripts, poetry and other imaginative writing' (*ibid*.: 85).

The orders for spoken language include the requirement that pupils should be taught to '[improvise], [rehearse] and [perform] play scripts and poetry in order to generate language and discuss language use and meaning, using role, intonation, tone, volume, mood, silence, stillness and action to add impact' (*ibid*.: 86).

Key Stage 4

The writing orders at Key Stage 4 include the requirement that pupils should:

> [read] a wide range of high-quality, challenging, classic literature and extended literary non-fiction, such as essays, reviews and journalism. This writing should include whole texts. The range will include at least one play by Shakespeare, works from the 19th, 20th and 21st centuries . . .
>
> (*ibid*.: 87)

As at Key Stage 3, the orders for spoken language at Key Stage 4 include the requirement that pupils should be taught to '[improvise], [rehearse] and [perform] play scripts and poetry in order to generate language and discuss language use and meaning, using role, intonation, tone, volume, mood, silence, stillness and action to add impact' (*ibid*.: 89).

Several of these quotations focus on the perfectly valid, indeed important activity of the reading and writing of scripted literary drama, an activity with which secondary English teachers generally feel comfortable but which is well away from the centre of the idea of drama as summarised or quoted in this and the previous sections. There is no point in finding detailed fault with individual requirements. Many of them are admirable in themselves. The problem resides in the fact that, put all together, they do not add up to a substantial, coherent, rigorous, iterative, developmental account of a subject in the school curriculum.

This is an unsatisfactory situation.

Drama in the school curriculum: another way

While drama in England continues to shelter within English, other educational legislatures have taken a different decision. In his 2008 paper quoted earlier, Jonothan Neelands offers a list.

> *Drama is included as a discrete subject and as a strand in the Arts in the National Curricula of a growing number of other national education systems. These include certain provinces and states within the USA, Canada and Australia; Cyprus, Taiwan, Hungary, Czech Republic, Norway, New Zealand, France, Malta amongst others. Drama is part of a statutory entitlement to the Arts in Scotland, Northern Ireland and the Republic of Ireland.*
>
> (Neelands, 2008: 1)

Let us take one English-speaking country from Neelands' list. The Australian Curriculum, Assessment and Reporting Authority (ACARA) is responsible for a recently introduced curriculum in Australia's schools. Here are three quotations from ACARA's website, drilling down from the curriculum as a whole, to The Arts, to Drama:

> *The Foundation – Year 10 Australian Curriculum is described as a three-dimensional curriculum that recognises the central importance of disciplinary knowledge, skills and understanding; general capabilities; and cross-curriculum priorities.*
>
> *Disciplinary knowledge is found in the eight learning areas of the Australian Curriculum: English, Mathematics, Science, Health and Physical Education, Humanities and Social Sciences, The Arts, Technologies and Languages. The latter four learning areas have been written to include multiple subjects, reflecting custom and practice in the discipline . . .*

In the Australian Curriculum, The Arts is a learning area that draws together related but distinct art forms. While these art forms have close relationships and are often used in interrelated ways, each involves different approaches to arts practices and critical and creative thinking that reflect distinct bodies of knowledge, understanding and skills. The curriculum examines past, current and emerging arts practices in each art form across a range of cultures and places.

The Australian Curriculum: The Arts comprises five subjects: Dance, Drama, Media Arts, Music, Visual Arts . . .

Drama is the expression and exploration of personal, cultural and social worlds through role and situation that engages, entertains and challenges. Students create meaning as drama makers, performers and audiences as they enjoy and analyse their own and others' stories and points of view. Like all art forms, drama has the capacity to engage, inspire and enrich all students, excite the imagination and encourage students to reach their creative and expressive potential.

(ACARA, 2016)

ACARA offers clear guidelines for the teaching of Drama from the foundation year up to Year 10: the entire school age-range. There is also guidance as to how Drama is to be configured or combined with the other four subjects in The Arts.

England embarrassed

The comparison between Australia's and England's approach to drama embarrasses the latter. The two countries are in different leagues in terms of substance, coherence, rigour and the understanding of iteration and development. It is too soon to say how successful will be Australia's attempt at giving full status to drama within the curriculum. However, the arrangements summarised here, which have been subject to extensive consultation between the Australian federal government and its agencies and the states and territories of Australia, and have been prepared with the active involvement of schools and teachers' organisations, have a good chance of doing what England has failed to do with its half measures and hopeful compromises: put drama firmly on the map.

An alternative

The proposals for drama in the alternative curriculum in Chapter 9 owe much to the Australian model. The proposals could be adopted and adapted for various purposes: as an alternative to the collection of references to drama in the new National Curriculum for English; as an aide-memoire for the use of drama in subjects across the curriculum; as a framework for teaching in schools where drama is already a freestanding subject; or as the basis of a future curriculum for drama as a foundation subject of the National Curriculum.

To conclude . . .

Across England, drama continues to be taught effectively and imaginatively by thousands of teachers, specialists or not, in a diversity of curriculum settings. Through the work of these teachers, drama makes its essential contribution to the education of children and young people as whole, social beings. Drama is a fundamental part of education for culture.

Learning *through* drama and learning *about* drama are equally valid approaches. There will be occasions when the one or the other approach predominates. There will be occasions when both are in play.

All subjects and areas of the curriculum are potentially capable of supplying content whose learning will benefit from the use of drama. For the teacher of English, the range of possibilities for the enrichment of learning through drama is wide.

Learning about drama will draw on a diversity of theatrical traditions, styles and techniques. It should also draw on traditions, styles and techniques which have developed in drama on film and television and which are developing in drama on recently invented digital platforms.

Drama's official status in the National Curriculum in England is a matter of unfinished business. At some point in the not too distant future, England's Department for Education should complete the business by according drama the status of a full National Curriculum subject. If this were to occur, it would not of course mean that drama ceases to be a key activity, an essential mode of learning, in English or in any other subject or area of the curriculum. It would simply mean that an activity which, along with music, image-making and dance, is as old as human civilisation itself, would finally have been accorded proper official recognition in England's schools.

6 Media

Andrew Burn

Summary of main points

In the past, media education has often been seen as a form of 'inoculation': of protection against the cultural, moral and ideological ill effects of the mass media. More recently, media education has struck a more positive note. Its emphasis is on the value of popular culture and on the importance of media forms such as cinema, television, comic books, video games, animation, advertising, news media and social media in representing our world.

Media education in the National Curriculum in England has been contained within English. This has provided positive opportunities for teachers and learners, raising the profile of moving-image texts, introducing the idea of multimodal texts, and emphasising the importance of digital media. However, media education's place within English has also caused problems: emphasising factual media at the expense of fiction; suggesting a 'suspicious' mode of reading media texts (in contrast to the 'appreciative' mode expected for literary texts); and restricting media education to the reading section of the curriculum, thus making it mandatory to 'read' media texts, but not to 'write' them.

In the most recent version of the National Curriculum for English, media education has effectively been expunged. It should be fully reinstated. Any adequate media curriculum should equally emphasise 'reading' (analysis of media) and 'writing' (production of media).

Media education can be a separate subject in the curriculum. That is how it is most strongly represented in the UK in post-14 education, in the form of specialist Media Studies and Film Studies syllabuses. While the popularity of these post-14 courses is welcome, media education is best located within English. This arrangement allows for a coherent approach to the study and making of texts and meanings across all media, which can extend and strengthen students' understanding of textual structures, contexts and functions. It is the arrangement most likely to provide entitlement to media education for all young people in the school system.

The study of media, drama and literature together within English allows teachers and students to explore the spectrum of cultural taste, from elite canonical texts through to popular cultural forms, and the increasing tendency for these to collapse into one another. The contrasting modes of engagement with texts characteristic of media and literary studies in schools, 'rhetorical' and 'poetic' stances respectively, are stronger if united.

A media education curriculum, involving 'reading' the media, 'writing' the media and engaging with the contexts in which media practices occur, must be recursive. It cannot artificially distribute certain kinds of work across 'ages and stages', but should suggest how the same work (for example, editing a film) might change, expand, become more challenging and diverse, as students get older, gain more experience and become more autonomous.

Media education: four patterns

A glance at the construction of media education in the English curriculum reveals four patterns which make useful starting points for a consideration of what is happening in media education now, and what might develop in the future.

The first pattern: media education as suspicious reading

The four patterns follow a common theme, set by the first pattern, in which media education has been constructed as a kind of suspicious reading, pushing teachers and students towards the scrutiny of newspapers and television programmes to detect bias, misrepresentation and other distortions of some imagined 'truth'.

Behind this suspicious reading lies a tangled history of protectionist impulses, clearly identified by David Buckingham in his *Media Education: Literacy, Learning and Contemporary Culture* (2003), and further explored below: impulses to protect young people from what are seen as the various debilitating effects of the mass media, whether such effects be cultural, ideological or moral. While these impulses may be considerably stronger in the US than in the UK (or indeed in European media education in general), they are nevertheless a factor in the institutional regulation of media texts for young people and in the value systems sometimes applied to schools' choice of texts.

The second pattern: media education's fact/fiction divide

The second pattern discernible in curricular constructions of media in English is that media have often been imagined as a genre of factual representation and communication: essentially, news media. It's as if the entire function of narrative texts and imaginative fiction is reserved for literature. Two histories are noteworthy here. One features F. R. Leavis, whose critical readings of media texts for school students never embraced the narrative structures of comic strips or the poetics of film, but rather made advertising their object of attack. Leavis notoriously invented many of the advertising texts he used, the better to exemplify their debased nature (Leavis and Thompson, 1977 [1933]).

The other history in this second pattern helps to explain how, regrettably, media literacy is now once again only being seen as a matter of how citizens retrieve and critically appraise factual information. This is the history of the computer. As Lev Manovich has memorably described, the computer, from its inception in the form of Babbage's Analytical Engine in the 1830s, has developed as a processor of information, in contrast to the history of photography (also beginning in the 1830s with Daguerre's daguerrotype), which is a history of cultural representations (Manovich, 1998).

As these two technologies have become fused in the multimedia computer, ICT educators are having difficulty understanding how the number-cruncher has become a tool of cultural production; while media and English teachers struggle with the implications of the cultural representations which have been their traditional stock-in-trade – films, poems, stories – becoming computable. It is partly for this reason that computer games, a cultural form which has always by definition been a set of computable representations, pose such interesting and challenging questions for media and English teachers as they consider how to teach such a form in the classroom.

In the wider world of policy, some politicians and officials have continued to be trapped by this division of media into, effectively, fictions on the one hand and factual information on the other. In Europe, at least, the fictions have been largely the interest of film educators, who have considered how cinema narratives can be critically explored in schools in much the same appreciative way that literature teachers deploy in their approach to literary fictions. Meanwhile, the policy-makers have been largely preoccupied with how factual information is conveyed to citizens through electronic media, particularly online.

So, the general effect of this fact/fiction divide in the educational and policy arenas is to overemphasise both the importance and the risks of factual information in young people's lives, and to almost completely neglect the most important uses young people actually make of the media: the music, dreams, fantasies, play, dramatic narratives, whimsical performances, album-making, aspirational self-representation, parodic invention and casual communication which make up most of their online lives.

The third pattern: media education as reading not writing

The third pattern in the construction of media in the English curriculum is that it represents, essentially, an act of critical *reading*. Media within English has been located within the reading section of the curriculum, with no equivalent provision made in the writing section. In England, it has been mandatory since the inception of the National Curriculum for English to teach young people to *read* the media (that is, critically interrogate it), but not to *write* it (that is, produce their own media texts) (Qualifications and Curriculum Authority [QCA], 2007). (But, as the section 'The present situation in England' below relates, even this requirement has been abandoned in the new National Curriculum for English.) There is a doubly suspicious stance here: a suspicion, again, of media texts, positioning them as objects of a critical gaze quite different from that envisaged for literature; but also a suspicion of young people's own media production work, implicitly devalued by comparison with creative writing.

There have been, indeed, criticisms of student media productions within the media education community, castigating some of them as incompetent and derivative, reproducing the very ideologies that teachers seek to expose (see Buckingham, 2003 for an extended account of this). But such pessimistic attitudes have largely been replaced in more recent years by positive accounts of the value of production work, based in rationales of conceptual learning, creative transformation and cultural practices of media production increasingly typical of young people's informal media cultures (Potter, 2005; Jenkins, 2006; McDougall, 2006).

The fourth pattern: media texts as poor relations of literature

Finally, successive versions of the English curriculum have demonstrated a suspicion of semiotic modes beyond language. Recent versions recognise the growing argument for a multimodal approach to textuality and literacy

(Jewitt and Kress, 2003; Kress and Van Leeuwen, 1996); but the occasional reference to multimodal texts arguably produces only internal contradictions within a conservative ring-fencing of language, buttressed by an increasingly unconvincing argument for language's superiority over other communicative modes.

This argument takes curious turns. In 2004–2005 a 'conversation' was initiated with stakeholders by the QCA, the government agency then responsible for curriculum development, about the future of the English curriculum. In its response document, the QCA argued, in reply to a number of submissions making the case for a version of the curriculum incorporating contemporary media texts, that:

Alongside views that media and screen-based texts [can] have their place in English 21 there is the caveat that these should never be at the expense of our rich book-based literary heritage – a point more fully elaborated in terms of the purpose and value of engaging with verbal language: the study of literature has one conspicuous advantage over the study of film and television media, in that it develops the skills of analysis, argument and discourse alongside language skills.

(QCA, 2005; my emphasis)

This position can be seen as a diluted residue of Leavis' attack on popular culture. The authors of the document here display a softened stance on the teaching of texts such as comics, films and television, allowing them a place as part of a wider cultural landscape; but there remains the firm belief that they need to be treated suspiciously, and to be seen as somehow thinner, more insubstantial, less nourishing than literature.

This chapter opposes the 'poor relation' view of media texts. There is no logical reason why the study of comic strip and animated film, for example, should not develop 'the skills of analysis, argument and discourse alongside language skills' just as effectively as the study of classic literature.

A model for media education

This section offers a model for media education, illustrated by examples.

Media and English have been kissing cousins ever since Leavis' launch of the 'inoculation' approach to media, as mentioned in the previous section:

the development of critical close reading skills in school students to protect them from the ill effects of the mass media. We have seen the three kinds of protectionism in the history of media education which Buckingham (2003) has identified: Leavis' cultural protectionism; the attempt of radical pedagogy in the 1970s and 1980s to protect young people from the ideological effects of the media; and the moral protectionism which Buckingham associates more with media education in America.

Let the cousins continue to kiss

Most media teachers in the UK would not now subscribe to any form of protectionism, taking instead a positive view of young people's media cultures and practices, not least because of a general shift towards forms of creative production enabled by the increasing availability of digital authoring tools. However, they would see themselves as teaching forms of critical awareness. In this section, I will focus on three aspects of media education which can inform English. It's important not to produce neat models of media education which emphasise difference from, even incompatibility with, English. Such models lead to media as a tacked-on appendage to the English curriculum, at best. More productive, maybe, is to muddle the boundaries, find common ground and use tensions to challenge each field of study to move beyond its limitations and prejudices.

The three areas I will focus on are *cultural distinction*, *rhetoric and poetics* and *creative production*. They roughly correspond to key concepts in the English curriculum as identified by the QCA (2007): cultural understanding, critical understanding and creativity. However, my emphasis here will be on the development of media literacy, which is also often understood in terms of this '3Cs' model (Bazalgette, 2008; Burn and Durran, 2007). In my model, a 'CRC' model, the concepts are rather differently understood, in ways which can usefully inform English teaching.

Cultural distinction

The simple way to state the problem here is to say that the English curriculum has traditionally been concerned with 'high' culture (though those teachers who come under the category identified in the Cox Report [The Cox Committee, 1989] as 'cultural analysts' have always contested the literary canon and the values associated with it); and to say that, meanwhile, media education has been committed to popular culture (though those who emphasise the importance of film sometimes observe their own kind of canon).

However, the official curriculum, oddly, renders the question of culture, high or popular, pretty well invisible. A search through versions of the National Curriculum for English for references to 'culture' or 'cultural' reveals only rather tokenistic references to multiculturalism, as if culture only becomes visible through contrast between ethnic groups. Contrasts between the cultures of different social classes, which might be expected to reveal something of the tension between popular and elite cultural forms and preferences, are not available as a mode of inquiry in the English curriculum.

So, for example, we are invited to consider Sujata Bhatt's poem 'Search for my tongue', in which the poet considers her bilingual tongue, split between English and Gujarati. The poem has been part of an anthology of poetry to be studied for GCSE English (Assessment and Qualifications Alliance, no date). But we are not invited to consider why some teenagers might prefer Marvel comics to Shakespeare, *Call of Duty: Modern Warfare* to the war poets, or *Hollyoaks* to Keats. Such contrasts do, I admit, run the risk of reducing the argument to tabloid knockabout of the 'Shakespeare or soaps?' variety, a hoary debate we have had many times before. Nevertheless, it seems important to acknowledge that these kinds of cultural distinction still exist and to consider how to approach them in the classroom. In any case, my argument is that we don't need to choose. We can, and should, have both extremes of the cultural spectrum and anything in between that suits our purpose and our students' interests.

Rhetoric and poetics

English and media education have quite different approaches to the characteristics of texts. Approaches to literary texts have often focused on their aesthetic form and have been characterised by what we might call a mode of appreciation, a *poetical* mode. By contrast, media texts have been approached in what we might call a *rhetorical* mode, exploring the politics of representation and interrogating the motivations of producers and audiences.

These two modes have long histories which can be traced back to Aristotle: we can detect the legacy of his *Poetics* in the English approach to literature, and the legacy of his *Rhetoric* in the media approach to the texts that fall within its domain. I simplify here for the sake of contrast; but, both in the habituated practices of the English and media classrooms, and in the curricular formations that have constructed literature as an object of reverence and media texts as objects of suspicion, something like this contrast seems stubbornly resistant to change. We need both rhetoric and poetics if we are to attend to the politics of representation in both media and literary texts, as well as to the aesthetic forms in which such representations are framed. Indeed, these should not be alternative, incompatible ways of looking at culture, but indivisible: two sides of the same coin. All rhetoric operates through aesthetic form and claims aesthetic value; all aesthetic form has a rhetorical, even political, purpose.

The rhetorical stance of media education is often encoded in the conceptual frameworks used to identify what critical understandings students might be expected to gain. There are several different versions of these, but they can generally be grouped under *institutions*, *texts* and *audiences*.

Institutions

The idea of media institutions is a staple of media education. It is rarely considered in the teaching of literature, though much of Dickens' work was structured by the contingencies of magazine publication, though the careers of the women writers of the nineteenth century were at the mercy of male publishers, and though the literary creations of modern novelists are commonly franchised by multinational media organisations. To move beyond the immediate pleasures of engagement with media texts in order to consider the shadowy regimes of production and distribution that lie behind them can seem dry, remote and hard to pin down. There are also uncertainties: what institutions are we talking about exactly? What do we need to know about them? Why do we need to know it?

Current approaches to media education would support a nuanced attitude to the question of the media industries. Buckingham (1998) argues, for instance, that we have moved beyond a paradigm of 'radical pedagogy' in which the role of education is to unmask bourgeois and capitalist ideologies. This is not to say that a degree of healthy scepticism is not warranted. There are good reasons why we might want young people to understand what commercial interests lie behind a McDonald's advert or a leader in a Murdoch- or Rothermere-owned newspaper. But institutions more typically have complex motives and socio-political functions.

To take an example, a class of Year 8 students is exploring the work of the games industry, and designing and producing their own video game.

In many ways, the games industry is similar to other media industries and often related to them through multinational corporations. An introductory activity draws attention to the ways in which media industries are represented in the packaging of games. In order to compare the book, film and game of *Harry Potter and the Chamber of Secrets*, for example, the teacher and students collect all the logos of companies represented on the covers and boxes of these texts, which include:

- Warner Bros (which owns the name of Harry Potter and associated items as trademarks);
- Electronic Arts (which published the game);
- Knowwonder Digital Mediaworks (which developed the game); and
- Bloomsbury (which published the book).

In addition, there are the logos of Ford (the texts include a flying Ford Anglia car), Microsoft, Times Educational Supplement (which had reviewed the book), Dolby sound (in the film), ELSPA (the European Leisure Software Publishers Association, which had rated the game as appropriate for children aged three-plus).

The project simulates aspects of the way the games development industry works; so, in designing and producing their own video game, students are asked to propose names for a game studio, to write proposals for a game for students of their age, to work collaboratively in pairs and as a whole class to design and produce a multi-level game, and to design posters and write press releases and magazine reviews of the game on its completion.

Texts

A rhetorical approach to texts will centre on the question of *representation*. This is a familiar word in media education and media studies; not so commonly found in English documents or conceptual frameworks. At one level, of course, representation means any semiotic act: any utterance, written word, image, dramatic gesture is a representation of some aspect of reality. The question to explore with students is the nature of the relationship between the representation and that 'reality', which is multiple, shifting and situated. We may explore Shylock as a representation of Renaissance ideas about Jewishness; but we cannot escape the fact that the actor depicting the role, the director behind him, and the audience in the theatre (or cinema) have more recent memories of the Holocaust and the Arab-Israeli conflict.

How, though, might students understand the detailed structure of texts which produce these meanings?

One approach is to focus on the signifying systems of particular media. Here is an example from film. A Year 8 boy is writing about what he has learned from re-editing a sequence from Baz Luhrmann's *Romeo + Juliet*. His task was to take a sequence of footage from the film, imported into the editing software Adobe Premiere, and to creatively rework it, adding different music, changing the order and duration, producing his own take on the play using these 'found' resources.

> *Also, at that point when the camera tracks up, it is the first time there has been any significant movement in it. The camera has stayed still to reflect the movement of the most important character in the sequence: like Mercutio, the camera has witnessed everything, but has done nothing about it . . . The final shot is of a new character to the sequence: Sampson. The camera is placed at an oblique angle to him. He is not an important character, he is at the side of the action. His emotion, his expression of fear and anxiety, needs to be acknowledged – not felt – by the audience. He simply watches – he does not act.*

(Josh, Year 8)

This kind of critical work, a fluid mix of technical production, aesthetic choices and critical reflection, is close to the kind of work a student might undertake in analysing literature. Media teachers would recognise it as a thoughtful reading of a filmic text, aware of both the grammar of the moving image and the meanings conveyed by it. English teachers would recognise it as an equally thoughtful reading of a sequence from *Romeo and Juliet*. It exemplifies the kind of thing I am thinking of as a 'poetics' of media education: an attention to the aesthetic features of dramatic texts which Aristotle codified, adapted for the photographic media of the early twenty-first century.

In this example, work in different media extends the understanding of textual structures that students might learn in English. To the metalinguistic lexicon of clause, sentence, paragraph, narrative, argument and so on is added the grammar of film (shots, camera movement, camera angle).

Audience

It is now orthodox for English teachers and media teachers to encourage students to create texts for a particular audience. But who that audience might be, or how we might get a concrete idea of her, him or them, is a slippery business. We can imagine, for instance, a series of concentric circles, the innermost of which is the students themselves. What are their reading/viewing/playing preferences? How do they make particular cultural choices? What kinds of pleasure do they derive from the texts they choose? In what social groups do they engage with these texts? What cultural practices do they engage in as audiences? The next circle outward might be a specific other audience, involving making texts for a class in a local primary school, for a parents' evening, for a local council meeting, for a visiting VIP. The outermost circle, one often used by media teachers, could be the socio-economic groupings of market research: are the students targeting their texts at the A1 or the C2 grouping, for example?

A project involving a Year 10 class was developed in collaboration with the UK charity organisation Comic Relief, much of whose work is channelled towards aid for Africa and support for sustainable development projects. In this case, Comic Relief wanted to link English schools with schools in Ghana to promote the idea of Fair Trade chocolate production. The chocolate was and is made by a London company, Divine Chocolate Ltd, 45 per cent of which is owned by the Fair Trade cocoa-growers' co-operative Kuapa Kokoo in Ghana. The teacher in the school featured here suggested an additional element to the project. Students would make a television advert for a new chocolate bar the company was launching: Dubble, marketed to children. Comic Relief agreed, and the school worked with Kika Dixon, the 'product champion' for Dubble at Divine, to develop a brief for a television advert. Kika visited the class and gave them the brief, just as she would to a professional advertising company. (A version of the project, including a video of Kika's project brief, is contained in the English and Media Centre's Media Pack for GCSE [Grahame, 2002].)

The project considered all three elements of representation: institutions and texts as well as audience. The intended audience for the chocolate bar was specified in Kika Dixon's original brief: '11- to 16-year-olds, boys and girls'. How would the students' work represent the target group and their interests, aspirations, preoccupations? How would it construct a mode of address which would be comprehensible, engaging and credible? How would it locate the viewer?

One group of four boys constructed their advert as a narrative of chocolate-eating, associated with lifestyle qualities (the brief wanted messages like 'cool, cheeky, delicious'). The group found this narrative easy and enjoyable to imagine, plan and construct. The boys decided early on to recruit a friend from their year group as the star of the advert and adopted an approach which several other groups also used: to show the boy buying the bar from the local corner shop, followed by some kind of transformation of his life.

The group found the Fair Trade message much harder to conceive and put across. The boys had real difficulty in imagining how the agency of African cocoa farmers might be represented. For them, as for other groups, part of this difficulty lay in a desire to represent Africa in a literal way. Eventually, they asked if they could take their camera out of school to the Botanical Gardens in Cambridge and film lush tropical vegetation which they hoped would represent cocoa plantations.

The result was a success. The music and its lyrics suggested a confident, urban teenage lifestyle, underlining the function of the boy as principal actor in the piece; the sequence cut to the rhythm of the music, suggesting his walk, his dance. The music and its rhythm were possibly stronger than any visual image in the first seconds of the ad, signalling the theme of the whole sequence as teenage identity and subordinating the bar and the Fair Trade message to the rhythm throughout.

Analysing audience behaviours is only part of the picture, however. Let us not forget effect. Do we really want a world where there are no media 'effects'? Of course, we don't want an entire generation uncritically swallowing the message that life without Coke or Playstation isn't worth living. But do we want students to be unmoved by the affective charge of horror or romance; unaffected by the polemic of Orwell's *1984* or Lennon's 'Imagine', unamused by the satirical humour of *The Simpsons*? The great nineteenth-century French magician, Jean-Eugene Robert-Houdin, argued that he much preferred to perform his illusions to intelligent people than to stupid people. Stupid people would always try to see how the trick was done, thereby making his job more difficult and destroying their own pleasure; while intelligent people would allow themselves to be duped, knowing that this was where the enjoyment of the experience lay. We could make the same argument about the media, while rejecting Robert-Houdin's crude dualism about people. We can know it is an illusion and still surrender ourselves to its spell. It is the paradox of Coleridge's 'willing suspension of disbelief'.

Creative production

Creativity in education is a highly contested idea, appearing in a bewildering variety of forms (Banaji and Burn with Buckingham, 2007). Here, I draw on the work of the Russian psychologist Lev Vygotsky, for whom the creativity of children and adolescents was closely related to play (Vygotsky 1998 [1931]). In playful activity, children learn the meaning of symbolic substitution through the manipulation of physical objects: Vygotsky's well-known example is a child using a broomstick as an imaginary horse. These symbolic understandings become internalised and develop into the mental processes which generate creative work. For Vygotsky, true creativity only develops, however, when the imaginative transformations of play are connected with thinking in concepts: in other words, with rational intellectual processes.

What might creative production look like in the English and media class-room? One example is drawn from a project in which a group of 30 11-year-olds make a machinima film.

Machinima is perhaps the most recent cultural form in the world of anima-tion. The word itself is a portmanteau combining 'machine' and 'cinema', with a substitution of the 'e' by an 'i', implying 'animation' and 'animé'. Machinima is defined by Kelland *et al.* (2005: 10) as 'the art of making animated films within a real-time 3-D environment'. It can be thought of as animation made from the 3-D environments and animated characters of computer games or virtual immersive worlds.

The students' film tells the story of a computer geek called Jeff, who meets an alien character, Dr T, in a videogame, travels with him to Cleopatra's palace, and eventually prevents his evil plan for world domination.

Martha and Rosa are editing the scene in which two characters, Jeff and Dr T, have arrived at Cleopatra's palace and have to convince her guard to let them in. They are editing to a printed script, which is a transcript of the impro-vised dialogue of the voice-acting group in the class. They tell me how they will edit a conversation sequence:

AB: If you were filming two people talking, how would you do it?
R: You'd put the camera there, and one of them would be there, and one would be there [indicating 'side by side' with hands].
AB: What's your other option?
R: You could put the camera on the person talking . . .
M: And then switch it round.

Here, Martha and Rosa first suggest a two-shot for a conversation and move towards the idea of shot-reverse-shot in response to my question. Elsewhere in my conversation with them, they show that they are quite confident about the idea of shot distance and its function of emphasis. They describe kinds of camera movement and the function of low- and high-angle shots to signify

Figure 6.1 Martha's and Rosa's shot-reverse-shot sequence, with the music track composed by another group.

power, although these have not been explicitly taught at this stage. When asked how these ideas could apply to their scene, they suggest that Cleopatra and the guard might be filmed from a low angle. When they move on to insert camera angles, they do exactly this. Figure 6.1 shows the two shots in which Dr T and Jeff meet Cleopatra's guard.

The imaginative processes here which create the characters, the story and the setting are articulated through the grammar of the moving image. The girls editing the sequence in Figure 6.1 are having to work out how to create the narrative tension in the encounter between Dr T, Jeff and Cleopatra's guard. To do this, they need to employ the familiar shot-reverse-shot sequence of film grammar. However, although in a sense this is 'old news', since it is a formula they view and understand on TV and film most days of their lives, in another sense they are having to create it from new. It is often argued that the continuity editing conventions of film are designed to be invisible, to produce an apparently seamless representation of reality which 'sutures' the viewer into its view. If this is true, it partly explains why, although students read the shot-reverse-shot convention repeatedly in their daily lives, when it comes to making their own films, it's as if they need to repeat a chapter of film-making history and discover it for themselves. This is creative work: a purposeful planning of how to represent a conversation through multiple points of view.

Recursive processes

The processes of learning in media education are recursive rather than linear. For example, in planning, shooting and editing a film, similar competences are called upon at increasingly sophisticated levels. These developing competences are also multimodal: Figure 6.1 shows how the girls have incorporated the music track composed and performed by another group. This raises the question of how media teachers might, as well as connecting with English and drama, collaborate more broadly across the arts.

To sum up, then, we can say that creativity in media production builds on playful experiment, and involves:

- imaginative work, bringing images, ideas, stories, sounds into being in ways that are new, innovative, valuable;
- the use of and transformation of existing cultural resources – visual, auditory, material;
- the use of physical and conceptual tools, many of which are exactly those explored in the rhetorical and poetic work described earlier.

The present situation in England

Across the four nations and regions of the UK, there have been specialist publicly examined media courses in secondary schools since the late 1960s. These courses have traditionally provided the concentrated models of media education, elaborated through examination syllabuses, training procedures and assessment mechanisms, which are a staple element of the kind of media education for which the UK is known and which are markedly different from other models to be found internationally, especially in Europe and the US (though more similar models exist in Canada, Australia and New Zealand).

Below the age of 14, provision in England and Wales has always been much weaker. Like drama, media education has existed in various versions of the National Curriculum as a sub-set of English, where, significantly, it has been located within the reading component. We saw earlier that though it has been mandatory for (some) schools to teach students how to 'read', or analyse, media texts, there has been no requirement to 'write', or make them. Apart from anything else, this position has been inconsistent with Ofcom's statutory responsibility to promote the creation of media texts alongside the critical understanding of them. In the primary curriculum, media education has been even more weakly represented than in the first three years of secondary education.

The disappearance of media from the new National Curriculum for English

In the new version of the National Curriculum for English in England (Department for Education, 2014a), media has been effectively erased from all four Key Stages. This can only be seen as a politically motivated act by the government. Its inclinations can be deduced from the report it commissioned into Cultural Education (Department for Culture, Media and Sport, 2012), which rehearsed the case for the arts in education, with a heavy emphasis on the existing National Curriculum foundation subjects, art and music, a brief consideration of the merits of drama and dance as independent subjects (subsequently ignored by the government), and a lengthy set of proposals for extra-mural activities to cover the other art forms. These activities included film education; but the word 'media' and the phrases 'media studies' and 'media education' were conspicuously absent from the report.

There exists, then, no core entitlement in England for media education for all children and young people; and no provision at all below Key Stage 4 and GCSE. This is a woeful state of affairs. An education system supposedly preparing future citizens to take part in a society whose media, in all its manifestations, will profoundly affect their professional, social and personal lives has opted to ignore that fact; and, as other chapters have noted, has opted to ignore virtually all forms of digital and electronic expression and communication.

Chapter 9 proposes a comprehensive provision for media education within English from 11 to 16.

To conclude . . .

English and media education belong together. They need and support each other; they stimulate and enliven each other; they also serve as correctives to each other's prejudices, restrictions of scope and intellectual limitations.

We need to move beyond the opposed stances of suspicion and reverence applied respectively to media texts and literary texts. So literature is out of its jacket, marked with the signs of its economic and material production, bleeding into other media, subject to the online transformations of fans able to rewrite the hallowed word with no respect for textual boundaries. Conversely, films, television drama, comic books and computer games have grown their own respectable histories, canons and heroic author-figures. They are collected, revered, curated, acknowledged by the institutions of high art which once reserved their attention for the traditional elite arts.

In this world of cultural reversals, English and media teachers owe it to their students to make common cause: to embrace models of literacy which collapse the boundaries between elite and popular culture, between today's and yesterday's cultural moment, between the meaning and the structure of texts, between texts' use of language and of other modes. Nothing will be lost, and there is much to gain.

At present, these intentions are impeded by the abandonment of any reference to media education in the National Curriculum for English.

7 Learners of English as an additional language

John Richmond

The numbers

The Distinctiveness of English as an Additional Language: A Cross-Curriculum Discipline (*Working Paper 5*), edited by Hugh South, was published in 1999 by the National Association for Language Development in the Curriculum (NALDIC). NALDIC is the principal professional association for teachers concerned with English as an additional language (EAL). The paper correctly states that in the year of its publication there were 'more than 500,000 bilingual pupils in the school population'. Much more recent figures compiled by NALDIC show that in 2015:

> There are more than a million children between 5 and 16 years old in UK schools who speak in excess of 360 languages between them in addition to English. Currently there are 1,061,010 bilingual 5–16 year olds in English schools, 29,532 in Scotland, 10,357 'newcomer' pupils in Northern Ireland and 31,132 EAL learners in Wales. So the number of EAL learners in UK schools doubled between 1999 and 2014, and is likely to continue to grow.
>
> (NALDIC, 2015)

This is a significant group: approximately one in six of the total. It is important that teachers understand both what these EAL learners have in common with learners for whom English is a mother tongue (EMT), and what is distinctive about their situation and their needs.

The common ground

To state what EAL and EMT learners have in common is the easier task. Both groups need an experience of learning in which the learner's prior knowledge, skill and understanding are creatively challenged and extended by the learning tasks and contexts the teacher provides, so that the new knowledge, skill or understanding which the teacher wishes the learner to acquire are accessible. The principles and the practices set out in all the preceding chapters in this book apply with equal force to EAL as to EMT learners.

The differences between EAL and EMT learners

Even a brief attempt to describe the difference between the positions of EAL and EMT learners will take a little longer. And there is no such thing as a 'typical' EAL learner. EAL learners differ from one another in their home languages, in the extent to which they are literate in those languages, and in their proficiency in oral and written English. Full and early bilingualism is increasingly common, and fluent literacy in both English and another language (or two) increasingly widespread.

However, here are five teaching principles which recognise the likely distinctive needs of the EAL learner as he or she strives to understand what is going on in the classroom and to meet the demands of the curriculum. They are drawn from a section in South (1999), the publication cited earlier.

How much does the learner know already?

First, teachers (which might mean classroom teachers, teaching assistants or teachers specifically assigned to support EAL learners) need a more precise understanding of EAL learners' prior knowledge of the content to be addressed, and of the degree of competence in English, with specific regard to that content, which the learner has. How much does he or she know already? What new aspect of competence in English, for example recognition of items of technical vocabulary, grasp of structure in laying out a piece of factual prose, understanding of the frequent use of the passive voice in scientific report or the past tense in narrative, does he or she need to be introduced to in order to make sense of the new knowledge?

The need for greater explicitness in presentation

Second, the context for the introduction of new knowledge, skill or understanding needs to be presented with greater explicitness for EAL than for EMT learners. As children progress through the school system, the curriculum typically becomes more independent of context, more abstract. Teachers need to work against this tendency with their EAL learners. Visual and graphic supports – for example sets of pictures, diagrams, maps or timelines – can help here. So can the teacher's more frequent and deliberate use of concrete examples and comparisons.

Production should be encouraged early

Third, while it is true that EAL learners engage in a great deal of what might be described as 'quiet learning' – learning which, while certainly not passive, is receptive and involves much listening and inference, they should also be encouraged to produce English, spoken, read or written, at whatever level of competence they can manage, from an early stage. It goes without saying that their efforts should be accorded generous praise.

The value of cross-language comparison

Fourth, and connected to the third principle, EAL learners (like learners of English as a foreign language and learners of a foreign language in school) are in an excellent position to develop metalinguistic awareness as their bi- or multilingual competence develops. If one can say more or less the same thing in more than one language, it is likely that one will sometimes want to describe how the two languages do a certain job similarly or differently. Similarity or difference may be in grammar or vocabulary or shades of meaning or direction of script. Teachers should draw EAL learners' attention to these similarities and differences, and encourage the use of linguistic terminology as appropriate to the learners' stage of development. This use can include terminology from the first language, especially if there is a teacher or another student who shares that language. It is easier to transfer a skill or a conceptual understanding from the stronger to the weaker language than to acquire it wholly through the weaker language. This is a good practical way to enhance pride in bi- and multilingualism, and to engage EMT learners in the discussion of these things too.

The need to keep a close check on progress

Fifth, teachers need to be aware of the progress EAL learners are making (or not making) from greater dependence (on contextual supports, on additional preparatory information, on adult help) towards independence in their learning. It may be argued that teachers need to be aware of this progress or lack of it with EMT learners too. They do. But because, typically, EAL learners need more support in the early stages, the gradual removal of that support, the gradual assumption that the EAL learner can cope without it, needs careful monitoring.

While it is true that most EAL learners can move quickly (within about two years) to a degree of fluency and comprehension enabling them to communicate with their EMT peers and to operate reasonably successfully in the classroom (the answers they give to a teacher's question, for example, show that they have some understanding of the topic being discussed), they are still a long way from having what Cummins (1984) describes as 'cognitive academic language proficiency' – the capacity to access and grasp the academic curriculum with the same likelihood of success as their EMT peers. It may take seven years, or longer, for them to achieve this proficiency. Hence the need for the teacher to maintain a close check on EAL learners' progress, so as to be sure that their rate of progress is not being held back by language issues where a specific intervention would clear an obstacle.

EAL learners and talk

Chapter 1 emphasised the fundamental role of the spoken language in all aspects of cognition and learning. It is *the* indispensable means of access to new knowledge, skill or understanding. And talk is the ground from which competence in literacy grows. Huge amounts of learning, much of it unconscious, occur as EAL learners listen to and absorb the English all around them, in school and in their world at large. This learning includes a developing grasp of the vocabulary, grammar and sound system of English, and all the paralinguistic and sociolinguistic customs and patterns (intonation, nodding and shaking of the head, turn-taking, polite ways of asking questions or of disagreeing, constructive ways of contributing to conversations) which EMT learners have usually acquired from early childhood.

It is vital that EAL learners are allowed the time and exposure for the essential receptive learning of all these things to take place. Teachers should not mistake silence for inattention. However, as the third of the teaching principles above says, EAL learners should 'also be encouraged to produce English, spoken, read or written, at whatever level of competence they can manage, from an early stage' and 'their efforts should be accorded generous praise'.

EAL learners and literacy

EAL learners with some experience of literacy in a language other than English are engaged in the complex process of simultaneously learning – as readers and writers – the writing systems of their first language and of English, and are making comparisons between them.

Nationally, EAL learners lagged behind first-language English speakers by a couple of percentage points in the 2014 Year 6 reading and writing tests in England, although there was large variation within and between language groups and within and between the local authorities and regions of England. In inner London, the same percentage of EAL and first-language English speakers (90 per cent) achieved level 4 in the reading and writing tests. Nationally, the two groups performed similarly on the grammar, punctuation and spelling test. Chinese girls consistently outperform everyone else, both EAL learners and first-language English speakers, although their advantage is narrowing. (See Department for Education, 2015b.)

Progress by EAL learners towards high levels of achievement in the reading and writing of English is increasingly notable in many schools. But there is still much to be done.

Reading

The reading classroom should contain books written in the first languages of EAL learners and in bilingual editions.

The left-to-right and top-to-bottom convention in English writing is just that, of course: a convention. Teachers should point it out as such to all the learners in a class. This understanding will be enhanced when there are EAL learners in the class who have some degree of literacy in writing systems which use other conventions.

Whereas first-language English readers can often infer the meanings of unfamiliar words from context, this has been shown to be a less reliable strategy for EAL learners (see, for example, Laufer, 2003). Bilingual books can help EAL learners check their understanding of the English. Encouraging young readers to read and talk about material written in their first language can have a positive consequence in terms of confidence and interest in reading books in English, as well as an immediate pay-off in terms of the experience of pleasure in reading and learning about specialist topics. There's also a significant body of research that shows that EAL learners develop their command of vocabulary in the additional language through extensive reading in that language, so they should not be confined to a diet of shortened and simplified texts (see, for example, Coady, 1997, and Day and Mamford, 1998).

Writing

The EAL writer is trying to make meaning in English writing as best he or she can, and trying to meet all the demands on a writer discussed in Chapter 3. It is likely that some features of her or his first language will appear in English writing. These first-language features are markers of the fact that the first language uses a particular form (usually a grammatical construction) to make meaning differently from the way the thing is done in English. What the EAL learner does *not* need at this point is more abstract, less experience-based instruction. It is very useful if the teacher knows enough about the student's first language to recognise the fact that the intervening feature has come from the first language, is able to point out why it is there in the English writing, and what its English equivalent is. In every other respect, the EAL learner needs the same balance of concern for content and support in the gradual acquisition of control of the writing system as the first-language English writer needs.

Literacy and more advanced EAL learners

More advanced EAL learners can derive especial benefit from conscious attention to the structures and styles of the more academic forms of writing with which their previous reading in English has not made them familiar. (The same could be said, of course, about many EMT readers.) See, for example, the Office for Standards in Education's 2003 report *More Advanced Learners of English as an Additional Language*:

> Pupils with EAL in most of the schools visited had below or well below average attainment at transfer in Year 7 and their attainment often remained below national averages at the end of Key Stage 3. By the end of Key Stage 4, most of these students had made significant progress, often attaining higher grades than predicted. However, in schools where they were not in the majority, they did less well in GCSE English examinations than English mother tongue speakers, and this remained true at A level.
>
> (Office for Standards in Education, 2003: 3)

The report concludes:

> *121. The support needs of bilingual learners do not cease once they become orally proficient in English. It is common for students learning English as a second language to achieve reasonable spoken fluency after 18 months to two years in the UK education system. Becoming skilled readers and writers in a second (or third) language, however, generally takes considerably longer.*

> *122. The higher up the education system, the greater the linguistic demands. For students to read and understand challenging material in GCSE courses and beyond, they need considerable first-hand experience of working on texts, guided by teachers who recognise the potential difficulties of such materials for bilingual students.*

> > *(ibid.: 31)*

In short, teachers' interventions should show the EAL learner characteristic structures and conventions of advanced written English in various genres and, when the learner is literate in a first language, invite comparisons with structures and conventions in that language.

8 Speakers of non-standard varieties of English

John Richmond

A linguistically complex competence

Many children and young people grow up in communities where the language of the home and the immediate community is a non-standard dialect of English or an English-based Creole, some of whose grammatical, lexical and sound features differ from their equivalents in Standard English. The linguistic situation of these children and young people is often complex. Some of them, for example those with a background in the Caribbean who also use the indigenous non-standard dialect of the place in the UK where they live, have access to more than one non-standard variety of English. (Multilingual children and young people use non-standard varieties of their languages too. Many of the Bengali-speaking children in schools in England, for instance, speak a form of the language significantly different from that of printed books.) These speakers may move between varieties of English or use mixtures of them as a result of often unconscious decisions made in context.

It is almost never the case nowadays that these students *only* speak a non-standard variety or varieties of the language. They are simultaneously aware of and influenced by Standard English. They come into contact with it through the media, through reading, in schooling: through their multiple contacts with the world beyond the home. And the language of the home is itself likely to use both standard and non-standard forms at different times.

The common ground which all varieties of English, including Standard English, share is vastly greater than the areas of difference.

Respect for difference

Schools and teachers have a responsibility to respect the language of a student's community and culture, whatever it is. In the past, some teachers have seen it as their responsibility to encourage or even force children and young people to speak in the dialect associated with success as they, the teachers, perceive it, and as other powerful forces, such as employers, are said to perceive it. At its crudest, this approach equates Standard English with correct English. Under the apparent – and usually sincere – benevolence of a desire for their students to do well, some teachers have been the transmitters of the message that, to the extent that their students' language differs from Standard English pronounced in the accent of a white middle-class southerner, it is inadequate, inappropriate or incorrect. And it has come as a shock to be told that a form or a sound that a teacher thought of as wrong or rough is simply somebody else's. Engendering enormous heat in the argument, underlying it really, have been the facts about class in Britain. It has been difficult not to make instant and persistent judgements about the quality or intelligence of a person on the basis of the way he or she speaks, rather than on the basis of what he or she says, because class divisions and suspicions have been, and to a great extent still are, deeply rooted in British society.

A dilemma

The worst examples of teachers' rejection or belittling of students' non-standard speech are probably behind us. However, today's teachers still face a dilemma: they wish to respect the language of their students' communities and cultures; they also acknowledge that Standard English, in its spoken as well as its written form, has a currency unlike that of any other variety of the language in many of the social contexts for which they are supposed to be preparing their students. How may this dilemma be resolved?

There is no value in the attempt by teachers in Early Years settings or primary schools to standardise non-standard features in a child's speech. However kindly the attempt, it is likely to be taken by children as a critical comment on their language and therefore on them. There are so many more important things to work on in the development of children's language and literacy up to the age of 11; and children during the primary years often come unconsciously to understand the choices to be made in those cases where the grammar of a non-standard variety is different from that of Standard English.

Language diversity as a part of knowledge about language

How should teachers in the secondary years resolve the dilemma just described? Answering the question will require a brief digression. Chapter 4 of this book, on grammar and knowledge about language, says that a characteristic of development in learners is the ability more and more to reflect consciously, abstractly, on language – their own and other people's – in use. This is why the government's new orders on the teaching of grammar have a wrong emphasis: primary-school pupils are to be taught an unrealistically large body of grammatical concepts and terminology, while secondary students are required merely to 'carry on the good work' – which, it is presumed, will have been done by the age of 11 – by applying these concepts and terminology to more advanced texts. The emphasis should be the opposite. Because secondary-school students are better able to reflect consciously and abstractly on language, there should be *more* analytical grammar teaching in the secondary than the primary years, not less.

Grammar teaching is best done as part of the teaching of a wider programme of knowledge about language, including teaching about language variety. In the context of such a programme, young people in secondary schools who have access to one or more non-standard varieties of English should be shown the standard equivalents of the non-standard forms in their speech, so that they are enabled to use oral Standard English for the purposes for which and in the contexts in which it is appropriate. In this way, young people come to understand that there are historical reasons for variety in English (and every other language): a 'double negative' or a non-standard verb inflection or an item of dialect vocabulary are not intellectual lapses. Older students have a good chance of seeing the value of the confident control of a wider speech repertoire, including Standard English, without that widening seeming to be a negative judgement on the language of their home background or of their peer group, and therefore a judgement on themselves.

Non-standard forms in writing

Some non-standard features find their way into the school writing of speakers of non-standard varieties of English. This writing, unless students are consciously using a non-standard variety as part of a story or playscript or poem, is in Standard English. Features of this kind are small in number, but they tend to be highly noticeable. Different ways of marking the past tense and the use of 'double negatives' are two common examples.

In working with students who have access to non-standard dialects or Creoles, it is useful if the teacher knows enough about a student's language background to recognise a non-standard feature when he or she sees one in the student's writing, to explain why it is there and what its Standard English equivalent is. The teacher needs to be able to distinguish between errors that any developing writer might make and examples of non-standard forms. The nature of the teacher's intervention, however, should be similar in the two cases: it should appeal to the student's developing knowledge of Standard English, derived from multiple encounters with it in speech and writing, while reassuring the student that progress towards competence in written Standard English will not be impaired by this extra complexity. The worst thing a teacher could do, of course, would be to communicate in some way that non-standard forms are 'bad' or 'wrong' or 'illogical'. There are cases ('hisself' versus 'himself' and 'amn't I?' versus 'aren't I?', for example) where non-standard forms are more 'logical' than their standard equivalents.

Meanwhile, it is important to remember, as already stated in the section 'A linguistically complex competence', that the similarities which unite all forms of English – standard and non-standard – greatly outnumber the differences between them. The fundamental principles about the teaching of writing apply with equal importance to young people who have non-standard forms of English in their language repertoire as to those who only have access to Standard English.

9 An alternative curriculum for English 11 to 16

John Richmond

Andrew Burn has written the proposals on media

General principles

The book so far has contained 'the argument': a statement or restatement of fundamental truths about how children and young people acquire competence and confidence as users of language, and how teachers can best help them to do so. In the course of the argument, there has been careful and sometimes stringent criticism of the requirements of the new version of the National Curriculum for English in England. This chapter contains a complete alternative curriculum for English 11 to 16, addressing the shortcomings of the new English orders, while incorporating material from that document which can be welcomed.

Continuity

As far as possible, the categories into which the alternative curriculum is divided are aligned horizontally (that is, across the modes of language). The proposals also allow for the fact that learning English and learning through English are essentially recursive processes in which common fundamental abilities and experiences are repeated in ever more demanding contexts as young people move through the school system.

The alternative curriculum combines Key Stages 3 and 4. Teachers are always dealing with learners at varying stages of development, even when they are in the same year group, and it is teachers who are in a position to judge when best to introduce new knowledge, understanding and skill to individuals or to the class as a whole. Development does not proceed at an even pace. Key Stages are administratively useful but educationally arbitrary divisions.

As an aside, we can note that the government itself is aware of the dangers of introducing too precise divisions, at least in the primary years. The National Curriculum orders divide Key Stage 1 into two separate years, and Key Stage 2 into two two-year periods. While seeking to justify the sub-divisions which it has introduced, the government acknowledges the practical difficulties which these sub-divisions bring:

> *The programmes of study for English are set out year-by-year for key stage 1 and two-yearly for key stage 2. The single year blocks at key stage 1 reflect the rapid pace of development in word reading during these two years. Schools are, however, only required to teach the relevant programme of study by the end of the key stage. Within each key stage, schools therefore have the flexibility to introduce content earlier or later than set out in the programme of study. In addition, schools can introduce key stage content during an earlier key stage if appropriate.*
>
> (Department for Education, 2014a: 17)

The same is true in the secondary years; hence the decision here to combine Key Stages 3 and 4.

Malleable material

This alternative curriculum is offered as malleable material rather than as a set of tablets of stone. To change the metaphor, there are likely to be equally good or better ways of 'cutting up the cake' of the curriculum than those proposed here. I offer one warning only: any attempt to cut up the cake which fails to spot that similar ingredients run all the way through it will lead only to incoherence.

In its wording, the alternative curriculum attempts descriptions of the kinds of classroom learning that effective teachers continually strive for. It will be noticed that the modal verb 'should' appears nowhere. Teachers are not helped by that kind of prodding. However, I would be insincere not to admit that, implicitly, these descriptions are desiderata, not plain statements of what is already happening everywhere.

This book has already acknowledged that not all of the requirements of the new National Curriculum for English are ill-judged; some we can actively welcome. With that partial welcome freely conceded, it may nonetheless be that schools not bound by the National Curriculum – academies and free schools – would prefer to base their English teaching on the proposals here rather than on the government's offering. I hope that even those schools still bound by law to follow the new National Curriculum might find practical encouragement in the realisation that, in those areas where the government's requirements are inadequate or misguided, there is an alternative.

And let me return to the 'purest of ironies' mentioned in the book's introduction. The government has an 'aspiration' that more and more state schools in England shall become academies. As we say in the introduction, in May 2016 it hastily backtracked from its intention, announced only two months previously, to *force* all schools to become academies by 2022. Nonetheless, its March 2016 White Paper retains the promise that academies can choose to treat the National Curriculum 'as an ambitious benchmark which autonomous academies can use and improve upon' (Department for Education, 2016a: paragraph 1.55a). This alternative *is* such an improvement.

Sources

Most of what follows is my or Andrew Burn's own devising. However, I acknowledge the following sources for wording in some of the sections of the alternative curriculum.

Talk

The former National Curriculum orders for speaking and listening for Key Stages 3 and 4, valid until July 2014 or July 2015 (QCA, 2007), have much to commend them. The new Key Stage 4 orders, valid from September 2015, also require a balanced variety of uses of the spoken language. The alternative curriculum for talk at Key Stages 3 and 4 is therefore not radically different from the best of what is offered in those documents.

Writing

The proposals for writing occasionally draw on forms of words which have been used at earlier stages of the preparation, introduction and continual revision of the National Curriculum for English, for example in the Cox Report (The Cox Committee, 1989).

Drama

The alternative curriculum for drama is indebted to three sources in particular for much of its wording: the objectives at 11 and 16 in *Drama from 5 to 16* (Her Majesty's Inspectorate, 1989: 3–5); the level descriptions for drama in *Drama in Schools* (Arts Council England, 2003: 35–40), which have been turned 'inside out' to create curriculum rather than assessment guidelines; and the guidelines for Drama in the Australian curriculum (ACARA, 2016).

The drama proposals could be regarded as a replacement for the collection of references to drama within the new National Curriculum for English, as an aide-memoire for the use of drama in subjects across the curriculum, as a framework for teaching in schools where drama is already a freestanding subject, or as the basis of a future curriculum for drama as a foundation subject of the National Curriculum.

Overlaps

The sections of the alternative curriculum are not watertight categories. Readers will quickly spot that there are overlaps between them. Those for talk, reading and writing have sub-categories linking each with the other two modes, and with drama. There are references to media elsewhere than in its own section. There are aspects of talk, reading and writing which point towards grammar and knowledge about language. These overlaps are deliberate; they are necessary characteristics of the whole reality that is language learning, however necessary it may be to divide the whole in order better to comprehend it.

Talk at Key Stages 3 and 4

Links with other modes

- Students read and hear literary prose, poetry, plays, essays, journalism and information texts which make increasing demands on their powers of inference, memory, comprehension and response. In their oral responses to these texts, these powers are exercised and tested using the full range of collaborative groupings available to the teacher, from pairs up to the class as a whole.

- Students are encouraged to articulate orally, in increasingly subtle ways, to other students in groups or to the class as a whole, why they chose topics for writing or structured a piece of writing – of whatever genre – as they did. They are supportive enquirers in discussing the writing of others.
- Drama and role-play, improvised or scripted, is in frequent use, both as activities in their own right and as supports to other elements of the English curriculum.

Discussion, argument and debate

- The exchange of opinion, information and argument, on social, environ-mental, moral and political topics affecting students in their lives in and beyond school, and moving into matters of local, national and international significance, is a staple of the oral work of the class. Formal debate is added to the repertoire of structures within which students engage in these exchanges.

Summary

- Students' skill in the oral summary of previous discussion or of information and ideas taken from educational resources is practised and extended.

Good listening

- Good listening is the focus of the teacher's attention and, as appropriate, praise. Good listeners give careful consideration to what other contributors have said, are willing to build on those contributions as appropriate, and – where a listener challenges another's contribution – are able to demonstrate, courteously but critically, why that contribution seems to the listener turned speaker to be incomplete, inadequately expressed or wrong.

Media

- The English classroom provides every opportunity, within the resources avail-able, for students to make use of modern media. Students respond orally to literary and informational ideas and stimuli they receive via the whole contemporary range of digital and electronic sources and platforms. They have regular opportunities to create products, individually and collaboratively, using these media.

Instrumental language

- In collaborative tasks of increasing complexity and length, requiring patience and stamina, students' ability to give and receive instructions, to plan together, to discuss ways forward in the task, to come to consensus even where there was initial disagreement, is exercised and tested.

Standard English

- Students for whom English is an additional language, or who use a non-standard variety or varieties of English in their everyday speech, are shown the standard equivalents of the non-standard or first-language-influenced forms they use, so that they are enabled to use oral Standard English in the many contexts in which it is appropriate. This is often best done as part of the specific study of varieties of English.

Oral performance

- Oral performance, whether individually or in groups, is a regular feature of the secondary English classroom. Performance takes the form, for example, of storytelling, prepared talks and improvised scenes, dramatic readings, or recital of poetry from memory. Performed reading, for example of poems, scenes from plays or passages of prose, may involve the use of recording equipment such as tablet computers and digital cameras, so that performances can be played back and evaluated.

Groupings for talk

- Students work in pairs, small groups and as a whole class.

Reading at Key Stages 3 and 4

The content of reading

- Students continue to develop their appreciation and love of reading, and read increasingly challenging material. The texts they read cover a wide range of genres: realistic contemporary and historical fiction, traditional stories such as myths and legends, plays, poetry, information texts and discursive writing. Students are introduced to journalism, to extended essays and reviews on literary, critical and social topics, to written advocacy and propaganda, and to some technical and other demanding factual material.
- Students' reading of imaginative literature includes some classics of the British, Irish and world-wide heritage of writing in English, including plays by Shakespeare and by major dramatists of subsequent centuries; examples of lyric and narrative poetry from the Elizabethan period to the present day; and some prose fiction (both novels and short stories) by major authors. The selection which teachers make aims for a balanced representation of different genres, historical periods and geographical, ethnic and cultural settings.
- In their reading, students make use of online sources and platforms, such as websites, wikis and blogs, as well as print.
- Students' own writing forms part of the class's resources for reading.
- Especially in classrooms where there are students learning English as an additional language, books are available in the students' first language(s) and in bilingual editions.

Students as critical readers

- Students are shown how to develop mature critical faculties as readers. These include:
    - identifying and interpreting themes, ideas and information in a text;
    - exploring structural aspects of a text, for example its form, setting, plot, characterisation, argument or powers of description;
    - analysing and evaluating a writer's decisions about vocabulary, style and grammar;
    - learning to discriminate between more and less effective examples of writing in a particular genre, and to articulate these critical judgements;

- comparing surface meaning in a text with an implied sub-text;
- placing written texts in their historical and social contexts, so as to understand why a writer has revealed, consciously or unconsciously, certain assumptions and attitudes.

- In reading poetry, students are shown the characteristics and learn the names of a variety of forms and techniques. They are shown how poets frequently use figurative, metaphorical and non-realist language to achieve effects.

Links with other modes

- All the other modes of language are continually in play in interaction with reading. Reading sometimes leads to writing. Discussion, role-play and drama are frequently used to interrogate, analyse, respond to and extend reading.

Groupings for reading

- The teacher continues to read aloud to students, engaging them in discussion of texts as the reading progresses. There are also frequent opportunities for pair and small-group discussion of texts. Students are encouraged to read widely and independently, and to keep a journal in which they record the details of their reading and their responses to texts.

Writing at Key Stages 3 and 4

The content of writing

- Students write across a wide range of forms: chronological accounts, descriptions, discursive essays, poems, prose stories, playscripts, diaries, letters, writing for formal or public purposes such as a speech, sets of instructions, writing in response to direct experience and to stimuli such as stories, poetry, films on television, DVD or online. Students' developing competence and maturity are evident in writing at greater length, with increasingly conscious control over the structure and organisation of different types of text. Students write to: report, narrate, persuade, argue, describe, instruct, explain; recollect, organise thought, reconstruct information from outside sources, summarise, hypothesise; express themselves in aesthetic and imaginative ways.

The distribution of writing

- The teacher is a vitally important audience for students' writing.
- The media by which forms of and purposes for writing are communicated include: handwritten scripts on paper, word-processing on screen, physical book-making, wall displays, poster campaigns, blogs, web publishing, emails, reading aloud, staged and filmed presentations.
- Students publish electronically, off-line or online, for example by having a class intranet or internet site where they can display their work, and where fellow students and the teacher can respond.

The composition of writing

- Students sketch, plan, draft, redraft, polish and proofread their writing, on paper or on a computer or using a combination of both, so that they achieve satisfaction in reading and presenting the finished article. The teacher, however, makes it clear that not every writer needs always to sketch and plan, and not every piece of writing needs to go through multiple stages of reworking.

Writing in multimodal contexts

- Language activities which combine speaking, listening, reading, drama and the use of digital technologies for writing occur frequently. Students come to understand that writing can be a preparation for other modes of language, or an outcome from the use of other modes of language, or a contributing element to productions and presentations in which more than one mode, both of language and of other forms of communication, are engaged.

Groupings for writing

- There is a balance between writing done individually by students and writing which contributes to a collaboration. Collaborative writing usually involves small groups of students working in a format which naturally calls for multiple contributions. Sometimes collaboration involves the whole class, as in the production of an anthology of imaginative writing.

- In the course of working collaboratively, students are shown how to be effective and supportive critics, editors and proofreaders of each other's work.

The writing system

Spelling

- Teachers draw students' attention to common spelling patterns in English. Some of the many English spellings which have to be learned a whole are displayed on the classroom walls, appearing in the context of meaningful sentences.
- Students use dictionaries, printed and electronic, appropriate for their age group, and appropriate spelling apps on tablet computers and other digital equipment.
- Students are encouraged to be independent in their efforts to spell conventionally, although the teacher should always be prepared to give spellings if students' independent strategies have failed.
- Students have personal spelling journals in which to note new correct spellings. They are shown how to practise them using the Look–Say–Cover–Write–Check routine.
- When students write on computers, they use the spellchecker (set to UK English spelling conventions), while being warned that spellcheckers are not infallible; they cannot detect homonyms or homophones.
- Students become familiar with the habit of proofreading the drafts of their texts.

Punctuation

- As well as discussing the use of basic features of English punctuation (capital letters, full stops, commas, question marks, exclamation marks, apostrophes and speech marks), teachers introduce students to more advanced conventions such as:

  - the use of quotation marks for citations, to reify words, or to acknowledge informality or unusual usage;
  - the use of dashes for parenthesis;
  - the use of the hyphen in compounds ('an in-form player', 'a black-and-white photograph').

- Discussion of the use of basic punctuation marks such as the comma leads students to understand explicitly what their functions are. Students' study of the use of punctuation marks in writing enables them to realise that sometimes a particular usage is a matter of style rather than correctness and that the use of punctuation marks has changed over time.

Layout

- Students are shown how writing is laid out in handwritten and word-processed prose and in printed books, including the use of paragraphs, chapters and sections within chapters. They learn about the layout of different kinds of poetry, of playscript, and of writing used in conjunction with illustrations, as in comic books.
- Students are introduced to conventions of layout in writing such as the indentation of quotations and the use of indented lists on separate lines to make reading easier.
- Students explore how handwritten, printed and on-screen writing can be combined with illustration (pictures, diagrams, maps) and with other modes (sound, colour, design elements such as font size and style) to communicate most effectively with the reader.

Handwriting, typing and word-processing

- The few students who for various reasons have not achieved a clear, relaxed and individual handwriting style by the beginning of Key Stage 3 are helped with letter formation by copying handwritten texts whose content is appropriate for their age and level of maturity.
- If students have not by the beginning of Key Stage 3 achieved the fluency in their use of a computer keyboard which enables them to type at least as quickly as they can handwrite, they are shown how to do so, using one of the online teaching packages available.
- Students are shown how to use the facilities of word-processing and web-publishing programs, including the shifting of text, use of italic and bold styles, underlining, choice of fonts, incorporation of illustrations, use of boxes and shading to help the reader.

Standard English

- When features of non-standard English or features deriving from the first language of an EAL learner are inadvertently used in students' Standard

English writing, the teacher points out those features, and says what their standard equivalents are.

- Students sometimes consciously use non-standard forms in their writing, for example in some poetry and in the dialogue of stories and plays.

Grammar and knowledge about language at Key Stages 3 and 4

Grammar

- Students are shown that many words operate in more than one word class.
- Students are introduced to the distinction within grammar between *syntax* and *morphology*.
- Students are shown examples of the *active* and the *passive voice* in sentences.
- Students are shown examples of *mood* in sentences: *indicative*, *interrogative*, *imperative*, *conditional*. They are shown examples of the small number of cases where English still uses the *subjunctive*.
- Students are introduced to the idea of the *complement* in sentences.
- Students are introduced to the idea of *noun*, *verb*, *adjectival* and *adverbial clauses*.
- Students are shown and helped to name some of the different kinds of *phrases* and *clauses*: for example, *relative clauses* as a sub-set of *subordinate clauses*, and *clauses* and *phrases of time, of place, of manner, of concession*.
- Students are shown the small number of *inflections* in English verbs, and introduced to the idea of *agreement* between subject and verb.
- Students are introduced to the distinction between *transitive* and *intransitive* verbs.
- Students are shown the purpose and use of *modal verbs*, and learn how to distinguish between *modal* and *lexical verbs*. They are shown how *modality* can also be expressed by *adjectives* and *adverbs*, and by *adjectival* and *adverbial phrases* and *clauses*.
- Students are helped to recognise and name the full range of *verb tenses*: *simple* and *continuous present*; *simple* and *continuous future*; *simple past* and *past perfect*; *future perfect*; *pluperfect*. In the context of the study of the *perfect tenses*, they are introduced to the function of *auxiliary verbs*.

- Students are shown how sentences can be analysed in three different ways: in terms of the *class* of each individual word in the sentence; in terms of the *dynamic* of the sentence (its *subject/object relations*; its use of *subordination*); and in terms of the way that a group of words, such as an *adjectival phrase*, can perform its grammatical function, even though – taking this example – it contains words of classes other than adjectives.

Knowledge about language

- Students develop their understanding of *text grammar*, becoming familiar with the terminology to describe a range of *genres* of writing and speech, and being helped to recognise *register* through observing some of the genres' typical characteristics. They are shown how *cohesive devices* hold a text together.
- Students are shown examples of *homophones* and *homonyms* or *homographs*, and are introduced to those terms.
- Students compare examples of different kinds of spoken language and written language.
- Students investigate the structure and presentation of *digital* and *multimodal texts*.
- Students study the spread of 'Englishes' across the world: dialects and Creoles, differences between Standard English and non-standard forms, differences between the standard forms of different countries. They are shown examples of writing by established authors which makes use of non-standard forms, for example in dialogue.
- Students' continuing study of etymology includes more of the historical reasons for today's English spelling: the historical and linguistic origins of words, borrowings from other languages, the efforts of some groups to reform spelling, the decisions of printers and scribes, the accommodation of the writing system to newly invented words.
- From their reading of pre-twentieth-century texts, students are shown some of the major changes in English grammar, punctuation, vocabulary and word meanings over the centuries. They study some contemporary trends and fashions in language, and the use of deliberate deviance from standard forms for special effects.
- Students study some of the connections between language and power, whether in interpersonal or mass uses of language.
- Students study some aspects of early language acquisition.

Drama at Key Stages 3 and 4

Making

- Students use drama as a mode of learning throughout the curriculum.
- Students try out a diversity of dramatic styles, including unorthodox approaches, in experimenting with improvisation and text.
- Students create and rehearse improvised and scripted dramas, for themselves and for others, which are entertaining, moving or surprising and which show increasing subtlety and complexity of structure and characterisation. In terms of content, this work may draw on the content of any subject or area of the curriculum to explore major issues of contemporary social, political or moral concern, or may be on lighter, comic or more personal and individual themes.
- Students give and accept suggestions and ideas during improvisations and rehearsals for presentations with tolerance and growing maturity.
- Students take on parts in scripted dramas which call for significant memorisation.
- Students experience the discipline and teamwork required to organise and rehearse a drama which must be performed to a deadline.

Presenting

- Students perform dramas in a variety of genres, making artistic choices and shaping design elements to intensify dramatic meaning for an audience.
- Students develop further skills in the use of voice, posture, movement and gesture which sustain and develop dramatic action and the presentation of character.
- Students work productively, imaginatively and thoughtfully as part of an ensemble, whether as performer, director, designer or stage manager.
- Students combine dramas with other art forms, including the visual arts, dance, music and poetry.
- Students integrate sound and silence, movement and stillness, light and darkness to make effective use of spaces where dramatic action takes place.
- Students make confident use of modern media and electronic technology to enhance and support their work in drama.

Responding

- Students understand and are able to define and give examples of some key concepts in drama, especially *fiction*, *symbol*, *character*, *role*, *situation* (or *setting*), *plot*, *dialogue*, *convention*, *genre*.
- Students develop a mature understanding of many of the techniques and styles of theatre and of drama on film, television and digital platforms.
- Students are introduced to some drama traditions other than the contemporary and other than the Western literary tradition.
- Students analyse scripted dramas in order to understand more deeply the dramatist's skill in construction of plot, development of character and the building up of dramatic tension.
- Students have opportunities to see, discuss and evaluate alternative interpretations of character or situation.
- Students benefit from extensive and varied experience of drama staged and performed by professionals, in school and out.
- Students continue to advance their powers of critical evaluation of their own and others' dramatic work, whether in school, at theatres or through film, television and other electronic media.

Media at Key Stages 3 and 4

Reading media

- Students experience, enjoy and discuss collective viewings of moving-image texts of many kinds (for example, cinema films, factual and dramatic TV programmes, YouTube clips, computer games).
- Students consider complex meanings such as ambiguity, through close analysis of media texts.
- Students research media institutions (broadcasters, news conglomerates, game companies) and their practices, motivations and functions.
- Students consider complex audience formations in relation to social class, gender and ethnicity; and how audiences are becoming producers in the digital age.

Writing media

- Students make media texts in different forms, developing more complex skills in filming, visual design of printed media, editing, game design and online media design (for example, navigation, hyperlinking, uses of widgets and plug-ins).
- Students develop complex representations of themselves, of their peers, of other individuals and groups in society, and of ideas.
- Students simulate media institutions (for example, film and television production companies, museums and cinemas, newspapers, film agencies and institutes, regulators, broadcasters, game developers, social media start-ups, archives) in their own productions.
- Students develop their understandings of media audiences: across social groups, over time, internationally, across and between different media.

Setting the media in their context

- Students explore, through research, simulation and creative practice, the wider contexts of media culture: taste, pleasure and cultural value; the functions of the media in entertainment, high art, popular culture, politics and education; the relationship between the media arts and the digital sciences (for example, in computer-generated imaging in films and in the programming of games).

10 Assessment and examinations at 16

John Richmond

General principles

Curriculum and assessment have an interactive and mutual influence on one another. A central principle ought to be: decide on your curriculum first; then decide how to assess progress within that curriculum effectively. Too often, the order of priority of attention to the two things has been the opposite. But even within a right understanding of the relationship, modes of assessment have a profound effect on what is taught and learned in the curriculum, and how it is taught and learned.

The introduction to this book noted the irony of the government's intention that the National Curriculum, currently a statutory document and one which has been laboured over in its many versions for many years, is effectively to become an advisory document if and when all state schools in England become academies. However, as also remarked in the introduction, and as the government is well aware, it is through the system of tests and examinations that a government can exert closer control over classrooms than through the requirements or advice of a curriculum statement.

In the book so far, there have been occasional references to current and planned examinations and other assessment arrangements at 16 in England. This chapter assembles in one place a critique of these examinations and other assessment arrangements; and offers practical, educationally prefer-able alternatives in every case where current or planned arrangements are unsatisfactory.

GCSE English Language and English Literature

The current subject content and assessment objectives for GCSE English Language and English Literature (Department for Education, 2013a and 2013b) took effect from September 2015.

Reading

There is much to welcome in the subject content and assessment objectives for reading. Students are encouraged to read widely and (in the case of English Literature but not English Language – a curious anomaly) for pleasure. An explicit link is made (again, in the case of English Literature but not English Language) between reading and the development of a student's own writing. In the English Language specifications, there is a demand that students study and critically analyse a diversity of literary and factual texts, across a range of genres, from the nineteenth, twentieth and twenty-first centuries, including online texts.

The reference to online texts to some extent makes good the absence of any mention of them in the Key Stage 4 programme of study, while highlighting more intensely the anomaly of that absence.

However, the fact that there is no prescription as to the number or kind of texts to be studied for English Language, and that 'All texts in the examination will be "unseen", that is, students will not have studied the examination texts during the course' (Department for Education, 2013a: 4), may lead teachers to make an unambitious selection of texts geared solely to the demands of the examination. There should be some prescription of literature in the English Language requirements – less of course in quantity than for English Literature: perhaps a Shakespeare play and a novel from the nineteenth, twentieth and twenty-first centuries and an anthology of poetry.

Apart from the privilege of taking pleasure in reading, students following the English Literature course are fortunate enough to 'have a chance to develop culturally and acquire knowledge of the best that has been thought and written' (Department for Education, 2013b: 3). Why are these clear benefits not also available, at least in some measure, to English Language students too? Virtually all GCSE students will take English Language, while a much smaller number will opt for English Literature.

English Literature requires that students study some set texts in detail. The requirements are these:

Students should study a range of high quality, intellectually challenging, and substantial whole texts in detail. These must include:

- *at least one play by Shakespeare;*
- *at least one 19th century novel;*

- *a selection of poetry since 1789, including representative Romantic poetry;*
- *fiction or drama from the British Isles from 1914 onwards.*

All works should have been originally written in English.

(ibid.: 4)

What has happened to the excellent requirement at Key Stage 3 that students study 'seminal world literature'? The exclusion of specific reference to world literature, written in English, particularly by twentieth- and twenty-first-century writers from America, Africa, Australia, New Zealand, the Indian sub-continent and the Caribbean, suggests a narrowing of the range likely to be offered to Literature students. It is they, if anyone, for whom the offer should be broader and should give some inkling of English literature's world status: an inkling which should be given to students in largely monocultural as well as in multicultural classrooms. And – as noted in Chapter 2 – someone's especial liking for the Romantic poets has promoted them above other equally worthwhile options.

Writing

The English Language subject content and assessment objectives for writing are brief:

- *producing clear and coherent text: writing effectively for different purposes and audiences: to describe, narrate, explain, instruct, give and respond to information, and argue; selecting vocabulary, grammar, form, and structural and organisational features judiciously to reflect audience, purpose and context; using language imaginatively and creatively; using information provided by others to write in different forms; maintaining a consistent point of view; maintaining coherence and consistency across a text;*
- *writing for impact: selecting, organising and emphasising facts, ideas and key points; citing evidence and quotation effectively and pertinently to support views; creating emotional impact; using language creatively, imaginatively and persuasively, including rhetorical devices (such as rhetorical questions, antithesis, parenthesis).*

(Department for Education, 2013a: 5)

These requirements are welcome. They demonstrate a clear understanding of the diversity of purposes for which, forms in which and audiences for which students by this age should be writing. They give teachers every encouragement to teach well.

Two major shortcomings

The two major shortcomings in assessment at GCSE are: the fact that since 2014 students' achievement in the spoken language has no longer counted towards their overall main grade in GCSE English Language; and that as from September 2015 coursework has no place in either the English Language or the English Literature examination. There is no legitimate justification for either of these changes.

The sidelining of spoken English

It is impossible to argue that our future citizens will not need a fluent and persuasive command of spoken English in their working and personal lives; it follows that such a centrally important competence should be assessed as an integral part of the major GCSE examination in English.

For decades, means have been found to assess students' achievement in the spoken language at 16. Spoken language, by its nature, may be harder to assess accurately than written language, but the presence of difficulty is no reason to duck the challenge. There is only one reason for the sidelining of the spoken language at GCSE: the government's true estimation of its importance by comparison with writing. Even to embark on such a comparison is absurd. Surely it is obvious that the spoken and the written language are of equal importance, and that competence in the one feeds into competence in the other. Students' achievement in the spoken language should be reinstated as a contribution to their main grade; I would suggest at 25 per cent.

The abolition of coursework

In removing coursework from GCSE English, the government has undermined a principle which, in theory, it enthusiastically supports: that young people should increasingly take responsibility for their learning and should show that they are capable of independent study and research. These qualities are valued in higher education, as Angela Goddard writes in Chapter 11, and they are clearly of great importance in many areas of the world of work. To remove the experience of coursework from the schooling of 14- to 16-year-olds is to deny them the opportunity to take a measure of responsibility for their learning, and to prepare them ill for future challenges in education and work.

The government is right to be concerned about the possibility that students will cheat, especially in the age of the internet, by passing off others' writing for their own. The facts, however, should have allayed this concern. The number of incidents of malpractice in all GCSE and A-level subjects across all the exam boards in 2014 actually decreased from previous years: 2,550 penalties were issued, representing 0.012 per cent of the total number of entries; that is, 12 per 100,000 (Office of Qualifications and Examinations Regulation, 2014d). This is 12 too many, of course, but it absolutely does not justify the abolition of coursework at GCSE. It should be reinstated; I would suggest at 25 per cent in both English Language and English Literature.

Thus, students' performance in final written papers would account for 50 per cent of the weighting in English Language and 75 per cent in English Literature.

To conclude . . .

Coursework should be restored to GCSE English Language and Literature, at 25 per cent of the total weighting.

Students' achievement in the spoken language should once more count towards the main grade at GCSE English Language, at 25 per cent of the total weighting.

There should be some prescription of the literature to be studied at GCSE English Language.

Seminal world literature should be part of the requirement for study at GCSE English Literature.

11 English 16 to 19

Angela Goddard

The structure of this final chapter is different from what has gone before. The curriculum 11 to 16 has been discussed in detail in Chapters 1 to 6; an alternative curriculum 11 to 16 proposed in Chapter 9; and assessment at 16 discussed in Chapter 10. It is much harder to separate curriculum and assessment at the 16-to-19 phase, where there is no National Curriculum as such, but where there are Department for Education subject criteria that define both course content and assessment for each qualification in English. For this reason, I discuss here the content and the assessment of English 16 to 19 together.

Summary of main points

At 16 to 19, there is no single subject called 'English'. At A-level, three different 'Englishes' have developed: English Language; English Literature; English Language and Literature.

Reform of AS-/A-levels (for courses beginning in 2015) has involved changes to both structure and content, with the aim of ensuring smoother transition for students going on to university.

Although one of the original aims of the reforms was to free up teaching time in order to deepen and enrich learning, the continuation of AS-level as a 'de-coupled' qualification has faced teachers with new constraints and presented learners with difficult choices.

Curriculum content for each of the 'Englishes' at A-level reveals some significant differences in ideology and approach, and in how the subjects connect with pre-16 curricula. There are missed opportunities to link with secondary-school English; and the reduction of coursework from 40 per cent to 20 per cent of the overall A-level does not reflect the high value that universities place on students' ability to work independently.

Assessment at A-level should (but currently doesn't) reflect the literacy practices of modern life and embrace new technologies.

It is very regrettable that the government has abolished Creative Writing A-level after a short but very popular life.

There are key aspects of English study at AS- and A-level that support employability and life skills. These should be part of any 16-to-19 course.

There is an urgent need for courses offering imaginative and purposeful English study at 16 to 19 that is more applied than that required by AS- and A-levels, and more challenging than that represented by qualifications promoting and assessing functional skills. The government has introduced new qualifications which go some way towards meeting this need. A still unmet need is for a GCSE-equivalent qualification, retaining the principle of imaginative and purposeful English study, intended for post-16 students who have not gained a level 2 qualification.

What is changing in the 'Englishes' at A-level?

Structural changes

A process of reforming A-levels began in 2013. The initial idea, proposed by the then Secretary of State for Education in England, Michael Gove, was to turn A-levels back into two-year, linear courses where all the assessments occur at the end. They had been changed from a linear system to a modular system in 2000 (in a government initiative called 'Curriculum 2000').

In the modular system, the overall A-level grade was the sum of its parts (normally between four and six), taken at stages throughout the course. After successfully completing a certain number of these parts (or units, as they were generally called), students could be credited with an AS-level ('Advanced Subsidiary') qualification, which could be used as a contribution to a full A-level, but which could also be taken away as a qualification in its own right. From 2000, it was common practice for students on A-level courses to take five AS-levels in the first year of their sixth-form studies, and two or three A-levels in the second year. Curriculum 2000 emphasised the need for students to broaden their experience of different subjects, and AS-levels were seen as a step in that direction.

'Decoupling' of AS-levels

AS-levels within the reformed structure (operating from 2015, first examined in 2016) no longer contribute to an A-level qualification; they are freestanding, separate qualifications, 'decoupled' from the A-level system. This means that if students want to take an AS-level and then decide to take the full A-level in that same subject, they have to take all the A-level assessments at the end of the course, even though they will have already been examined on the same subject content at AS-level (because AS-level is a sub-set of A-level in terms of content). However, A-level examinations are not allowed simply to repeat the AS formats even where the same content is being covered, as they must operate at a more demanding level. They inevitably introduce new elements, too. So from the perspective of a student who has taken AS-level examinations and then goes on to take A-level examinations, there is potentially some misleading familiarity. For example, a task that looks familiar from AS-level might require a different approach at A-level.

Weighting of coursework reduced

The contribution of coursework (in the reformed system called 'Non-examined assessment') to the overall A-level grade has been reduced from 40 per cent to 20 per cent.

Devolved powers

The structural changes described above apply to England only, because the Secretary of State and all the bodies associated with qualifications taken in England – the Department for Education, the exams regulator Ofqual, and the English exam boards AQA, OCR and Edexcel (Pearson) – have no jurisdiction over how exams are run in Scotland, Wales or Northern Ireland. Each of these parts of the UK has been given devolved powers and is following its own distinctive pathway in terms of educational policy. Scotland is continuing the system of Highers that has been in existence for many years, based on different curricula from those of A-levels. Wales is not reforming its English A-levels at all for its own Welsh candidates, who are obliged to take the qualifications offered by the Welsh exam board, WJEC. However, WJEC has also created a new entity called Eduqas, which is offering reformed A-levels in English to candidates in England. Northern Ireland has its own exam board, CCEA, and the current plan is not to reform. CCEA only offers English Literature A-level, and not the other two 'Englishes', English Language and English Language and Literature.

Implications for teachers of the structural changes

Initially, the idea of A-levels as linear courses was seen as freeing up teachers to teach a wider range of subject knowledge in greater depth, because there wouldn't be the constant punctuations of modular assessments, with their associated revision time and study leave. But this is only going to be the case where there are separate AS- and A-level classes.

At an early stage of the reform process, when schools and colleges were digesting what the structural changes would mean for how they organised their learning, it seemed as though the AS-level qualifications might be completely sidelined and drop out of use. Indeed, a survey conducted by the Universities and Colleges Admissions Service in 2014 (Universities and Colleges Admissions Service, 2015: 3) reported that only half the schools surveyed were going to offer AS-levels, as a result of a combination of practical problems and lack of clarity about the implications for students either way. However, there have also been some powerful drivers making a case for the continued importance of AS. Having no interim qualification is a worrying idea for schools and colleges, with the prospect that some of their students might end up with nothing to show for two years of study. The academic year 2015/2016 also sees the requirement for learners to be in education or training until the age of 18, so there is an urgent need for more routes for learning and more types of qualification other than A-level, not fewer. Headteachers, MPs and universities themselves have all raised concerns about the status of AS.

Universities – the very sector that the A-level reforms were supposed to please – have traditionally relied on AS results as a predictor of the future performance of their applicants. In 2014, Cambridge University signalled its view of the value of this qualification for its selection processes:

High profile critics [of the reform] include Cambridge University, which wrote to all schools and colleges in November [2014] urging teachers to continue to offer AS-levels. The prestigious institution has previously said that for admission to its courses, AS-levels are the best predictor of how well a student will perform in every subject except maths.

(*Belfast Telegraph*, 2015)

It therefore looks likely that AS will continue to be offered in many schools and colleges, and equally likely that teachers will have mixed classes, since running separate classes will be expensive, particularly for smaller institutions. But balancing the needs of both AS- and A-level students will require considerable skill, and there will be no unimpaired expanse of time in which teachers can plan creatively, as was initially imagined. The knowledge that some or even most of a class needs to be prepared for a 'decoupled' assessment at the end of the first year immediately puts constraints on what can be covered, when and for whom. In all the 'Englishes' there are certain areas, books and skills specified as part of AS-level courses. In these cases, the AS curriculum will be the driver of the A-level. If non-examined assessment applies only to A-level and not to AS, there will be pressure on teachers to leave the course-work to the second year of the course, which is hardly ideal.

The problem with 'decoupling'

English is a subject where learning takes place in a recursive way. This means that learners return to aspects of the subject repeatedly, developing deeper and more sophisticated levels of understanding and skill. It is not the kind of subject where learners can 'tick off' aspects as they go and move on to the next discrete area. A problem with modular systems is that they tend to compartmentalise learning, so teachers of English at 16 to 19 have had to find ways to counter this effect in the modular courses that were running under the previous system. Initially, therefore, teachers of English welcomed the idea that the reformed courses would enable them to teach their subject in a way that allowed the recursive nature of the subject free rein. However, the retention of the AS qualification as a 'decoupled' element has now severely constrained how the subject can be taught, because it has created a number of different groups within classrooms who will all need to be accommodated and supported:

* AS-level students who pass the AS and leave the group after a year;
* AS-level students who pass the AS and decide they like English enough to want to do an A-level; they now have a qualification but one that doesn't 'count';
* A-level students who take no exams until the end of the two-year course.

This is not simply a question of what to do, when. It is a question that affects how students are to make sense of the assessments they are facing, and how they are going to see themselves as learners. For example, which situation of the following two would you rather be in?

* You take your AS exams and, as a result, get some feedback on your performance. In the following year, you take exams that cover the same ground and that seem similar but they are in fact different.

Or:

* You have no possibility of any interim qualification, but you can approach a single version of the final exams, with no confusion resulting from previous assessments.

In some schools and colleges, all the A-level students are being funded to take AS assessments as a kind of 'mock'. In these cases, all the students, not just some, will be going over previous content in the second year, but via new exam formats. This will be less complex for teachers to manage. But they will still be teaching a second-year group whose existing qualifications don't count towards their final grade, which will be a new experience for everyone concerned. It might also be the case that early failure or poor performance at AS will discourage students from continuing. In the previous modular system, where earlier assessments counted, poor performance could sometimes act as a spur to galvanise students into action to make up lost ground in the second year.

The problem with different systems across the UK

Teachers of students in the 16-to-19 phase feel an obligation to help their students with university applications. Even before the 2015 reform, many felt out of touch with the contemporary higher-education scene (see Goddard and Beard, 2007). With some A-level subjects reformed and others not, and with some parts of the UK operating non-reformed and others reformed versions of the same subject, the picture is considerably more challenging than it was. Whereas schools across the UK are required either to take reformed A-levels or non-reformed ones (or Highers), depending on where they are located, universities have no such regional constraints, although there are complexities around tuition fees, of course. But it is unclear what difference it would make to a student's chances if he or she applied from one area to another: for example, if a Welsh student applied to an English university. In theory, universities in England should look more favourably on applicants with reformed qualifications, since they are supposed to be more rigorous and robust. However, all the qualifications, old and new, have the same names and so in reality many admissions tutors are unlikely to know the difference.

Changes to content

As well as bringing about structural changes, the reform process has required universities to be more closely involved in shaping the subject content of A-levels. Regulation of content and structure, previously overseen by one educational body, has been split between two separate organisations.

The Department for Education is responsible for content; the Office of Qualifications and Examinations Regulation (Ofqual) is responsible for structure. It has been the Department's responsibility to revise subject content, with help from higher education, and Ofqual's responsibility to devise a structure for assessment: for example, to decide on the overall length of exam time allowed, the coursework/exam balance, the definitions and weightings of the assessment objectives. Ofqual has had to ensure that any specification devised by exam boards meets both the subject criteria and the structural requirements. This continues to be the situation at the time of writing, where many more subjects are going through the reform process.

The problem with dividing structure from content

The difficulty with the plan just described is that structure and content are closely interrelated. Structure determines how content can be managed so as to offer students a coherent, whole experience of learning. Unfortunately, no one from the two organisations has actually sat down and linked the two elements to see how they would work together in practice. The job of making something coherent out of the various conditions and requirements in content and structure was passed to the exam boards.

   The next three sections discuss the merits and shortcomings of the content of each of the three 'Englishes' at A-level. For reasons of space, the detail of the content and of the associated assessment objectives in each case are not included here. They are available online, at the URLs given.

English Language A-level

Subject content and assessment objectives

The subject content for English Language A-level (Department for Education, 2014d) is available at www.gov.uk/government/uploads/system/uploads/attachment_data/file/302109/A_level_English_language_subject_content.pdf. Its assessment objectives (Office of Qualifications and Examinations Regulation, 2014a) are available at www.gov.uk/government/uploads/system/uploads/attachment_data/file/371216/2014–05–23-gce-subject-level-guidance-for-english-language-may.pdf.

Links with higher education

English Language draws on some elements of academic linguistics. For example, the concept of 'language levels' has been a staple of linguistics courses since it was first proposed by de Saussure; and language levels have been part of English Language A-level, albeit in different configurations and in a more restricted way, since the inception of the subject. Being able to separate out aspects of language and focus on them one by one can be useful to students; it stops them being overwhelmed by trying to analyse everything at once. The separations also reflect the kinds of modules that many traditional university courses favour; to this extent, they help students' transition to higher education.

At both AS- and A-level, the emphasis is on how the different language levels can be applied. This is a positive aspect of the reformed curriculum. Taken as a whole, the subject-content statements align English Language most strongly with sociolinguistics and text/discourse analysis, which are appropriate connections accessible to a wide range of students. The study by Goddard and Beard (2007: 18) on student transition from A-level to university showed that the AS-/A-level English Language students who were the subject of the research were planning to apply to a very diverse range of courses in universities: 74 different subjects were mentioned by the students as areas they were thinking about. It is therefore important that language study at AS- and A-level continues to have broad relevance; this need is well met in the statements referring to 'historical, geographical, social and individual varieties of English' and 'attitudes towards language and its users'. These applied aspects of language are relevant in any workplace as well as to other academic subjects.

Links – and missed connections – with English up to 16

Language as a communication skill

The subject-content document emphasises the importance of building on GCSE work. This is harder to see in reality, but there are some connections. One positive aspect of continuity with GCSE is in the recognition of language as a communication skill, although the descriptive terms used at AS- and A-level are different from those used at GCSE. The modes that are familiar throughout the National Curriculum and at GCSE, of speaking, listening, reading and writing, are replaced at AS- and A-level by descriptions of skills that cut across those domains. But there is one assessment objective, AO5 ('targeted in the range 10–15%' of the total), which focuses solely on using English to communicate:

> *Demonstrate expertise and creativity in the use of English to communicate in different ways.*
>
> (Office of Qualifications and Examinations Regulation, 2014a)

There is no reference in the assessment objectives to Standard English, neither is there any particular emphasis on the secretarial aspects of writing such as punctuation and spelling. Of course, accuracy is important at post-16, as is the appropriate use of Standard English, but the idea of skill as expressed in AO5 is in the demonstration of variety (using English in *different* ways), in controlling whatever style is chosen (*expertise*, which is understood to include accuracy) and in showing *creativity*, which means being able to inject some flair and refreshment into traditional genres.

Despite the differences in wording, we can at least see here one common thread linking English pre- and post-16, in the idea of students as producers of original language.

Language as a topic

Unfortunately, there is now no common thread linking AS- and A-level with GCSE when it comes to the much larger matter of language considered as a topic. This thread links AS- and A-level upwards but not downwards. University linguistics courses are not usually concerned with students as producers of language, beyond their academic writing for assessment. Higher education treats language as a topic, and so do large elements of AS- and A-level English Language. This is by far the biggest difference between post-16 language study and GCSE.

It would undoubtedly help students to bridge the gap between GCSE and AS-/A-level if they were able to study language as a topic in some modest way during their earlier school years. In fact, before the recent changes to GCSE and the removal of coursework, there was an opportunity for this, in the study of spoken language as a coursework option. Its demise represents a lost connection, making the transition for 16-year-olds even more of a culture shock.

The absence of any study of language as a topic up to 16, apart from the study of grammar, represents a particularly sad loss, because there are so many interesting aspects that could be explored. Language varies and changes, language is acquired, language is a human construct and a form of behaviour, language is valued in different ways, language is a symbolic system existing alongside other modes of communication with which participants make meaning. But unless learners in primary or secondary schools happen to have had a teacher who is interested in language as a phenomenon, they are unlikely to have encountered any of these ideas before they come to A-level.

Metalinguistic awareness and the place of terminology

An understanding of how language structures work relies on an incremental process of acquiring metalinguistic awareness. Unfortunately, the new National Curriculum for English requires an overemphasis on language structures – in particular, grammar, spelling and grapho-phonic rules for reading – in the primary years, and much less in the secondary years. This would mean that, if the requirements of the new National Curriculum were followed exactly (which is doubtful), in five or six years' time those students beginning AS- or A-level in English Language would have to think back to their primary-school days to remember the aspects of grammar they learned then; if, indeed, they managed to comprehend them at all at that earlier point.

Readers of Chapter 4 will have seen that, as well as recommending that the balance between the amount of grammar taught in primary and in secondary schools should be reversed, so that less is taught at primary and more at secondary level, the chapter proposes a modest 'knowledge about language' curriculum at Key Stages 3 and 4, along lines very similar to those sketched in the paragraph before last.

English Literature A-level

Subject content and assessment objectives

The subject content for English Literature A-level (Department for Education, 2014f) is available at www.gov.uk/government/uploads/system/uploads/attachment_data/file/302110/A_level_English_literature_content.pdf. Its assessment objectives (Office of Qualifications and Examinations Regulation, 2014c) are available at www.gov.uk/government/uploads/system/uploads/attachment_data/file/371213/2014–05–23-gce-subject-level-guidance-for-english-literature-may.pdf. (The assessment objectives also appear in the section 'Assessment at A-level' below.)

Fitting it all in

The central aims and objectives of the subject content for English Literature, taken as individual statements, are perfectly reasonable, and it is hard to imagine how any teacher of English could object to them. Yet in combination they read as a battery of requirements that make it difficult to see how the first central aim of the course can be achieved: that students should be interested in and enjoy their studies. The specification developers have been engaged in a kind of Rubik's cube activity, where far too much creative energy has been spent working out how to fit everything together.

The consequences of 'blue-riband' status

The criteria for English Literature are both more extensive and more specific than for English Language. In the latter, for example, no attempt is made, rightly, to specify historical periods or particular theoretical approaches. By contrast, in the light of the great diversity of theoretical approaches within the academic field of literary study (as outlined, for example, in Eaglestone and Kövesi, 2013), the English Literature criteria have attempted a sort of marriage between different perspectives, but with one particular perspective dominating the others, making coherence difficult to achieve. The more specific requirements to do with the study of certain kinds of canonical writers, certain time periods and, especially, the requirement to analyse an 'unseen' text, all derive from the liberal-humanist work of F. R. Leavis and others in the Cambridge University English School of the 1930s. Leavis proposed the notion of 'The Great Tradition' of literary works, knowledge of which constitutes a form of cultural capital. 'The Great Tradition' harks back to the original idea of 'the admiration of great works' that was the starting point for the study of English (Literature) on the first university courses.

'Doing an unseen'

This same idea still underlies contemporary lists of 'classic' literature and is expressed in the requirement at AS- and A-level, GCSE English Literature and, to a lesser extent, GCSE English Language, to study particular authors, movements and historical periods. Liberal-humanist values also stressed the personal aspect of responding to literature, the idea of finding passion within oneself as a reader in appreciating the beauty of literary works. An associate of Leavis at Cambridge, I. A. Richards, devised an activity that encapsulated this kind of personal response, calling it 'practical criticism'. The idea was to strip away contextual knowledge and respond to the text simply from an aesthetic point of view. This has come to be known in school-based practice as 'doing an unseen': an individual responds supposedly naturally to a text that he or she has never seen before, with the notion that this somehow creates a level playing field on which students can show off their critical skills. The 'unseen' is a required part of GCSE and A-level assessment in English Literature.

If we step out of the liberal-humanist tradition and into any other, the 'unseen' looks like a very peculiar creature indeed. For example, the Russian formalist school associated with the literary critic Mikhail Bakhtin (see, for example, Bakhtin, 1981) stressed the intertextuality of all communication and the way in which all language is drenched with cultural knowledge, so that any act of communication involves a history of usage. In short, there is no context-free text, ever. And the language of literary criticism is in itself a semantic field that has to be learned and applied. The ability to put on a convincing display of emotion as a result of an encounter with a literary text one has never seen before is the result of extensive schooling and socio-cultural knowledge. While universities have moved on from the pure 'practical criticism' seminar, it lives on in the school system, in an age obsessed with exam results and league tables, as a supposed counter to plagiarism and cheating, or to unfair levels of preparation for exams. Go online and Google 'doing an unseen' if you still believe that this activity is about a student responding naturally to a literary text.

Interestingly, English Language A-level regularly involves students commenting on material they have never seen before. Texts and data appear in test conditions, but their role is completely different from their literary relative: it is to exemplify a topic area and help to keep the student grounded in answering questions. Where texts are set for analysis, examiners go to great lengths to explain in detail where the text is from and what it is. It would be difficult to find two more radically different understandings of why a student should be presented with texts and data they have never seen before.

But isn't it just about books?

One of the problems with debates about the merits of individual books is that they make the subject seem to be just about books, not about learners' skills or even about how books relate to each other (despite these being in the subject criteria). The endless focus on individual books and writers produces particular ways of thinking about the subject amongst its practitioners at school level. Ask a group of A-level English Literature teachers what they are currently 'doing' with their classes and you will invariably be told the name of a text, a set text. It is very rare that you will be told about any of the following, which are all activities that you might hope the subject would include:

- trying out different ways of reading texts;
- looking at different theoretical approaches to reading;
- considering certain critical traditions and ideologies;
- reading a text for the fun of it;
- doing some creative writing;
- blogging as part of a reading group that extends beyond the classroom;
- individualised study, where each student is being supervised doing something different, customised to their needs.

And ask the same group of teachers what they did themselves for A-level, and they will again rattle off a list of eight or so set books. In contrast, teachers of English Language A-level appear to see their subject as very skills-based: for example, to do with developing language awareness, text-analysis skills, understanding different modes of communication and writing in different ways (Goddard and Beard, 2007: 19).

Original writing – not required on board

One of the desirable activities in the list above is 'doing some creative writing'. This would seem logical, given that, of all the 'Englishes', English Literature is the one associated most strongly with creativity. But although the requirement to develop and credit students' skill in using English is part of English Language and of English Language and Literature, it is not a fundamental part of English Literature, where writing skills are seen only as a way of showing knowledge of the field of study; they are not separately named in the assessment objectives, as they are in the other 'Englishes'. This means that the use of English in English Literature is associated solely with essay writing and discursive argument (or with re-creative tasks that constitute a literary-critical method).

Perhaps the traditional idea of 'admiring' great literary works is also still having an effect here, in suggesting that literary texts constitute a sort of hallowed ground that no apprentice writer such as an A-level student should be allowed to approach.

One result of the narrowness of the English Literature curriculum in its exclusion of students' original writing was the arrival of a new A-level subject altogether, Creative Writing, which began in 2013. This subject has proved popular at 16 to 19, as it has been for many years in higher education, showing that there is both professional confidence in teaching the subject and student interest in learning creative skills.

Creative Writing A-level's brief life

It is dismaying, therefore, that the government has decided to abolish Creative Writing A-level so soon after its introduction. It will be examined for the last time in 2018, with one opportunity for a re-sit in 2019. The government justifies its decision by pointing to its effort to 'streamline' the range of qualifications on offer, and by suggesting that there is overlap between Creative Writing and the English A-levels. The latter of these justifications is clearly fallacious. Creative Writing was introduced precisely because English Literature makes no space for original writing. The original writing allowed at English Language and English Language and Literature tends to be more pragmatically oriented. Creative Writing has been the one place at A-level where original literary writing is required and encouraged. There has been an outcry at the government's decision, though no change of mind so far on the part of the government.

English Literature and transition

Problems of transition in English Literature revolve around what practices – what approaches to literature – have become embedded at the respective stages. So, for example, if GCSE is approached as the study in isolation of a series of canonical works of literature, one after another, and this continues to be the students' experience at AS-/A-level, then there is arguably good transition (of bad practice) between those phases and a chasm a mile wide between A-level and undergraduate study. On the other hand, if the obsessive focus on what people read (rather than how they read) can be put in its rightful place as one consideration rather than the only one, then the very good aspects of the AS-/A-level subject content – including how meanings are made in a wide range of texts, how texts connect with each other and the importance of context – provide a good platform for transition to university.

English Language and Literature A-level

Subject content and assessment objectives

The subject content for English Language and Literature A-level (Department for Education, 2014e) are available at www.gov.uk/government/uploads/system/uploads/attachment_data/file/302108/A_level_English_language_and_literature_content.pdf. Its assessment objectives (Office of Qualifications and Examinations Regulation, 2014b) are available at www.gov.uk/government/uploads/system/uploads/attachment_data/file/371198/2014–04–09-gce-subject-level-conditions-and-requirements-for-english-language-and-literature.pdf.

The relationship with the other two 'Englishes'

English Language and Literature has common ground with English Language in including students' own writing skills and in using the language levels of linguistics; it has common ground with English Literature in focusing on how meaning is shaped in texts and in the importance of contexts. There is a requirement that non-literary material should be studied (unlike English Literature) and that two out of the three literary genres of prose, poetry and drama should be studied (unlike English Language). Literary and linguistic approaches need to be integrated, but there is no requirement about how this should be done. There are no requirements to study particular authors or time periods, and no requirement to include an 'unseen'. However, there is an expectation, as with English Literature, that literary texts be 'of proven worth'.

English Language and Literature appears to have escaped the detailed requirements to cover texts published before or after certain dates; instead, there is a more sensible general requirement to study texts written 'at different times'. Shakespeare is not compulsory, although exam boards are likely to include Shakespearean drama because of its cultural salience.

The parameters above offer relative freedom. But in other ways, English Language and Literature is highly constrained. For one thing, it is overcrowded.

This is a characteristic typical of many joint or interdisciplinary courses, where subjects are added together and in the process become bigger than the sum of the two halves. For example, there is a requirement to study a minimum of six texts, which seems unfair when half of an equivalent English Literature set-book diet would suggest a minimum of four.

Another problem confronting this joint subject is the vagueness of the terminology applied to it. The requirements stipulate that at least one of the texts should be 'non-literary'. What does that mean, exactly? Non-fiction? But some non-fiction is deemed 'literary' in its style. Does 'non-literary' include or exclude non-fiction? The terms 'non-fiction' and 'non-literary' come from different academic fields. 'Non-fiction' was coined, evidently, to contrast with fiction, and therefore refers to prose texts. 'Non-literary' refers to texts beyond non-fiction, including all those everyday texts, for example speech, that surround us on a daily basis and are not classed as 'literary'. This of course begs big questions about what 'literariness' is in the first place.

Dumbing down . . . or up?

English Language and Literature is in a unique position to explore notions of 'literariness' and creativity because of the requirement to bring different types of material together and to view them alongside one another. As suggested earlier, English Literature A-level offers no opportunity to integrate any material that isn't canonically 'literary'; and English Language A-level has no particular focus on literary material, instead analysing a wide variety of texts and prioritising big sociolinguistic topics, such as language and gender. Insofar as there is scope for innovation across the subject area, the combined subject seems to offer most potential.

However, there were some strongly conservative voices during the reform process that objected to studying everyday texts at all and particularly to the idea of bringing everyday texts alongside canonical pieces of literature. For example, Petrie's (2014) article in the Mail Online calls the proposed new A-levels 'A-levels in Idiocy' and misquotes past exam questions that asked students to analyse non-literary texts. The full texts of these questions can be found in Clayton (2014); and in his blog, the academic linguist David Crystal explains why analysing everyday communication is a challenging academic task. His article is entitled 'On dumbing up' (Crystal, 2014).

English Language and Literature and transition

This subject is in a difficult position in trying to build from GCSE, because in the reformed GCSE system there is no combined subject: English Language and English Literature exist as independent qualifications at that level. In spite of this, many English teachers will naturally range across language and literature in practice, because literary texts are a stimulating source of language use. However, Eaglestone and Kövesi (2013) worry that, as English Literature GCSE is not compulsory, more and more students will drop the subject, leaving the study of English Literature at 16 to 19 and thereafter facing an uncertain future. If this occurs, the combined A-level subject will also be adversely affected.

In terms of transition upwards from A-level, English Language and Literature is also in a complex position identity-wise. If university departments perceive the subject to be literary, it may feature as part of their UCAS entry requirements for English Literature courses. If departments perceive the subject to be linguistic, it may feature as part of their UCAS entry requirements for English Language courses. In reality, broadly based university English departments offering a wide range of courses on both literary and linguistic routes tend to include all the 'Englishes' on their lists of UCAS entry requirements or preferred subjects, in an attempt to be inclusive.

Assessment at A-level

Subject content is of course not the end of the story, because specifications have to be expressed in ways that allow fair assessments to take place at the required stages. Ofqual regulates on a wide range of aspects of assessment, including:

- the weighting allowable for coursework;
- the relative weightings of assessment objectives for each of the subjects;
- parameters for the number of hours exams can last;
- parameters for the numbers of papers allowed;
- how questions can be expressed;
- how mark schemes work;
- how the subject content – all of which must feature in assessment – will be covered.

Of these, the most problematic for the A-level 'Englishes' are two areas: the coursework regulation and the assessment objectives.

Coursework

Across all the 'Englishes', coursework (renamed 'non-examined assessment') most readily fulfils those parts of the Department for Education's requirements that A-level students 'undertake independent and sustained studies' and make connections between different parts of their studies. These are not requirements at AS-level, so coursework looks destined to become an activity at A-level but not at AS-level.

But the issue of coursework is problematic because its weighting has been reduced across the 'Englishes', to 20 per cent of the overall A-level from a previous maximum of 40 per cent. This change goes against all available evidence that the coursework element of English study at 16 to 19 – with its emphasis on developing the ability to do independent work and pursue individual research plans, to undertake critical thinking, to produce a sustained piece of academic argument, draft, scrutinise and redraft original writing – was the part of the A-level English curriculum most valued by universities. A requirement at an early stage of the reform process was for all the exam boards to engage with higher-education partners in order to ascertain their views about different aspects of A-level provision, and the coursework element was universally seen to be a key factor in smoothing the transition from A-level to undergraduate study.

Worries about cheating

The issue at the core of the decision to limit coursework is nothing to do with pedagogy and everything to with concerns about cheating. Of course, plagiarism and other forms of cheating need to be taken seriously. But no one ever suggests publicly that universities should drastically reduce or even remove the assignments they set and revert to exams because of the same concerns. In many universities, tutors never get to know their students in anything like the way teachers do in schools and colleges; it can be the case that a higher-education tutor sets an assignment for hundreds of students whom they only meet once. In contrast, teachers at 16 to 19 are expected to sign a paper to authenticate the A-level coursework produced by students they know well, and the students themselves sign to say that the work is their own.

One way to minimise opportunities for plagiarism is to set assignments that involve students in collecting and analysing their own material; and this has been the case in many different specifications, including (from the start, in the early 1980s) A-level specifications in English Language, where students have to investigate language by collecting their own data. This can be an opportunity for students to explore aspects of their own language experiences and environments by standing back and observing with a researcher's eye; or they can investigate an area completely new to them. Agreeing research plans with their teachers involves students in thinking about methodologies, ethics, practical concerns such as time management and the meeting of deadlines, as well as academic conventions such as transcription and how to use secondary sources appropriately. Writing up a research report is a valuable skill to learn in itself.

It is clear from reading exam boards' Chief Examiner reports that students can often give their teachers new insights into language use: for example, the use of English in a bilingual household, the use of different dialects and occupational registers, applications of new technologies and aspects of language impairment. There is no reason why such rich opportunities for learning should be denied or downgraded because of fears that a small number of students might be dishonest. To repeat figures already quoted in Chapter 10, the numbers of incidents of malpractice in all GCSE and A-level subjects across all the exam boards in 2014 actually decreased: 2,550 penalties were issued, representing 0.012 per cent of the total number of entries, or 12 per 100,000 (Office of Qualifications and Examinations Regulation, 2014d).

The A-level reforms were supposedly designed to prepare students more effectively for higher education. The limitation of coursework does precisely the opposite. In effect, because there is now no coursework of any kind at GCSE, students will be taking their first tentative steps towards independent work of this kind only very shortly before encountering it as the main form of assessment at university.

Assessment objectives

Regardless of the assessment vehicle involved, marks are awarded to student work in the 'Englishes' via assessment objectives, with each subject having its own range.

Assessment objectives, like their degree-level equivalents, 'learning outcomes', attempt to break down achievement into a set of component parts, with the expectation that this will help to increase the transparency of markers' judgements. A positive way of looking at this atomisation is that a student who is lacking in one aspect can still be credited in others. For example, a student might be able to label some features accurately, but not be able to explain in any detail what they contribute to the overall meaning of a text. The opposite could also be the case: a student might be able to say some useful things about a text's overall messages without being able to label features accurately.

Assessment objectives have often been misappropriated. There is nothing wrong with them as statements about what students should be able to do. But they are supposed to be an assessment tool for markers to use. They are not supposed to be a teaching tool or a cognitive model for how people actually interpret texts. But as marking schemes have become shared multi-purpose public documents, with the benign intention that they demonstrate transparency in assessment processes, they pop up frequently as starting points in classrooms rather than as end points in exam boards. This turns a subject that should be experienced holistically into a set of mechanical exercises. And, sadly, no marker is likely to respond well to a mechanical performance, so the whole enterprise is self-defeating.

The same is true of any rigid framework for answering questions; for example, the much-quoted 'PEE' structure (point-evidence-explanation) for making points in GCSE written answers produces an unnatural, robotic writing style that is alienating to read.

A further intrinsic problem is that, at A-level, assessment objectives (this time very much unlike the learning outcomes in universities) are required to have precise weightings every time they are used. Here, for example, are the assessment objectives for English Literature:

		A-level	AS
AO1	Articulate informed, personal and creative responses to literary texts, using associated concepts and terminology, and coherent, accurate written expression	Each of AO1, AO2 and AO3 can be targeted in the range 20–30%	Each of AO1, AO2 and AO3 can be targeted in the range 20–30%
AO2	Analyse ways in which meanings are shaped in literary texts		
AO3	Demonstrate understanding of the significance and influence of the contexts in which literary texts are written and received		
AO4	Explore connections across literary texts	Each of AO4 and AO5 can be targeted in the range 10–15%	Each of AO4 and AO5 can be targeted in the range 10–15%
AO5	Explore literary texts informed by different interpretations		

Figure 11.1 Assessment objectives for English Literature.

Source: Office of Qualifications and Examinations Regulation, 2014c.

(As may be seen, AOs 4 and 5 have much lighter weightings than AOs 1, 2 and 3.)

An activity might have more or less AO1, AO2 and so on. Quantification at this microscopic level can amount to trying to measure the unmeasurable, because the central skills of literary analysis are interrelated. The holistic very quickly becomes the fragmented, especially when atomistic assessment is the favoured model because it can look more scientific and therefore 'rigorous'.

There is currently a centralising mind-set pervading educational assessment, requiring everyone to do the same thing. Different subjects need to be treated differently. Creating precisely weighted equations between questions and assessment objectives may work for mathematics and scientific subjects. Treating English as if it were mathematics doesn't work.

Where should assessment be heading?

End-of-course assessments of linear courses, reductions in coursework, the limiting of opportunities for re-sits: all these point backwards to a former time. Pen-and-paper assessment hasn't changed in decades. As you read this, how long has it been since you sat and wrote anything for hours at a time, using a pen? Most of us spend most of our writing time at a keyboard of one kind or another. Keyboards have fast become the norm, and even in classrooms, tablets and iPads are replacing paper notebooks (the term 'notebook' is so e-oriented that I had to preface it with the modifier 'paper'). Spelling routines are memorised partly by the habitual movements of the muscles in our hands, so – for most of us – this means movements across a keyboard rather than joining letters together with a pen. Writing digitally means that we get used to drafting and editing as we go, rephrasing, reorganising and reshaping until we have produced something that we are happy with. But we still insist that students go and sit in an exam room for several hours and, using a pen, produce legible coherent pieces of writing in a paper booklet.

One of the oddest aspects of the current situation is that almost every aspect of national assessment is online – apart from the writing by the students themselves. Exam papers are produced largely online; teachers and markers are standardised online; most students' writing will be marked online within the next couple of years, scanned onto computer systems so that the handwriting can be read electronically.

Other ways of doing things

Denmark does things differently. Since the 1990s, Danish students have been able to type their exam answers on computers. In 2009, students were allowed full access to the internet during their final-year exams, in a trial which planned to include all schools by 2011. The Danish education minister, Bertel Haarder, was quoted as saying:

> *Our exams have to reflect daily life in the classroom and daily life in the class-room has to reflect life in society . . . The internet is indispensible, including in the exam situation. I'm sure that it would be a matter of very few years when most European countries will be on the same line.*
>
> (Hobson, 2009)

Norway also trialled a similar scheme in 2009.

What about cheating? In the Danish model, the emphasis of the assessments is on sifting through and analysing information, not on regurgitating facts and figures. One of the students interviewed by a BBC journalist covering the initial pilot commented: 'It'd be difficult to cheat because you don't have time, you're under pressure, and you have too many tasks' (Hobson, 2009). The Norwegian model goes further. All students are given a laptop for their studies at 16, which they bring into the exam room for their assessments. They log into a special controlled space where they download the exam material. With their own laptops, they work in a virtual environment familiar to them, rather than on a computer they are not used to. The Norwegian system involves a set of monitoring software called 3ami, developed by a UK company.

Negative and positive arguments for change

The subject criteria for English Language A-level require students to understand multimodal texts. They are able to produce multimodal texts as part of their coursework. Exam papers for English Language regularly include website material that has been captured via screenshots, reset by typesetters and turned into paper. In English Language and English Language and Literature exams, students may be asked to 'write' website material on paper in the exam booklet. This is an absurd situation. We in the UK must have the technological expertise to set up robust monitoring systems within the computer-based working spaces that are required to run online exams. After all, we have already made money from this expertise by selling our educational technology to Norway.

Aside from being able to experience and produce multimodal texts properly, there are other reasons for using computers in exams. For many years, English Language A-level students have had to work on spoken language in exam conditions by reading and interpreting transcripts. Aspects of spoken language such as non-verbal behaviour, prosodic features such as intonation, paralinguistic effects such as whispering or laughter or breathy voice, the pragmatics of simultaneous speech, and the particular pronunciations of regional speakers and of young children, all have to be imagined via transcription symbols and keys. This can turn interpretation into a sort of literary-critical exercise where one has to imagine the voices behind the words.

Think how much more interesting, realistic, genuine and immediate would be the experience of hearing speech or – even better – hearing and seeing speech unfold within video, so that the spatial and temporal aspects of the interaction could be appreciated. Visually impaired students often have particular expertise in hearing the subtleties of voices: imagine how much better this facility would be for them, compared with reading a transcript written in an enlarged typeface. The study of language change would be transformed, as students would be able to hear how texts sounded up to 150 years ago. These ideas are focused on English Language, but the other 'Englishes' would benefit too. Poetry could be heard, drama could be seen as well as heard, a prose text could be run alongside a film clip. English could finally escape the page.

16-to-19 qualifications other than A-level

The chapter so far has been concerned with AS- and A-level. It is important to remember, however, that there are many thousands of 16- to 19-year-olds in schools and colleges who are not taking those courses, but who need a worthwhile qualification of some kind either in English, or which involves the use of English in achieving a qualification with another name.

Level 3 qualifications

The government has introduced two new sets of advanced qualifications, with the same level-3 status as A-level, and intended to attract the same esteem. These are Applied General qualifications and Tech Levels.

Applied General qualifications – these are rigorous advanced (level 3) qualifications that equip students with transferable knowledge and skills. They are for post-16 students wanting to continue their education through applied learning. They fulfil entry requirements for a range of higher education courses, either by meeting entry requirements in their own right or being accepted alongside and adding value to other qualifications at the same level.

Tech Levels – these are rigorous advanced (level 3) technical qualifications, on a par with A levels and recognised by employers. They are for post-16 students wishing to specialise in a specific industry, occupation or occupational group. They equip a student with specialist knowledge and skills, enabling entry to an apprenticeship or other employment, or progression to a related higher-education course. In some cases, these qualifications provide a 'licence to practise' or exemption from professional exams. Tech Levels are one of three components of the new Technical Baccalaureate (TechBacc) performance table measure.

(Department for Education, 2015d: 8)

Tech Levels can contribute to a Technical Baccalaureate (TechBacc). This is:

a performance table measure that will report the number of students achieving a Tech Level, an approved level 3 maths qualification and an Extended Project qualification.

(*ibid*.:10)

The Extended Project qualification:

develops and tests students' skills in writing, communication, research, self-discipline and self-motivation. Such skills are in high demand by industry and academia. The extended project component also gives students the opportunity to undertake research projects with an industry focus, relevant to their vocational programme. It encourages students to explore further aspects of the occupational area and equips them with a breadth of knowledge and understanding to strengthen their employability.

(Department for Education, 2014g: 6)

It sounds excellent. It sits uneasily with the government's recent decision to abolish coursework at GCSE and severely to reduce it at A-level.

Up-to-level-2 qualifications

Many students who enter post-16 education without a grade C or better at GCSE English (a level-2 qualification) retake the course, in the hope of getting at least a C grade the second time round.

The government is rightly insistent on the importance of English and mathematics in the education of all 16- to 19-year-olds, at whatever level:

> all students aged 16 to 19 studying 150 hours or more, who do not hold a GCSE at A*–C or equivalent qualification in maths and/or in English, are required to study these subjects as part of their study programme in each academic year. This requirement is a 'condition of funding'.
>
> All full time 16 to 19 year old students starting a new study programme with a grade D in maths or English must enrol on GCSE courses. This requirement does not apply to students on traineeships. Students with prior attainment of grade E or below can study other maths and English qualifications such as Functional Skills, ESOL and Free Standing Maths qualifications recognised by the funding condition as 'stepping stone' qualifications on the journey towards achievement of a GCSE.
>
> (Department for Education, 2016c: 8)

Several of the examining bodies regulated by the Office of Qualifications and Examinations Regulation offer these 'stepping stone' qualifications. Functional Skills courses in English, mathematics and ICT, for example, operate at three levels: entry (itself divided into sub-levels 1, 2 and 3), level 1 and level 2.

In the case of English, the course is divided into three familiar parts: reading; writing; and speaking, listening and communication. As the word 'Functional' suggests, the focus of study is on practical, real-life rather than aesthetic uses of the language; there is no study of imaginative literature, for example. The outcome of the examination is a simple pass or fail; there are no grades.

Until August 2014, a level-2 pass was considered the equivalent of a grade C at GCSE. Since September of that year, a level-2 pass has lost that equivalence and has been considered another stepping stone, beyond level 1 and entry-level passes, towards the achievement of a grade C.

A GCSE-equivalent qualification designed for post-16

The Association of Colleges and the National Institute of Adult Continuing Education have been lobbying the government and the Office of Qualifications and Examinations Regulation to design and introduce new qualifications 'which are rigorous and related to the world of work', as the quotation below will show. One such qualification could be a GCSE course aimed specifically at post-16 students. This group includes adults, including those learning English as an additional language and mature students who were not successful at school, as well as young people aged 16 and 17 who have not achieved at least a C at GCSE in Year 11 of their schooling.

The argument in favour of a different kind of GCSE course, particularly with regard to 16- and 17-year-olds with recent experience of failure or limited success at GCSE, is that simply to serve up the same menu again a short time later is hardly motivating. There are tasks which could be undertaken and texts which could be studied which are more suitable for an older age group than for 14- to 16-year-olds. A different kind of course could be offered without compromising on the proper degree of demand which the examination should make on students.

As part of its manifesto before the May 2015 general election, the Association of Colleges put its case thus:

Meeting the English and maths challenge

Our ask

To enable colleges and schools to meet the OECD challenge, the next Government should develop new English and maths qualifications which allow students aged 16 to 19 and adults to gain the skills that businesses need.

In detail

Only 59% of 16-year-olds achieve a grade A*–C in GCSE English and maths. The Coalition has launched significant reforms to GCSEs (including to English and maths) in an effort to make them more rigorous and to ensure that they are an accurate portrayal of ability. These new GCSEs will be taught from September 2015 and graded 1 to 9, with 9 being the highest. Whilst recognising the principle behind these changes, and the intent to raise standards, we believe that even fewer young people will achieve a 'good' GCSE grade in English and maths.

These young people will, however, still need to continue with English and maths after the age of 16 in order for them to understand the application of literacy and numeracy skills (both in and out of work) and to secure a good job. The vast majority will study these subjects in an FE college, often alongside a vocational qualification.

Unfortunately, many young people dislike English and maths, often because of the way it has been taught in schools and because the current GCSE seems distant from the real world outside the classroom.

We are clear that it is not in these students' best interests, especially those furthest away from achieving a current GCSE grade C, to be asked to take the GCSEs again and again.

Therefore, the next Government should work with businesses, large public sector employers such as the NHS and local councils, and colleges to develop new English and maths qualifications, which are rigorous and related to the world of work. These qualifications might also be appropriate to 'adult returners', i.e. those people who left school perhaps many years ago but want to improve their English and maths for personal or career reasons.

(Association of Colleges, 2015)

This seems a wholly reasonable proposal. The argument for introducing a GCSE-equivalent qualification (which would have to have a different name), designed to meet the needs of post-16 students, is strong.

Technical Certificates

Technical Certificates are another 'up-to-level-2' qualification. They:

provide students aged 16 to 19 with a route into a skilled trade or occupation where employers recognise entry at this level (for example, most construction trades, care work and hairdressing). They will also provide access to Tech Levels or an apprenticeship.

(Department for Education, 2016c: 5)

Key competences for life and work

So there is a developing range of courses and qualifications for students at 16 to 19: as well as AS- and A-level, there are Tech Levels, Applied General qualifications, the TechBacc, GCSE (but not yet an examination of equivalent status tailored to the needs of post-16 students), Functional Skills English, Technical certificates. All require the use of English in some measure, and rightly so. What employment context, what aspect of citizenship, does not require good language and communication skills? Key competences, at whatever level of achievement, include: to read for pleasure and for information; to write fluently, plainly and correctly; to use the spoken language to state a point of view, to transmit information and to collaborate with others. They should be built into all 16-to-19 qualifications, at all levels, both the more academic and the more work-oriented.

To conclude . . .

The 'decoupling' of AS- from A-level is regrettable and has brought various practical problems with it.

The reduction in the weighting of coursework at A-level is a backward step. Concerns about potential cheating are understandable, but the most recent evidence is that the number of students who cheat is tiny: certainly not large enough to offset the argument in favour of the encouragement of independent study.

There are pluses and minuses in terms of coherent transitions between GCSE and A-level and between A-level and higher education. Much more could be done to improve the coherence of these transitions.

A-level English Literature has not yet escaped an over-preoccupation with *what* is being read; there needs to be more concern with *how* texts are read, and the 'how' needs to go beyond the limitations of the liberal-humanist admiration of great works.

There is no provision in A-level English Literature for original writing by students, and it is deeply regrettable that the government has abolished A-level Creative Writing after its short and popular life. That decision should be reversed.

A-level English Language and Literature offers a worthwhile combination of language and literary study, but the syllabus is overcrowded. It could usefully be pruned.

Separate, weighted assessment objectives are not an appropriate means of assessing the quality of continuous writing.

Much more could be done to bring examination-setting and assessment into the twenty-first century. The technology exists for students to consider and respond to texts presented to them multimodally.

Now that all young people in England are expected to be in education or training until the age of 18, there is a need for courses which require a more applied study and use of English than that required by AS- and A-levels, and which are more challenging than qualifications promoting and assessing functional skills. The government has introduced reforms which attempt to meet this need.

The most urgent unmet need concerns post-16 students, whether 17-year-olds who have taken GCSEs only recently, or older students, who for one reason or another have not achieved a level-2 qualification. The government should move quickly to establish a GCSE-equivalent qualification (which would for obvious reasons require a name not including the words 'secondary education') suitable for these students.

References

The combined reference list for this book and its sister volume, *Curriculum and Assessment in English 3 to 11: A Better Plan,* is available online at www.routledge.com/9780415784498.

Index